Explaining Language Structure through Systems Interaction

Typological Studies in Language (TSL)

A companion series to the journal *Studies in Language*

Volumes in this series will be functionally and typologically oriented, covering specific topics in language by collecting together data from a wide variety of languages and language typologies. The orientation of the volumes will be substantive rather than formal, with the aim of investigating universals of human language via as broadly defined a data base as possible, leaning toward cross-linguistic, diachronic, developmental and live-discourse data.

Volume 55

Explaining Language Structure through Systems Interaction
Zygmunt Frajzyngier and Erin Shay

Explaining Language Structure through Systems Interaction

Zygmunt Frajzyngier
Erin Shay
University of Colorado

John Benjamins Publishing Company
Amsterdam / Philadelphia

∞™ The paper used in this publication meets the minimum requirements of American National Standard for Information Sciences – Permanence of Paper for Printed Library Materials, ANSI Z39.48-1984.

Library of Congress Cataloging-in-Publication Data

Frajzyngier, Zygmunt.
Explaining language structure through systems interaction / Zygmunt Frajzyngier, Erin Shay.
p. cm. (Typological Studies in Language, ISSN 0167–7373 ; v. 55)
Includes bibliographical references and indexes.
Grammar, Comparative and general. 2. Structural linguistics. 3. System theory. I. Shay, Erin. II. Title. III. Typological studies in Language; v. 55

P151. F677 2003
415-dc21 2003058313
ISBN 90 272 2963 5 (Eur.) / 1 58811 436 8 (US) (Hb; alk. paper)

John Benjamins Publishing Co. · P.O. Box 36224 · 1020 ME Amsterdam · The Netherlands
John Benjamins North America · P.O. Box 27519 · Philadelphia PA 19118-0519 · USA

Contents

Acknowledgments

Work on this book was supported in part by the Centre National de la Recherche Scientifique (CNRS) of Paris through a research associateship granted to Frajzyngier. As part of this grant, Frajzyngier spent the summer of 2001 working in Nice. Much of the hitherto unpublished data on Chadic languages used in this book were gathered by Zygmunt Frajzyngier and Erin Shay under grants from NEH and NSF (grant No. BNS-84 18923) and under other grants to Frajzyngier. Some data were gathered with the support of the University of Colorado's Committee on Research and Creative Work. Frajzyngier worked on some elements of this book while a guest researcher at the Max Planck Institute for Evolutionary Anthropology in Leipzig. To all these institutions go our sincere thanks.

Certain issues discussed in this book were presented by Frajzyngier in four graduate courses conducted at the University of Colorado in Boulder between 1997 and 2002. Individual issues were presented through talks by Frajzyngier at the Max Planck Institute for Evolutionary Anthropology in Leipzig; at the Universities of Frankfurt, Konstanz, Zurich, Amsterdam, Bayreuth, Nice, and Lyon; and at the Langage, Langue et Cultures d'Afrique Noire (LLACAN), CNRS. In addition, issues from Chapter 10 were presented at the Third Congress of African Linguistics in Lomé, Togo. Certain issues from Chapter 5 were presented at the Second Congress of African Linguistics in Leipzig. Elements from Chapter 8 were presented at the Conference on Functional Linguistics at the University of New Mexico, Albuquerque, in 1995. Elements from Chapter 7 were presented at the 2nd Conference of the Association for Linguistic Typology at the University of Oregon, Eugene. We would like to thank the students at the University of Colorado and audiences at various talks for their important critical input, for the questions they raised, and for the suggestions they made.

A work of this type would not have been possible without the generous sharing of information and advice from colleagues around the world: Gideon Goldenberg, Hebrew University of Jerusalem; Robert Nicolaï and Michel Denais, CNRS, Nice; Frank Lichtenberk, University of Auckland, New Zealand; Marianne Mithun, University of California, Santa Barbara; Scott DeLancey, University of Oregon, Eugene; Henry Tourneux, CNRS, Paris; Karen Ebert, University of Zurich; Maher Awad, University of Pennsylvania; Toshi Asano, Immanuel Barshi, Barbara Fox, Saeko Ogihara, David Rood, Chia-Ying (Charlene) Lee,

Gilana Rivkin, Alanna Van Antwerp, and Faridah Hudson, all of the University of Colorado; Trefor Roberts, Denver; Gareth Roberts, Wales; Vera Podlesskaya, Institute for Oriental Studies, Moscow; Flor de Lys Houston, Ohio; and Olga and Valentin Okorokov, Longmont, Colorado.

We are very grateful to Edith Moravcsik, University of Wisconsin, Milwaukee, for directing us to literature that we might otherwise have omitted and for her critical comments, questions and suggestions. These prompted us to tighten up several hypotheses and to provide additional supporting arguments.

Although many people and institutions helped us in our work, none of them bears any responsibility for mistakes and errors of fact, interpretation or conclusions. To our families we express thanks for their support and understanding. May this little book be an expression of our gratitude.

Abbreviations

The list includes abbreviations used in morpheme-by-morpheme glosses and in formulas. We did not unify glossing for data coming from different sources. Consequently, the same function may be represented by different glosses in the book.

1	First person
2	Second person
3	Third person
ABS	Absolutive extension
ACC	Accusative
ACT	Active
ADJ	Adjective
ADV	Adverb
AFF	Affected argument
AGAIN	Verbal extension coding repetition of the action
ALL	Allative
APPL	Applicative
ART	Article
ASSC	Associative
AWAY	Verbal extension coding movement away
BEN	Benefactive/dative
CLAS	Classifier
COLL	Collective
COM	Comment-on-focus marker
COMP	Complementizer
COMPL	Completive
COND	Conditional
CONJ	Conjunction
COP	Copula
D.HAB	Dependent habitual aspect
D.PVG	Distal extension: Point of view of goal
D:SO	Distal extension: Point of view of source
DAT	Dative

DEF	Definite
DEM	Demonstrative
DEM.R	Remote demonstrative
DET	Determiner
DIMIN	Diminutive
DOWN	Movement down extension
DU	Dual
Eng.	English
EP	Epenthetic
EXCL	Exclusive
F	Feminine
for	Preposition coding benefactive
Fr.	French
FREQ	Frequentative
Ful.	Fula (Fulfulde)
FUT	Future
GEN	Genitive
GER	Gerund
GO	Goal orientation
HAB	Habitual
HAU.	Hausa
HON	Honorific
HYP	Hypothetical
ICP	Intransitive copy pronoun
IDEO	Ideophone
IMP	Imperative
IMPF	Imperfective
IN	Verbal extension indicating movement inside
INCEPT	Inceptive
INCL	Inclusive
INF	Infinitive
INN	Verbal extension coding movement to or from an inner space
INTERJ	Interjection
INV	Inverse
IO	Indirect object, indirect object marker
IRR	Irrealis
LLC	London–Lund Corpus
LOC	Locative

M	Masculine
N	Noun
N	Neuter
NEG	Negation
NOM	Nominative; nominalized
NORM	Normative
O, OBJ	Object, object marker
OBL	Marker of oblique case
OUT	Verbal extension indicating movement from inside out
P	Person; plural
PART	Partitive
PAST	Past tense
PEJ	Pejorative
PL	Plural
PM	Previous mention
PO	Potential object extension
POL	Polite form of address
PRED	Predicator
PREP	Preposition
PRES	Present tense
PRF	Perfective
PTCL	Particle
PTCPL	Participle
PROH	Prohibitive
PROX	Proximate previous mention; proximate deixis
PURP	Purpose; purposive marker
PVG	Point of view of goal
Q	Interrogative marker
QUANT	Quantifier
REF	Referential
REFL	Reflexive
REL	Relative
REM	Remote previous mention; remote deixis
RESP	Respect
RHET	Rhetorical
S	Sentence
S	Subject; singular
SEQ	Sequential marker

SG	Singular
SO	Point of view of source
Sources	Sources for Polish Frequentative Dictionary (Electronic data)
STAT	Stative
SUBJ	Subjunctive
TEMP	Temporal
TR	Transitive
TENT	Tentative
UNSP	Unspecified argument
UP	Verbal extension indicating movement upward
V	Verb
VENT	Ventive
VN	Verbal noun
VOC	Vocative

Chapter 1

Introduction: Theoretical and methodological foundations

1. The aim and organization of the present work

The present work proposes a framework for describing language forms and functions through the description of relationships among lexicon, morphology, syntax, and phonology. The proposed theoretical framework is based on the following components:

- The notion of formal coding means, which participate in various formal and functional systems;
- The principle of functional transparency (defined in Section 4 of this chapter);
- The notion of functional domains (defined in Section 6 of this chapter); and
- The notion of systems interaction in the coding of functional domains (defined in Section 7 of this chapter).

In this chapter we describe the theoretical importance of each of these components. We also describe the implications of the proposed approach for linguistic typology. The remainder of the book is divided into two parts. In Part I: Coding Means, we discuss the formal properties of the various coding means, including their possibilities and limitations, and discuss some of the functions coded by those means.

The following coding means are discussed in the first part of the work:

Lexicon (Chapter 2)
Linear order (Chapter 3)
Coding through inflection (Chapter 4)
Coding through phonology (Chapter 5)
Coding through agreement (Chapter 6)
Nominal classification as a coding means (Chapter 7)
Subject-to-object raising and the domain of modality (Chapter 8)

In Part II, Selected Functional Domains, we apply the proposed approach to several functional domains that have been at the center of linguistic research for the last forty years and to some domains that are only now emerging as objects of interest. We demonstrate how various means interact in the coding of selected functional domains. In each chapter we discuss the means used by various languages to code functions within a given functional domain. We demonstrate that the coding devices in a language interact within their functional domains and that this interaction is governed by the principle of functional transparency. We postulate that the occurrence or non-occurrence of certain formal devices in a given language may be attributed to the inherent limitations of these devices, the functional repercussions of these limitations, and the existence of other coding means in that language. The following functional domains are discussed:

Coding locative predication (Chapter 10)
Coding semantic relations: The case of indirect affectedness of the subject (Chapter 9)
Reference systems (Chapter 11)

In Chapter 12 we present our conclusions and provide a brief discussion of several open questions.

The work is typological in that it draws data from languages from different families representing different types of lexical, morphological, and syntactic systems. Since our main aim is the study of the interaction of various systems within a single language, we have limited our data to a relatively small number of languages: English, Polish, Russian, French, Welsh, German, Spanish, Mandarin, Japanese; Hausa, Gidar, Lele, Hdi, Mandara, Mina, Hona, East Dangla (Chadic); Arabic, Hebrew, Amharic (Semitic); Songhay (Nilo-Saharan); Lango (Nilotic); Kiyaka (Bantu); Krongo (Kordofanian); Dahalo (Cushitic); Malay and Tagalog. The methodological advantages of this limitation are as follows: For many of these languages, we have firsthand knowledge and are able to check the data in natural discourse. Much of the data for Polish, English, Russian and various Chadic languages come from natural language corpora. For other languages, we have access to native speakers with whom we can check the relevant data. In this way we are not limited to published sources and are able to keep our reliance on elicited data to a bare minimum. Our experience, and the experience of other linguists working with hitherto-undescribed languages, indicates that elicited data often yield forms that are not attested in natural discourse and are therefore not products of the grammatical system of the language (Grinevald 1995).[1]

The present work represents a methodological innovation in that it uses two types of cross-linguistic data. The first type comes from closely related languages spoken within a relatively confined geographical area. Differences among such languages, unlike their similarities, cannot be due to common retention or to common innovation and so must be due to other, language-internal factors. The second type of data comes from unrelated languages of different language families. Here, similarities cannot be attributed to common retention and therefore must result from common innovation, which may be due to common structural properties of the languages in question. If the differences found among closely related languages correspond with the similarities found among unrelated languages, it can be concluded that these correspondences reflect systems interactions among the various coding means.

The purpose of the following introduction is to provide a significant preview of things to come later in the book.

2. The notion of language as the object of this study

Within the proposed approach there exist no functional domains, individual functions or individual meanings, except as they are coded by the formal means of a given language. In other words, language is viewed as a means of creating meaning. This contrasts with approaches in which language is viewed as a means of connecting meaning with phonetic realization. For a review of such approaches, cf. Jackendoff (2001: 267–93). In our view, meaning does not exist as some universe outside of language but exists only within a given language and only to the extent that the language codes it through some formal means. Consequently, it is natural that different languages code different meanings in their grammatical structures and in their lexicons. Given similarities in human cognitive abilities, experiences, and cultures, it is also entirely possible and natural that related and unrelated languages will code similar or identical functions.

Showing that different forms have the same function is not a simple matter. The fact that a linguist labels a certain form 'passive', 'reflexive', or 'causative' often means nothing more than that the form shares some functional properties with forms so labeled in some other language(s). But whether these perceived properties are actually central to the functions of the given form in the target language is rarely addressed.

The proposed approach allows us to offer an explanation for similarities and differences among languages, not only in the internal structure of their grammatical systems but in forms of discourse as well. Similarities and differences alike result from the coding means available in languages and from the functional domains these means encode. All languages share one property, however: They obey the principle of functional transparency.

3. The principle of functional transparency

We propose that a fundamental principle for explaining language structure and language use is the principle of functional transparency. This principle applies to any instance of language use by fluent speakers and it applies at every level of linguistic structure. The principle is motivated by the hearer's need to understand the utterance. The language structure provides the speaker with the means to satisfy this need in accordance with the principle of functional transparency. The principle has two components:

1. Every utterance must have a transparent function within the discourse; and
2. Every constituent must have a transparent function within the utterance.

'Transparency' has to do with the hearer's ability to identify the role of an element within the functional domains coded through grammatical means in the language; it does not have to do with the hearer's understanding of the role of these elements with respect to some real world. We provide here a few illustrations of the principle of functional transparency in the domain of discourse, followed by an illustration of the same principle within the domain of the clause.

Every utterance in discourse must be transparent with respect to its relationship to preceding and following discourse. Continuation of the same discourse topic is the morphologically and syntactically unmarked situation. A change of discourse topic is coded by syntactic, morphological or periphrastic means. In written English, the graphic division into paragraphs signals the independence of chunks of discourse:

I married my partner on Saturday.

We have had a very eventful two-and-a-bit years together and just before I was diagnosed, we decided to get married and try to lead quieter lives together.

I am very grateful that she decided to go ahead with the wedding.

I am a very lucky man to enjoy her support and company and it was a pleasure to be able to tell her so in front of so many family and friends.

I almost managed to get to the end of my speech without my voice cracking.

Our daughter had a whale of a time, grinning merrily at all the cameras and objecting only to our attempts to put flowers in her hair just before we walked up the aisle with her.

(From Ivan Noble's diary, BBC World Service)

In conversation, connections within discourse are marked by other means, viz. rhetorical questions or particles such as 'and', 'so', 'well'. Compare the following fragment of discourse from the London–Lund Corpus (LLC):[2]

4_7_0 <632 b> ^how /old is she# .
4_7_0 <633 a> *^fift\een#*
4_7_0 <634 c> *^fift/een#*
4_7_0 <635 c> ^she got ^she . ^her “!father was :f\ined#
4_7_0 <636 c> ^fifty ‘pounds for :her . playing tr\/uant {at ^sch\/ool#}# .
4_7_0 <637 c> ^**so** he t\old her to ‘sort of . you ^kn/ow#
4_7_0 <638 c> if you ^do it once m/ore#
4_7_0 <639 c> I‘m ^chucking you !\out# .
4_7_0 <640 a> ^and she d\/id it#

4_7_0 <640 a> ^**and** she d\/id it#
4_7_0 <641 a> *^**so** he _chucked her :\out#*
4_7_0 <642 c> *^so he _chucked her \out#*
4_7_0 <643 c> **and** she ^hasn‘t been !s\/een for a’bout ten ‘days you know# .
4_7_0 <644 b> **well** ^what did he ex!!p\ect if he((‘d)) ‘chucked her _out# -

At the clausal level, the principle of functional transparency has two aspects. The first is purely formal: The role of every constituent in the clause must be transparent to the hearer. This aspect of transparency is achieved either through the inherent properties of lexical items in the clause or through the system of grammatical means, which may include affixes, adpositions, linear order and free morphemes with grammatical functions. The second aspect of the principle of functional transparency is that it is fully determined by the functional domains grammaticalized in the language rather than by some putative language-independent needs of the hearer. The grammatical means of a given language code functions within language-specific domains such as modality, deixis, aspect, the relationship between arguments and the predicate, and so forth; in fact, all of the domains grammaticalized in the given language. As an illustration, consider the coding of modality.

In some languages the principle of functional transparency requires the speaker to indicate whether the clause expresses his belief in the truth of the proposition. This is the unmarked modality in languages from many families (Frajzyngier 1985d). In languages with a grammaticalized evidential system, such as Tuyuca (Barnes 1986), the domain of modality requires the speaker to indicate the source of the assertion. Evidence for the existence of the transparency principle in the domain of modality is that a single utterance cannot be marked for two opposite values within the same functional domain. Thus, a clause cannot be marked as a statement about the truth and a question about the truth at the same time. The closest one can come to this is a request for confirmation of one's belief in the truth of the proposition. This is the function of English tag questions:

2_8_2 <710 B> [@:m] +- -+ ^hy'drology is the :sc\ience of — ^science of the"!qu\antity of 'water I 'think#
2_8_2 <711 B> is ^probably — the !b\est way of p/utting it#
2_8_2 <712 B> ^**wouldn't you** *. ((**th/ink#**))* (London–Lund Corpus)

Conversational implicatures and indirect means of expression do not affect this component of functional transparency. In fact, conversational implicatures exist precisely because the function of every utterance is transparent within the domain of discourse: The hearer can discover the actual function of an utterance by comparing its role in the domain of discourse (conventional meaning, in Grice's terms) with its role in the actual conduct of the conversation.

In the domain of the relationship between predicate and noun phrase(s), the principle of functional transparency provides that the function of every noun phrase within the functional domain of the clause be transparent to the hearer. If a clause expressing some relationship between its predicate and noun phrases contains a noun phrase whose role in the clause is not transparent with respect to the functional domains encoded in the language, the clause is ungrammatical. Consider the following utterance:

2_13_0 <710 A> +I'd ^l\ike to get back to S/ete#+ (LLC)

While the full meaning of 2_13_0 will not be obvious to a person who does not know what Sete is (and recall that 2_13_0 is a spoken, not a written, utterance, so the clue offered by capitalization is not available to the hearer), the sentence is nevertheless grammatical. Adding another subject pronoun, or a noun not marked by a preposition, anywhere within the utterance makes the utterance ungrammatical:

(1) *I'd ^l\ike to get back to S/ete#+ Paris
*Paris +I'd ^l\ike to get back to S/ete#+
*he +I'd ^l\ike to get back to S/ete#+
*I'd ^l\ike to get back to S/ete#+he

The reason that (1) is ungrammatical is that it is the role of a constituent, rather than its meaning, that must be transparent to the hearer.

4. Semantic underpinnings of the principle of functional transparency

4.1. The scope of functional transparency

Recall that the principle of functional transparency requires the role of every constituent in the utterance to be transparent within the applicable functional domain encoded in the language; it does not require that every constituent satisfy the hearer's need to understand the role of the constituent in some real world. Upon hearing an utterance, the hearer uses his/her knowledge of the grammatical means and functional domains of the language to establish to what domain the utterance belongs. The same operation is repeated with respect to each constituent of the utterance, i.e., the hearer establishes the functional domain of each constituent. The meaning of an utterance is not the sum of the meanings of its constituents, as demonstrated in Frajzyngier (1987), but is established by calculating the place of the utterance and its constituents within the functional domains coded by the language.

As an illustration, consider two clauses with virtually identical constituents in English and German. If the meaning of the clause were the sum of the meanings of its constituents, the two clauses would have identical meanings:

(2) ^Mallet has pro:duced a [@:m] a {re!v\ised} consti:t\ution#

A German translation including the same constituents could have the following form (translation courtesy of Eckart Schütrumpf, p.c.):

(3) Mallet hat eine revidierte Verfassung hearausgebracht.
Mallet have:3SG INDEF revised constitution produce:PAST

Although the two sentences have the same components, their meanings are not identical because the English sentence codes different functional distinctions from those coded by the German sentence. The form 'has produced' codes aspect in English, while the German form *hat herausgebracht* codes past tense. Evidence that the two clauses code different meanings is provided by the fact that the English sentence cannot be followed by the clause:

... but it has been lost.

The German sentence, on the other hand, can be followed by the clause:

... aber sie ist verloren gegangen.

Decoding the English sentence requires knowledge of the English tense and aspectual system, while decoding the German sentence requires knowledge of the German tense and aspectual system. The two systems code different distinctions. The decoding of meaning is therefore not a direct path from form to function but rather a path from form to functional domain. Only after a form has been analyzed for its role in a functional domain can it lead to other functions, which may include meaning in the outside world.

4.2. How is functional transparency coded?

The functional transparency of a constituent within some functional domain may result from an inherent property of a lexical item or may be coded by other means available in the language. Many languages contain two broad categories of morphemes, those whose role in an utterance is determined by their inherent properties and those whose primary function is to code the role of some other element in the utterance. For example, consider adverbial expressions in English. English has a class of inherent adverbs that are not marked by prepositions when functioning adverbially, though they may be marked by prepositions when their function is to code spatial relations. In contrast, a lexical item that is not an inherent adverb must be marked by a preposition when used in an adverbial function. In (4a,b), the inherent locative adverb 'here' is unmarked, while in (4b), the inherent noun phrase 'a bad mood' is marked by the preposition 'in'. Eliminating the preposition 'in' would result in an uninterpretable sentence:

(4) a. 1_1_0 <453 B> ((she said well)) ^what have you !!g\ot#
1_1_0 <454 B> ((and he said)) I've ^got some **:h/ere#** -
b. I hate sitting around **here** because I'm **in a bad mood**. I'll go home. (Miller and Weinert 1998: 40)

Two crucial notions must be borne in mind with respect to the concept of functional transparency. First, functional transparency applies only to those domains that are grammaticalized in a given language; it does not imply that the hearer will necessarily be able to decode the real-world function of every element in an utterance. Consider the problem of grammatical relations in Mandarin. Some linguists postulate that Mandarin codes the category topic (Hockett 1955; Chao 1968), while others postulate topic and subject (Li and Thompson 1989). In either case, it appears that the language has not grammaticalized either the subject–object dichotomy or the agent-patient dichotomy, as there are no means of coding these categories (Chao 1968). Since these roles have not been grammaticalized in the language, they do not have to be transparent to the hearer:

(5) Jeh gua chyj heen tyan.
DEM melon eating very sweet
'This melon eating very sweet, __ tastes very sweet.' (Chao 1968:70)

In Chao's view, the following examples represent noun deletion and the absence of the possessive forms of the pronouns. In our approach, these sentences represent the absence of a distinction between subject and object in the language and the omission of possessive pronouns:

(6) Ta sh g Ryhbeen neu.ren.
3SG COP CLAS Japan woman
'He is a Japanese woman.' for 'His servant is a Japanese woman.'

Ta sh ig Meeigwo janq.fu.
3SG COP CLAS America husband
'She is (a case of being married to) an American husband.'
(Chao 1968:71)

(7) Woo lao naw-binq.
I all the time disturb-sickness
'I am bothered by sickness all the time.' (Chao 1968:72)
(Glosses courtesy of Chia-Ying Lee, p.c.)

Thus, the principle of functional transparency operates only for the domains actually coded in Mandarin and not for some general system of functional or semantic relations. These may be the categories of topic and comment, as proposed by Hockett (1955); Chao (1968), and Li and Thompson (1989), or they may be other categories as yet unidentified, but they are not the categories subject vs. object or agent vs. patient.

The second crucial notion pertaining to functional transparency is that of scope. The scope of the principle of functional transparency is not the whole language but only the functional domain of the utterance. For example, a language that has grammaticalized the distinction between subject and object in the indicative clause may not have grammaticalized this distinction in other types of clauses, so the scope of functional transparency will vary with the type of clause. Consider the case of the relative clause, which functions as a comment on the head of the relative clause. In a number of languages, the distinction between the categories subject and object in the head of the relative clause may be neutralized when the subject and object have the same person, gender, and number (examples courtesy of Gideon Goldenberg, Hebrew University of Jerusalem; glosses and morphemic division by the authors of the present work):

(8) ya-yyä-w lij
REL-see-3M child
'the child whom he saw' or 'the child who saw him' (Amharic)

yä-gäddäluwachäw säw-och
REL-kill:3PL:3PL man-PL
'the men who killed them' or 'the men whom they killed' (Amharic)

ha-ish asher ra'a
DEF-man REL see
'the man who saw' or 'the man whom he saw' (Hebrew)

al-rajulu lladhi ra'a-hu
DEF-man REL see-3M
'the man who saw him' or 'the man whom he saw' (Arabic)

There is a similar ambiguity in contemporary spoken French, this time resulting from the phonological fusion of two words. The phonetic form [lom kila vü] can mean either 'the man whom he saw' or 'the man who saw him', the two meanings represented by the written forms:

(9) l'homme qui l'a vu
l'homme qu'il a vu (we are grateful to Michel Denais, CNRS, Nice, for drawing our attention to this ambiguity in French)

Relative clauses in Semitic languages (and in French) can of course be disambiguated by a number of means, but the point is that relative clauses in some Semitic languages do not have to be disambiguated. Thus, the principle of functional transparency should not be construed as implying that no clause may be ambiguous or that every expression must be universally transparent in some general sense; rather, the principle of functional transparency operates within the grammatical system of an individual language and with respect to a specific functional domain.

We show in the present work that the presence of various formal means in languages, including adpositions, inflectional marking on lexical categories, and agreement, is motivated in part by the principle of functional transparency.

5. The coding means

Many contemporary theoretical approaches assume a dichotomy between phonology and syntax wherein the former is responsible for the phonetic realization of structures formed by syntactic rules. Syntax, in turn, is understood as a set of rules for forming various kinds of phrases. In our approach there is no place for such a dichotomy or for the perception of syntax as a set of rules for forming phrases. Instead, phonology, inflectional and derivational morphology, and linear order are all viewed as means of coding the functional domains grammaticalized in the language.

While different languages make use of different formal coding means, all coding means belong to one of the following formal domains (understood in the very broad senses given below): lexicon; inflectional and derivational morphology; linear order; and phonology. Other formal means, such as gestures, could be incorporated into the model without altering its precepts. Within each coding means are various subtypes, each having a distinct function in a given language. Several formal means may be combined in the coding of a single function. The first part of the book contains a description of each of the coding means, whose important characteristics are summarized here.

5.1. Independence of coding means

The notion of the existence of coding means implies perforce that these means are independent; that is, that the use of a given means is not triggered by any other element occurring in the clause. Any member of the class of lexical morphemes, such as a noun, a verb or an adjective, is an excellent example of the notion of independent coding means. Nothing in the following example predicts or triggers the use of the pronoun 'he', of the noun 'streptococcus', of the adjective 'violent', or of the determiner 'some':

> 1_8_0 <1033 A> it was ^some _((violent)) _streptoc\occus {that he'd ^g\ot# (LLC)

We extend the notion of independent coding means to encompass all derivational morphology; most inflectional morphology, including agreement; linear order; and some phonological phenomena, namely those that are not controlled by the phonological environment. Treating derivational morphology as an independent coding means is as non-controversial as treating the lexicon as an independent coding means: The speaker may, but does not have to, derive a given lexical category from another or add to the utterance another lexical item within the same category.

A form whose presence is entirely determined by some other element of the utterance is not an independent coding means but rather a redundant consequence of the deployment of some other means. It remains an open question whether there are any such forms in individual languages. However, given the contemporary state of linguistic theory we must justify why, contrary to both old and recent scholarly tradition, we consider agreement, inflectional case marking, and a host of other inflectional phenomena to be independent coding means rather than the result of such processes as government and agreement. We defend the independent nature of each of these coding means in separate chapters. In this section, we choose one instance from English to illustrate the proposed methodology for establishing whether a given form is an independent coding means or simply the result of the use of some other constituent in the utterance.

The basis of the methodology is this: Given an utterance involving two forms A and B, the only way to prove that form A triggers form B is to show that form B occurs in the utterance if and only if the form A also occurs in the utterance. If form B occurs in the utterance in the absence of form A, then form B is an independent coding means. Within the contemporary literature, English pronouns are often invoked as examples of case assignment, where the case assigner is held to be a verb or a preposition. Using the proposed methodology, we show that accusative marking on pronouns in English (form B) is not triggered by the presence of a verb or preposition (form A) in the clause.

In standard spoken and written English, pronouns usually have accusative case when they follow a verb or a preposition. For this reason, verbs and prepositions are often analyzed as case assigners. In many instances, the accusative case indeed appears to be the automatic outcome of the pronoun's position after a verb or a preposition:

1_3_0 <291 A> ^they ought to ^ch\/uck **her** _out in the _world
1_1_0 <77 A> [@:] I ^did get a !p\ostcard fr/om **him**#
1_3_0 <685 A> and I was ^jolly gr\ateful for **them**#

However, the fact that the pronoun occurs in the accusative case when following a verb or a preposition is just a distributional statement; it does not by itself indicate a cause-effect relationship. In fact, accusative case on pronouns in English is an independent coding means. One piece of evidence for this hypothesis is that a pronoun following a verb may occur in the nominative case. Kortmann (2002) cites the following forms from the Southwestern dialect of England:

I used to go to my uncle's and help **he**.
Work didn't frighten **we**, we knew we had to do it…

A pronoun following a verb also is in the nominative case when it is the subject of the subsequent clause:

2_13_0 <1080 B> ^you for!get **he** *!!\is* one# (LLC).

^I ((sylls)) always th\ink# — -
1_3_0 <852 A> **they** ^always ((sort of [@])) pre:c\eded their rem/arks#
1_3_0 <853 A> with ((things)) ^this sort of [@m] .
{auth:\oritative} en!d\orsement# (LLC)

A pronoun after the verb *to be* may be in either the nominative or the accusative case:

But for the present, gentle reader! and
Still gentler purchaser! the Bard-that's **I**-
Must, with permision, shake you by the hand
(Byron, Don Juan, Canto the first, CCXXI, McConell 1978:230)

1_5_0 <14 A> cos *^l\ectures#
1_5_0 <15 A> are ^rather a !waste of* t\ime#
1_5_0 <16 A> ((^/are **they**#)) (LLC)

1_10_0 <998 b> well if you can really very handsomely lend me your/- car on Wednesday that's **me** for Wednesday really

An additional piece of evidence for the independence of accusative-marked pronouns and putative case assigners is that a pronoun in the accusative may occur in an environment in which it is not preceded by either a verb or a preposition and there is no verb or a preposition in the utterance to assign the accusative case (the two clauses below occurred together in discourse, though their numbering, taken directly from the LLC, is incorrect):

6_2_0 <578 a> you'll ^learn to 'drive at the :same t\ime#*
6_2_0 <575 (b> **me** to 'drive **((while I'm th\ere#))** (LLC)

Accusative case marking on pronouns in English thus does not meet the 'if and only if' condition specified above: Form B (in this instance, a pronoun in the accusative case) does not occur in an utterance if and only if form A (in this instance, a 'case-assigning' verb or preposition) also occurs. Accusative case marking on pronouns does meet the criteria for an independent coding means: Form B can occur in an utterance in the absence of form A.

It is theoretically possible that a given form, such as a case-marked pronoun, could represent an independent coding means in one environment and yet be merely triggered by the presence of some other constituent in another environment. This hypothesis is undesirable for pre-theoretical reasons, as it proposes two different sources for the same form and an analysis that postulates multiple sources for a single form cannot be theoretically constrained. Having multiple sources for a single form also would place a considerable burden on the hearer to decode the meaning of linguistic structures, in effect defeating the purpose of linguistic structures. Nevertheless, since pronouns having the accusative form in English usually occur after verbs and prepositions in standard written and spoken English, we must show why this is so.

5.2. Agreement and government do not exist, but disagreement and insubordination are not tolerated

The general principle proposed in the present section is that while there is no agreement and no government in the sense that one form triggers changes on another form, **disagreement** is not allowed. If two constituents A and B are part of the same construction and there is a feature X coded on the form A, the form B cannot code feature Y if features X and Y both belong to the same domain. Consider a language in which nouns, verbs and adjectives code number, either singular or plural. If a noun is marked singular, the adjective must also be marked singular, because plural marking would constitute conflicting coding of a feature in the same functional domain:

Los géneros se manifiestan en múltiple concordancias.
DEF:PL gender:PL REFL manifest:PL in numerous:PL agreement:PL
'Genders are revealed by numerous agreements.' (Najlis 1973: 19)

*Los géneros se manifiesta en múltiple concordancias.
DEF:PL gender:PL REFL manifest in numerous agreement:PL
for 'Genders are revealed by numerous agreements.'

In a language in which verbs and adjectives code number but nouns do not, coding number on one category and not coding it on another category does not constitute conflicting coding. This is the case in Pero (West Chadic), which does not code the category number on nouns; consequently, a noun is neither inherently singular nor plural. Verbs code the number of the subject of an intransitive verb or the object of a transitive verb. A noun occurring with a verb in the singular is construed as singular and a noun occurring with a verb in the plural is plural:

(10) Gbáalì tóɗɗ-áanì.
calabash break-STAT
'The calabash is broken.' (STAT = 'stative')

Gbáalì tóɗɗò-t-áanì.
calabash break-PL-STAT
'The calabashes are broken.' (Frajzyngier 1989a)

A similar situation obtains in other languages that do not code number on nouns (cf. Corbett 2000 for a review of cases where nouns are not coded for number).

We can now return to the question of accusative case in English pronouns. Old English, like other Indo-European languages, used to have a case system that affected both nouns and pronouns. It is very likely that nouns following prepositions were also marked by different cases. The case system on nouns is now almost completely atrophied, with the exception of the genitive. The decline of the case system has been compensated for by the deployment of linear order to code grammatical relations, with the position after the verb coding the object. The elimination of the case system on nouns has left prepositions as the only markers of all other relationships among nouns or between the predicate and a noun. In this way, the position after the verb and the position after a preposition have become coding means.

It happens that pronouns have preserved not one but three cases: nominative, genitive, and accusative. The function coded by the position after the verb overlaps with, but is not identical to, the function that was coded by the accusative case in Old English (the claim that the number and type of distinctions coded by a three-case system must be different from those coded by linear order is supported in Chapter 4 of this book). In standard spoken and written English, use of a pronoun in the nominative case in the position after the verb when the pronoun and the verb belong to the same clause would constitute coding of conflicting features. This is because the position after the verb codes one function (object) while the nominative form of the pronoun codes another function (subject). (Instances of nominative coding on a post-verbal pronoun within a single clause, such as those identified in Kortmann 2002 (above), indicate that the dialect in question has a different set of coding means and a different type of systems interaction from that found in standard English and so would have to be examined separately.) The independence of coding via case marking and coding via the position after the verb allows for nominative case marking on the pronoun to code the pronoun after the verb as subject of the succeeding clause, a type of coding that would be impossible if accusative case marking were, in fact, an automatic result of the position of the pronoun.

5.3. Lexicon

The lexicon is understood here to comprise only free lexemes, including those that carry only a functional load. Bound morphemes are discussed within the domains of inflectional and derivational morphology.

Within the present approach, each lexical item may have two functions: to code a slice of the common cognitive state of the speaker and hearer (traditional 'lexical meaning') and to code a function in some functional domain grammaticalized in the language. We differ from many contemporary theories in that we do not subscribe to the notion that the lexicalization of some portion of the cognitive state determines the categoriality of a given lexical item.

The defining characteristic of a lexical category or subcategory is its role in a functional domain. This approach is similar to that taken in Frajzyngier (1985a) but differs significantly from superficially similar approaches in Hengeveld (1992) and Croft (2000).

Within the proposed approach, the functional domain of a verb, in a language that has grammaticalized this category, is the proposition, and the function of the verb is predicate of a proposition. The functional domain of a noun is also the proposition, wherein the noun carries the function of argument. A noun that performs some other function, e.g. that of modifier, usually must be coded for this function by one of the means available in the language, such as linear order, case marking, and/or adpositions. However, a noun performing a modifying function does not have to be marked if the head it modifies is marked as a modified element. This is what occurs in the 'construct state' in Hebrew and other Semitic languages:

(11) dabar 'word'
dbar elohim
word God
'word of God' (Kautzsch-Gesenius 1910: 247)

susim 'horses'
susey par'oh
horses Pharaoh
'the horses of Pharaoh' (Kautzsch-Gesenius 1910: 248)

The proposed approach differs from that taken by Hengeveld (1992), who states that the function of a lexical item is determined by its role in a construction and who consequently conceives of the simultaneous lexicalization of various functions. If 'construction' is understood in the usual sense of the term, viz. as a composition of one or more forms that together carry a function, then Hengeveld's description cannot be true, since it can be shown that the form of a construction may vary with the lexical items that occur in it. We discuss this issue at length in Chapter 10, where we demonstrate that in Mina, a Central Chadic language, the form of a locative predication depends on the inherent characteristics of the lexical items used in it. If the verb in a locative predication is not inherently locative, the language requires that the construction contain a local predicator. If the nominal complement in such a construction is not inherently locative, the construction must contain a locative preposition. If both verb and noun are inherently locative, however, neither the predicator nor the locative preposition is used. A similar situation exists in English, where a noun functioning as a locative complement usually must be marked by a locative preposition. However, when the locative noun 'home' functions as the complement of a directional verb of movement, no preposition is used. This is because 'home' in English is inherently locative:

1_9_0 <1221 B> ((I)) ^staggered thr/ough it# -
1_9_0 <1222 B> "^flew 'back '**home** the :next !d\ay# . (LLC)

1_10_0 <955 A> *and then ^you'll be 'coming '**home** in the 'after:n\/oon#

2_1_2 <1209 a> what did you travel ((**home**)) first or something of *that order*

With a predicate that is not a verb of movement, the noun 'home' must be preceded by a preposition:

1_9_0 <1314 a> and this also cleared ((out)) the problem that we've had for ages [@ @] **at home** because (LLC)

2_1_2 <1246 a> because you knew the .sort of layout of the library and *you ((felt **at home** there))*

Our approach differs from that of Croft (2000 and elsewhere) in that we do not propose universal prototypes for the categories noun, verb, and adjective. We do not assume that all languages distinguish among verbs, nouns, adjectives, nor do we assume there to be a finite list of possible lexical categories. Instead, we seek the fundamental defining criteria of each proposed lexical category in a given language in hopes of discovering true cross-linguistic identity of categories. If we take the defining criterion of a category to be its role in some functional domain, then cross-linguistic categorial identity will be found when:

- The languages examined have the same functional domain(s);
- The functional domains have the same subdomains; and
- The lexical items in question have the same function(s) within the same domain and subdomain.

If lexical items from different languages do not meet these criteria, the lexical items do not represent identical categories. The typology of lexical categories becomes an interesting enterprise under such conditions since it may reveal which functional domains are most often or least often lexicalized across languages. It may also reveal the implications of various lexicalizations. Evans (1999), on kinship verbs, represents a move in this direction.

It should be noted that the inflectional properties often invoked as the defining features of lexical categories cannot be fully relied upon because the same inflectional properties can occur with different lexical categories in the same language, e.g. case inflection on nouns and adjectives in Polish and Russian, number coding on verbs and nouns in Chadic languages, and tense coding on nouns and verbs. On the other hand, derivational morphology, especially that which changes the categoriality of a lexical item, is an important indicator of the inherent lexical category of that item.

5.4. Inflectional and derivational coding

We use the term inflection to mean coding on nouns, verbs, and other categories, including adjectives, adverbs, complementizers, and prepositions. In our understanding, inflection does not change the categoriality of a lexical item. Derivation either changes the categoriality of a lexical item or produces another lexical item within the same lexical category.

We consider inflection to be an independent coding means; in other words, inflection is not triggered by any other component of an utterance. Abundant evidence for the correctness of this approach is provided cross-linguistically by the presence of inflected lexical items in utterances lacking any potential trigger of inflection.

Inflectional morphology interacts with other coding means. Its presence in a language has important effects for all aspects of that language, though the actual functions of inflection differ from language to language. In some languages (e.g.

Bantu languages, Hdi (Central Chadic)), inflection on the verb codes the grammatical and/or semantic role of a noun phrase. In such languages, verbal inflection as a coding means interacts with prepositional and linear order coding. In some languages (e.g. Gidar (Central Chadic), Bantu, some Slavic languages), verbal inflection also has functions within the domain of reference, where it codes the subject or object of the clause as being 'known' (cf. Chapter 11) or having been previously mentioned in discourse.

The availability of inflectional coding increases the number of coding means and thereby the number of functions that may be coded. The genitive case in Polish codes the non-affected or partially affected object. Objects of negative clauses are coded by the genitive case:

(12) Nie ma **znaczenia**
NEG have:3SG:PRES significance:GEN
'It has no importance.' (Sources)[3]

Czy-ż nie zgadywałem **twoich** **życzeń**.
Q-EMPH NEG guess:FREQ:PAST:1SG:M 2F:GEN:PL wish:PL:GEN
'Wasn't I guessing your wishes?' (Sources)

The genitive is also used to code the partitive function:

(13) Ale **chleba** dajcie.
but bread:GEN give:PL
'But give [us] some bread!' (Sources)

Cf.:

(14) Ale **chleb** dajcie.
but bread:NOM give:PL
'But give the bread!'

The genitive case in Polish thus codes a category, non-affected or partially affected object, a category not coded by the grammatical system of English.

The presence of inflectional coding in a language affects the forms of discourse in that it affects the minimum number of lexical items required in a clause. We illustrate this here by comparing discourse examples from Polish and English.

In a language with inflection, a category whose inherent function is that of the modifier of a head can occur without its head. In Polish, possessive pronouns and adjectives can occur without their heads because they code gender and number:

(15) Moi **starzy** mówią
1SG.POSS.M.PL old:PL say:3PL:PRES
'My old folks say' (Sources)

(16) Nie twoja rzecz.
NEG 2SG:POSS:F thing
'None of your business.' (Sources)

Ale **moja,** rozumiesz.
but 1SG:POSS:F understand:2SG
'But it is my business, do you understand?' (Sources)

The fact that Polish nouns and adjectives can occur without their heads affects the form of answers to specific (wh-) questions in Polish:

(17) Która godzina. **Szesnasta pięćdziesiąt osiem?**
what hour sixteen fifty eight
'What time is it?' '[It is] 16:58.'

(18) Którą zabawkę teraz trzymasz w prawej ręce? **Lalkę.**
what:ACC toy:ACC now hold:PRES:2SG in right hand:LOC doll:ACC
'What toy are you holding in [your] right hand?'
'[I am holding] a doll.' (Sources)

In English, in contrast, possessive pronouns or bare adjectives cannot serve as arguments without a head noun:

(19) *my old says
*my says
*old says he does not…
*but my, you understand

Such clauses are grammatical only with a head noun:

10_4_3 <950 a> **the ^old man** 'Archie was 'going to :f\ight his 'way/ b/ack#.

2_3_0 <230 a> well we had some pretty dreary **old men** in* the First World War didn't we

Deletion of the heads results in ungrammatical clauses:

(20) ***old** was 'going to :f\ight his 'way/ b/ack# .
*well we had some pretty dreary **old** in* the First World War didn't we

These discourse differences between Polish and English are a direct result of the fact that Polish codes the domains of gender and number on adjectives and possessive pronoun while English does not. We discuss the consequences of inflectional coding in greater detail in Chapter 4. In Chapter 7 we discuss other implications of inflectional coding on nouns, adjectives, and pronouns.

The term inflection, as used in the present work, also subsumes all phenomena traditionally referred to as agreement. We take agreement, like all other types of inflectional coding, to be an independent coding means, in that it is not triggered by some element in the clause. Evidence for this is that agreement may be marked on the verb or on some other constituent in the absence of any potential agreement trigger elsewhere in the clause.

Nichols (1992) has observed that the presence of coding on the verb correlates with verb-initial or verb-final position in the clause. Indeed, as shown in the present work, inflectional coding is one means that may be used to code grammatical relations when linear order is limited to a single position (see below). Yet another function of inflection has to do with the coding of categoriality. The present work offers a new analysis of third-person singular agreement in the English present tense. We propose, contrary to both traditional and contemporary approaches, that this phenomenon is not triggered by the presence of a third-person subject but is instead a means of coding the categoriality of constituents in the present-tense clause. In this analysis, verb agreement in English is a coding means that is in complementary distribution with other coding means in the same domain, such as subject pronouns and forms of verbal inflection.

In Chapter 4 we discuss the formal properties, functions, and systems interaction of inflection. We illustrate two fundamental properties of inflectional coding: its potential richness as a coding means and the ways in which inflectional properties affect the forms of discourse. While this chapter is devoted to the formal and functional properties of inflectional coding, the pervasive effects of the presence of this coding means in a language make it crucial to the discussion in many other chapters.

5.5. Linear order

Both formal logic and many contemporary syntactic theories use linear order as a means of representing semantic or grammatical relations. For Chomsky, linear order has always served this function but with the tacit assumption that this is also the way languages code grammatical and semantic relations (cf. Chomsky 2000: 23 and n. 22). In the proposed framework, linear order is shown to be just one means of coding functions in various domains; it is explicitly not a means of putting words together or, in more sophisticated terms, of building linguistic constructions. The narrower term 'linear order' refers here to the order of morphemes within a construction. These morphemes may be bound or independent, i.e. separate words. In the latter case, linear order refers to the traditional term 'word order'. In the approach we propose, linear order is a coding means with a variety of functions within a language and across languages.

Although linear order has been the subject of numerous studies, and although linear order was for some time the fundamental way of representing linguistic structures in the generative tradition, there have been no studies examining the foundations of linear order coding. In Chapter 3 we discuss the prerequisites and constraints involved in coding through linear order and examine the implications of those constraints.

For linear order to be a viable coding means, the clause must contain an identifiable reference point with respect to which the linear order may be stated. If the subject and object are marked as such by morphological or phonological means, their identity does not have to be coded by linear order. However, one cannot state that coding through linear order involves simply putting A before B or B before A unless A has formal characteristics that distinguish it from B. It is these distinguishing characteristics that make A (or B) available as a reference point. If A and B do have different characteristics, then linear order is used to code the relationship between A and B rather than the categorial identity of A and B.

The reference point for linear coding could be a lexical category, such as a verb, or it could be a phrasal, clausal, or sentential boundary, provided these are overtly marked in the language. The choice of reference point depends to a large degree on the morphological characteristics of the language. There can be only one potential instantiation of the reference point per construction. The fact that there is often only one verb per clause explains why the verb serves as the reference point in so many languages from different language families.

We show in Chapter 3 that coding through linear order is inherently limited in that a maximum of two categories can be coded through linear order: one preceding the reference point and the other following the reference point. Consequently, a construction cannot have more than two instantiations of the item(s) whose function is coded by linear order.

Functions coded by linear order vary from language to language. In English, linear order in the formal domain of the clause is used to code the grammatical relations subject and object. Altering the linear order of (13) results in an ungrammatical utterance:

(21) 'I've told the truth.' (AP, June 23, 2000)
*I've the truth told.
*The truth, told I've.
*Told I've the truth.

While a clause with a fronted object, such as the following, is possible, these seem to occur mainly in linguistics textbooks:

(22) 'The truth, I've told.'

In Polish, linear order in the domain of the clause codes the speaker's assumptions about the hearer's state of knowledge with respect to the content of the clause, a domain sometimes called 'information structure'. Changing the word order in Polish results in a sentence that reflects a different set of anticipations about the hearer's reaction to the content. Putting the object before the verb places it in contrast with some other potential object(s):

VO order:

(23) Jak powiem **prawdę**, nie spodoba się to obywatelowi
when tell:FUT:1SG truth:ACC NEG please:PRF:3SG REFL DEM citizen:DAT
kapitanowi.
captain:DAT
'If I tell the truth, you, citizen captain, will not like it.' (Sources)

OV order, second clause:

(24) A oto jak wygląda prawda obiektywna.
CONJ DEM how appear truth:NOM objective
'That is what the objective truth looks like.'

OV order:

(25) Z mojego punktu widzenia **prawdę subiektywną**
from my point view:GEN truth:ACC subjective:ACC
zasugerował nam hipnotyzer.
suggest:PRF:PAST:3SG:M 1PL:DAT hypnotist
'From my point of view, the subjective truth was suggested to us by the hypnotist.' (Sources)

Interestingly, linear order presents a richer system of coding means in a language that also has inflectional means. This follows naturally from the fact that in a rich inflectional system the role of every element in the functional domain of the proposition is coded by inflection, leaving linear order available to code information structure or some other function. In the domain of information structure, the coding potential of linear order is much richer than that provided by a binary distinction between focus and topicalization. Consider the following sentence:

(26) Staszek odrzucił twoje nęcące propozycje.
Staszek reject:PAST:3M:SG 2SG:PL:ACC attractive:PL:ACC propositions
'Staszek rejected your attractive propositions.' (Sources)

The five components of this sentence may be ordered in 120 different ways (5 factorial, or $5 \times 4 \times 3 \times 2 \times 1$), giving potentially 120 different meanings. The actual functions of various word orders in Polish have yet to be described and we are not in position to list them here. One functional possibility offered by the availability of multiple linear orders is that of placing every noun phrase and prepositional phrase in the clause in contrastive focus:

(27) Ty mnie, na polskiej ziemi, polskiego słowa
2SG:NOM 1SG:ACC on Polish:ADJ:F soil Polish:ADJ:M:GEN word:GEN
zabronisz.
forbid:FUT:2SG
'Are you going to forbid me the use of a Polish word on Polish soil?' (Sources)

A more precise rendering of this example would be:

(28) You [of all people] are going to forbid me the use of a Polish [and not some other] word on Polish [and not some other] soil?'

Putting stress (loudness accompanied by a pause) on *mnie* 'me' in this sentence also puts *mnie* in focus, yielding the following meaning:

(29) You [of all people] are going to forbid me [of all people] the use of a Polish [and not some other] word on Polish [and not some other] soil?'

5.6. Phonology

The well-known functions of phonology include providing for the unique representation of morphemes and coding various types of modalities. To these we add the function, relatively neglected in the literature, of coding syntactic structures. As a case study, we examine the coding of phrase-internal and phrase-external positions in Mina, a Central Chadic language. The coding of these positions allows the hearer to decode the internal structure of a sequence of morphemes. Specifically, vowel retention codes phrase-final position while vowel deletion codes phrase-internal position. This distinction allows different phrasal organizations to code the difference between a fronted focused element and a fronted topicalized element as well as allowing clause-internal elements to be marked for focus. For example, retaining the final vowel of a morpheme preceding an adverb sets the adverb apart as a separate phrase and thereby marks it as focused:

(28) Sə lím-é [**gwáɮá mùmbùrkó**].
1SG see-GO elephant yesterday
'I saw an elephant, just yesterday.'

Deleting the final vowel of the preceding morpheme indicates that the adverb has the same information value as the other elements of the clause:

(29) Sə lím-é [**gwáɮ mùmbùrkó**].
1SG see-GO elephant yesterday
'I saw an elephant yesterday.'

6. Functional domains and subdomains

6.1. The theoretical foundation

The existence of functional domains is implicitly accepted in many theoretical frameworks, and some domains have been described in modern grammars of individual languages. When linguists talk about aspectual systems or tense systems, for example, they are talking about functional domains. The difficulty with functional domains is not that they are not recognized but that there is no rigorous methodology for determining which functional domains and subdomains exist in a language. In addition, a number of contemporary syntactic theories do not distinguish between the functional domain and the means of coding the domain. The categories AUX, COMP, INFL, CASE, as postulated at various times in the generative tradition, reflect a lack of distinction between means and functions, as do discussions implying that pronouns and agreement or AGR are functional domains. A clear understanding of the notion of functional domains and a clear distinction between the means of coding and the functional domains encoded will allow for a better understanding of the structure of language and of the synchronic and diachronic processes that operate in language.

Following Frajzyngier and Mycielski (1998), a functional domain D is defined as follows:

a. A functional domain D is a class of mutually exclusive types of expressions constructed by a set of specific means of coding M (D).
b. The types of expressions within the functional domain D have a specific pragmatic, semantic, or syntactic function in common.
c. A functional domain D is a class of types of expressions with a certain set of meanings D* such that D* is disjoint with E* for any functional domain E ≠ D of the same language.

Various systems interact in forming the subdomains of a given domain. A functional domain may include subdomains, which either form a nesting system or are disjoint. The description of a functional subdomain must include a statement of the larger functional domain of which it is a part. In the following figure, the largest rectangle represents a functional domain. Each rectangle within it represents a functional subdomain:

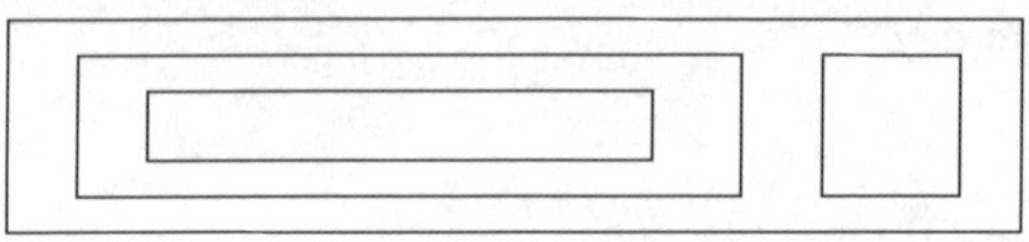

As proposed in Frajzyngier and Mycielski (1998), the core of the description of a grammar of a language L should consist of at least two components:

1. A list of functional domains D_1, D_2, . . . , defined by means of their sets of meanings $(D_1)^*$, $(D_2)^*$, . . . ;
2. Alternative descriptions of D_1, D_2, . . . , by the system of means M (D_1), M (D_2), . . . of coding used in D_1, D_2, . . . ;

6.2. Methodology for the discovery of functional domains

A study of the functions of a given coding means in a language typically proceeds as follows: The researcher gathers as many tokens of the given means as possible, produces a taxonomy of these functions, and attempts to discover what these functions have in common. The hard part of this procedure is to determine whether one is dealing with different functions or with several instantiations of the same function. Usually, this question is answered by means of some tacit and intuitive analysis of the real world described by the linguistic constructions in question.

This methodology, used in descriptions of individual languages and in cross-linguistic typological studies, can produce useful information for the study of grammaticalization, metaphorical extensions, and polysemy. When it comes to functional domains, however, the methodology may fail to recognize that various tokens of a given means in fact belong to different functional domains. Applying this methodology to the form 'that' in English, for example, will yield tokens of 'that' as deictic pronoun, determiner, remote anaphor, and complementizer. All of these functions are undoubtedly linked by some grammaticalization chain, but in the grammar of contemporary English these functions belong to two different functional domains, the first three to the domain of reference coding and the fourth to the domain of modality in embedded clauses (Frajzyngier 1995a).

A better method of establishing the functions of a linguistic form is to examine the relationship between that form and other forms within the language. If the forms, or coding means, are in complementary distribution, they probably code different subdomains or different functions of the same domain. Two formal means that code subdomains of the same functional domain cannot co-occur within the same syntactic unit. Two means that co-occur within the same utterance code different domains unless the two means are a complex means of coding a single domain. In short, one must look at the function of a given means in contrast with other means available in the language rather than simply listing the types of constructions in which the means in question can occur.

In Chapter 9, we use the proposed methodology to illustrate the difference between the assumption of a function and the discovery of a function. This is done by exploring the functions of the dative case in a number of languages. We demonstrate that the function of the dative case, examined in the context of other cases within the same system, is to code indirect affectedness and that this function subsumes the functions of benefactive and recipient. We demonstrate the dative case does not code a possessive function, as is claimed in König and Haspelmath (1998).

It cannot be assumed that morphemes with similar translations or similar positions in a grammatical paradigm code similar functions. Evidence is provided by pronouns in English and Polish. Pronouns in these languages are similar in that they code the features gender (for the third-person singular), number, and person, but they actually belong to different subdomains within the domain of reference. Pronouns in English code coreference when preceded by an antecedent having the same person, gender and number, while pronouns in Polish code switch reference with respect to the antecedent. Consider the third-person singular masculine pronoun in English:

1_1_0 <74 A> [@:] **he** ^should have had **his** . dissertation \/in#
1_1_0 <75 A> ((at the)) be^ginning of M\/ay# .(LLC)

The Polish equivalent of this utterance does not have the third-person subject pronoun:

(30) **Powinien** był ukończyć swoją dysertację na początku
should:3SG:M be:3SG:M finish his dissertation at beginning:LOC
maja.
May:GEN
'He should have finished his dissertation at the beginning of May.'

Adding a subject pronoun yields a very different meaning:

(31) **On** **powinien** był mieć swoją dysertację na początku
3SG:M should:3SG:M be:3SG:M have his dissertation at beginning:LOC
maja.
May:GEN
'**He** should have had his dissertation at the beginning of May [others may have had a different deadline].'

Compare also the following natural written discourse example from Polish, in which the first reference to the third-person masculine subject is through the pronoun *on*, while the second reference to the same subject has no pronoun. In the English equivalent, the third-person masculine pronoun must occur twice:

(32) Hela moja złota, **on** ma prawo być, nawet **powinien** być.
Hela my golden 3M:SG have right be even should:3SG:M be
'Hela, my love. He has the right to be. Even more, he should be!' (Sources)

Similarly, the first-person singular pronouns 'I' in English and *ja* in Polish do not have the same functions. Consider again the quote from the Associated Press:

(33) "I've told the truth." (AP, June 23, 2000)

This sentence must be translated into Polish without a pronoun:

(34) Prawdę powiedziałem. or Powiedziałem prawdę.
truth:ACC say:PAST:1SG:M say:PAST:1SG:M truth:ACC
'I told the truth.' 'I told the truth.'

Use of the first-person pronoun in the Polish sentence renders a very different meaning:

(35) Ja powiedziałem prawdę.
1SG say:PAST:1SG:M truth:ACC
'I have told the truth [others may have told lies].'

Thus, the function of the subject pronoun in Polish is quite different from the function of the subject pronoun in English (for a discussion of this and related phenomena, cf. Frajzyngier 1997b).

7. Systems interaction in the coding of functional domains

Systems interaction in the coding of functional domains follows from the definition of functional domains. Coding means within a given functional domain have complementary functions such that if function (F_1) is coded by one means (M_1), it is not also coded by another means (M_2) in the same functional domain in the same construction. If several coding means have functions within one functional domain, these means are in complementary distribution such that each means codes a different subdomain. Before we discuss the implications of and potential counterarguments to the notion of systems interaction, we illustrate the principle by showing interactions in two domains: the coding of adverbial phrases and the coding of grammatical relations.

Consider the interaction between lexical and syntactic means in the domain of adverbial phrases in English. Names of weeks are inherently adverbial and do not have to be preceded by a preposition:

1_5_0 <305 A> but ^if you worked :Saturday :mornings h\ere#

2_7_0 <869 C> ((the)) ^last 'time I went to 'work was :Monday n\ight# .

These items can be preceded by a preposition, a construction whose function may have to do with placing the adverb in focus:

(36) "On Monday [not some other day], I worked all morning"

(37) "Monday, I worked all morning" is not as readily accepted by native speakers as means of placing 'Monday' in focus

3_2_1 <181 A> ^come d\/own# .
3_2_1 <182 A> ^on !Monday 'go back :((Th\ursday)) night#
3_2_1 <183 A> something of ^th\at kind# .

Other adverbs have been lexicalized by adding a preposition to a noun, such as 'today' and 'tomorrow'. Adverbs so lexicalized do not require additional marking for the adverbial function:

1_10_0 <272 b> she tried to throw out establishment **today** —

5_12_0 <1055 b> ^well I have a !meeting **tomorrow** 'morning in{Golden Squ\are} :[?]in Nov\ello's# -

An expression that is not an inherent adverb of time must be marked by a preposition, e.g. 'in the evening', 'at night', 'within a week', or by some other means:

3_2_1 <365 (A> *[@:]* . and you're getting ^married **in** the :third week of : \August#

Another means of coding a noun as an adverb of time is to add a temporal adjective:

1_7_0 <5 A> and ^**last** night :after you'd g/one# -

One cannot predict *a priori* which means will interact in the coding of a given function. Consider the coding of grammatical relations in specific interrogative clauses in Gidar. Grammatical relations in the indicative clause are coded by the linear order Subject Verb Object. In a specific interrogative clause, the question word is fronted regardless of its grammatical role. The specific interrogative words *náwá* 'who' and *mə́* 'what' code a distinction between human and non-human participants but do not code grammatical roles, so these roles must be marked in some other way. This is done through the use of different third-person subject pronouns. Gidar has two third-person singular masculine and plural subject pronouns, *à* and *də̀*. If the third-person subject of the comment clause is marked by *à*, the argument represented by the question words *náwá* or *mə́* is interpreted as object (QS is a marker of the specific interrogative):

(38) Mə́ à-zə́m dì?
what 3M-eat QS
'What did he eat?'

M-yí à-ná dì?
what-COP 3M-say QS
'What did he say?'

If the third-person subject appears as *dә̀* rather than *à*, the question is about the subject of the clause:

(39) Mә́ **dә̀**-zә́m háy ná-w dì?
what 3M-eat corn GEN-1SG QS
'What ate my corn?' (upon seeing damaged corn in the field)

Mí **dә̀**-tóŋ dә̀ dá-k dì.
what:COP 3M-enter ASSC REM.DEM QS
'What (animal) has entered over there?'

The question words *náwá* 'who' and *mә́* 'what' in adjunct roles are coded by the appropriate prepositions:

(40) **Ví mì** kә̀-dà rg-á háy vá-n púm dә̀ púmmò dì.
for what 2SG-D.PROG thresh-OBJ corn DEF-M morning ASSC morning QS
'Why are you threshing this corn so early in the morning?'

Thus, the coding devices of subject pronouns and prepositions interact to code the role of the questioned argument.

We can now turn to the implications of and potential problems with the systems interaction principle. We are grateful to Edith Moravcsik for posing the challenging questions that led to the development of this section.

The principle of systems interaction, as formulated above, implies that within a given functional domain and a given construction there obtains a one-to-one relationship between a linguistic form and a function. Systems interaction excludes the possibility of having one function coded by different means within the same construction (redundancy), although, as we have shown above, disagreement among means coding overlapping functions is not allowed. The evidence for this constraint is provided in virtually every chapter of the present book. It has been claimed in the literature that the same function could be coded by different means in the same construction, an example being the co-occurrence of definite markers and proper nouns (Haspelmath 1999). But these are only apparent counterexamples. In languages in which such constructions are possible, the first task is to discover what the marker referred to as definite actually codes. In Mupun, a West Chadic language, the 'definite' marker codes previous mention. A noun that has been previously mentioned in discourse may be coded by a definite marker regardless of whether the noun is an ordinary noun, a proper name, or a toponym.

However, a single function may be coded by more than one means provided these means occur in different constructions. In fact, this is the very basis of systems interaction. For example, in Chapter 10 (locative predication) we show that in Mina (Central Chadic), if the locative function in a given construction is not coded by lexical means it is coded by grammatical means, which include a locative predicator for predicates and locative prepositions for nouns.

A single coding means may have more than one function only if each function belongs to a different functional domain. In the domain of a proposition, the phonological form *that* in English functions as a deictic noun. In the domain of reference it functions as a determiner. In the domain of modality it functions as a *de dicto* complementizer (cf. Frajzyngier 1992). Although *that* is polyfunctional in the language, it has only one function in each of the functional domains listed. Discussions of the functions of a given morpheme within a whole language rather than within a single functional domain are useful in providing preliminary data for the study of grammaticalization, but they are not particularly useful for the study of the functions of a given morpheme within various constructions. Such a study is meaningless unless one also studies other morphemes coding functions in the same domains.

The possibility of structural ambiguity, wherein one coding means has different functions within a single domain, is explicitly excluded by the principle of systems interaction. Non-structural ambiguity, such as that resulting from lexical polysemy, is possible, but this type of ambiguity does not affect the structure of the language.

8. Toward a new methodology in typology

Although the proposed framework is a methodology for the description of individual languages, it has considerable implications for linguistic typology. The Systems Interaction framework, unlike many contemporary theories, does not assume *a priori* the existence of any specific formal or functional categories, nor does it make use of the notion of prototypical grammatical categories. Instead, it proposes a methodology for discovering functional categories by examining all of the coding means available in the language and the relationships that obtain among them. The explanatory power of the framework lies in its ability to establish well-defined, language-specific formal and functional categories and to describe these categories in terms that facilitate cross-language comparisons. A further benefit of the approach is that it contributes to explaining the existence or non-existence in a language of one or another formal means, a phenomenon that any linguistic theory must address at one time or another.

Many current typological studies rely heavily on categories that are based, whether explicitly or not, on some notion of prototype. A study that starts with the question, 'How does language L code domain D?', is likely to garner all kinds of expressions, each of which may pertain to the function in question but which, taken together, do not necessarily form a functional domain. Such typological studies of reflexives, definiteness, passives, or nominal and clausal conjunctions start with a presumed prototypical function of reflexive, definite, passive, etc., and examine how such functions are coded and in what way languages depart from the assumed prototype.

We do not consider this method reliable, because quite often such studies are based on non-explicit analyses of functions drawn from a very limited number of languages. Postulated prototypical grammatical categories are inevitably based on the languages with which the linguist is most familiar. In the past, prototypical functional categories were based on Latin and Greek. In contemporary approaches, prototypical categories are drawn from English, a handful of other Western Indo-European languages, and Japanese (notably for the category 'topic'). Languages from other parts of the world are used as sources only if the relevant prototypical function does not occur in English.

The extension of the notion of prototype to cross-linguistic typology of grammatical categories has several drawbacks. First, comparison across languages is based on some perceived semantic similarity between two or more forms. However, there is no way of knowing whether this semantic overlap represents the central function of these forms or whether it is only marginal. As an illustration, consider the traditional assumption that reflexive forms code coreferentiality. The fallacy of this approach is demonstrated in Frajzyngier (1999), where it is shown that the fundamental function of reflexive forms in a number of languages is to code the point of view of the subject rather than to code coreferentiality. An analysis based on the assumption that the central function of reflexive markers is to code coreferentiality would overlook this insight.

The traditional use of the prototype in typology is illustrated by the following fragment from Lyons (1999):

> Noun phrases with 'the' and 'a' and their semantic equivalents (or near equivalents) in other languages can be thought of as the basic instantiations of definite and indefinite noun phrases, in that the definiteness or indefiniteness stems from the

> presence of the article, which has as its essential semantic function to express this category. (Lyons 1999: 2).

This definition does not provide a language-independent definition of definiteness. Instead, it assumes that there is a prototypical function of definiteness and a prototypical means of coding this function. Lyons maintains this approach even though he acknowledges:

> [T]hat articles can encode more than definiteness or indefiniteness, and that they have been argued to have quite different principal function, at least in some languages. (Lyons 1999: 2).

Such approaches assume that the essential function of a form is that which has been established for the language with which the researcher is most familiar, that this function is somehow prototypical, and that other functions of the form are less prototypical. This approach is useful for picking up similarities among languages, but it has the crucial side effect of ignoring the actual range of functions of a given form within the grammatical system of its own language. Moreover, this notion of prototype is often based on intuition rather than on an analysis of individual languages.

There is a more reliable, though more difficult, way to conduct typological research. A methodology that brings with it no assumptions about the existence of prototypical categories must discover, language by language, what functional domains and subdomains actually exist across languages. Such a methodology does not attempt to extend to one language either the prototypical or the actual functions of a category found in another language; instead, it leaves open the possibility that languages may have different categories and that these categories may have different boundaries even if the categories are similar in some respects.

The starting point in a typology of this kind will be a statement about the functional domains that have been grammaticalized in the languages in question. These domains could include grammatical relations, semantic relations within a clause, functional domains encoded in the noun phrase, and many others. The list of functional domains will be long, but it will be finite for each language. Once these lists have been prepared, the possibilities for typological research are many. The next step might be to compare the internal structure of a given domain across languages. In Chapter 11, we illustrate the application of this methodology to the functional domain of reference. We demonstrate that some languages (e.g. Gidar) have separate subdomains of previously mentioned and 'known' (cf. Ebert 1971 on Frisian), while other languages (e.g. English) distinguish only between the definite and the indefinite. Still other languages (e.g. Mina) code remote previous mention, the domain of known referent, the domain of deduced referent, and the domain of deixis. Such findings clearly provide interesting and useful restraints on the types of typological generalizations that can be made concerning the domain of reference across languages.

9. Conclusions

Language is a complex organism consisting of forms that interact with one another in the coding of various functions. The ability to explain these interactions contributes greatly to our ability to explain why a language is as it is; in other words, why it has certain kind of constructions and not others. The Systems Interaction approach is a methodology for studying these interactions. In addition to providing a framework for describing individual languages, Systems Interaction lays the foundation for a new direction in typology. Research within the Systems Interaction framework shows that the number and type of functions encoded by the grammatical system of a language is highly dependent on the coding means available within the language, an insight that will lead to the discovery of new cross-linguistic generalizations.

Our study contributes new analyses of specific problems in individual languages, e.g.:

- the function of third-person agreement in English;
- constraints on and properties of ditransitive verbs in English;
- the function of nasal alternates in Polish pronouns;
- the function of final vowel deletion in Chadic languages;
- the function of consonant mutation in Welsh;
- the functions of agreement on prepositions and complementizers in Chadic languages;
- the functions of genitive case in nominative-accusative languages;
- non-referential functions of the definite article in English;
- the modal functions of subject-to-object raising in English and other languages;
- the functions of dative case in Polish.

Our study also presents new cross-linguistic analyses of theoretical issues, including:

- a new interpretation of phenomena attributed to agreement;

- a new interpretation of phenomena attributed to government;
- a principle regarding 'disagreement';
- prerequisites for and implications of linear order coding;
- defining characteristics of lexical categories;
- a methodology for discovering and demonstrating the functions of linguistic forms.

CHAPTER 2

Interaction of the lexicon with other coding means

1. Introduction

The aim of the present chapter is to show that the existence of lexical categories and subcategories (as opposed to the existence of individual lexical items) is motivated by the internal organization of a language rather than by supposed universal cognitive requirements. In this model, the defining characteristics of lexical categories and subcategories are based on the grammatical systems of individual languages. Accordingly, languages with similar grammatical systems will have similar lexical categories. While this approach does not preclude cross-linguistic typology, it does require that such a typology be based on language-specific characteristics rather than on *a priori* assumptions about the existence and nature of lexical categories.

The first part of the chapter proposes a model of lexicalization that provides language-independent criteria for determining what lexical categories exist in a language. The proposed model is open-ended and allows for the possibility that a language may have lexical categories other than nouns, verbs, adjectives, adverbs, and adpositions. The ideophones found in African and Asian languages are one such example (cf. Voeltz and Kilian-Hatz 2001). Another example is the category of local predicator, as described in Chapter 10. The model also allows each lexical category in a language to be described independently of all other categories within the language. The proposed approach allows us to treat lexical categories (e.g. nouns, verbs, adjectives, and adverbs) and lexical subcategories in a unified fashion. A lexical subcategory is a member of a larger lexical category, such as noun or verb, that is marked differently from other members of the lexical category by having different syntactic or morphological properties. Any lexical category may contain subcategories that code specific semantic functions or that allow for the formation and functioning of other coding means. We illustrate the proposed model with an examination of the category adjective in Mupun, a West Chadic language.

The second part of this chapter illustrates how the methodology may lead to the discovery of a lexical subcategory, in this case the subcategory of inherently locative nouns in Gidar.

2. Relationship of the proposed approach to some current approaches

In traditional approaches, lexical categories were described in terms of their relationship to reality or to the external world. This approach has long been abandoned, although traces of it linger in some current works, especially those that invoke cognitive explanations for linguistic categories. In the discourse approach, as advocated by Hopper and Thompson (1984) and Thompson (1988), lexical categories are determined by their role in discourse. This approach also is demonstrably not sufficient, as shown in Frajzyngier (1985a, 1986). The basis of our argument against the discourse approach is that in the same discourse conditions and in the same types of constructions, some lexical categories may be used and others may not. Whether or not a lexical item may be used depends solely on the inherent properties of the lexical item, not on discourse conditions. In counterexpectation predications in Polish, for example, there is a rule that the predicate must be at least as predicative as the subject. The hierarchy of predication is Noun<Adjective<Verb. Here are examples of counterexpectation predications in which the subject and the predicate have the same inherent predicativity. In the first example the predicate is a pronoun, in the second a noun, and in the third an adjective:

(1) Kto wy, a kto my....
who 2PL CONJ who 1PL
'Who are you and who are we?' (Sources)

(2) Jestem tylko zwykłą kobietą, a on pisarz, literat.
be:1SG only ordinary woman CONJ 3M writer man of letters
'I am just an ordinary woman. But he is a writer, a man of letters.' (Sources)

(3) Stary a głupi.
old CONJ silly
'He is old and yet he is silly.'

One can have a noun in the subject function and an adjective or a verb in the predicate function, since both are more predicative than the subject:

(4) Profesor a głupi.
professor CONJ silly
'He is a professor and yet he is silly.'

(5) Tancerz a śpiewa.
dancer CONJ sing
'He is a dancer and yet he sings.'

One cannot, however, reverse the order of the constituents, since the subject would then be more predicative than the predicate:

(6) *Śpiewa a tancerz.
sing CONJ dancer
'He sings and yet he is a dancer.'

(7) *Głupi a profesor.
stupid CONJ professor
'He is stupid and yet he is a professor.'

Hengeveld (1992) claims that lexical categories are determined by the types of constructions in which they occur, but we demonstrate here that the inherent properties of lexical categories affect the forms of constructions coding various functional domains. As an illustration, consider the modifying function in a language. If the modifier is an inherent adjective, the modifying construction will have a different structure from the one in which the modifier is not an inherent adjective. Compare modifying constructions in English:

(8) a new house
*a built house
cf. a house which is built

In agreement with Croft (2000:86) we take '[lexical] syntactic categories as being language specific'. However, Croft states that:

> [W]e discard the assumption that syntactic structures are made up of atomic primitives (language-universal or language-particular). Constructions, not categories and relations, are the basic, primitive units of syntactic representation. The categories and relations found in constructions are derivative. (Croft 2001:45–6)

In contrast, we propose that lexical categories are indeed primitive rather than derived means of coding, in the same sense in which linear order, morphology, and phonology are primitive coding means.

In what follows we rely extensively on the contrast between the lexicalization and the grammaticalization of a function. The term 'lexicalization' means that a function has been encoded in lexical form (cf. Frajzyngier 1986, 1988 for specific studies). The term 'grammaticalization' means that a function has been encoded in the grammatical system through phonological, morphological, linear order or other means. The general principle is that if a function F has been lexicalized, no grammatical means is used to code F when the lexical form coding F is used. If a lexical item is used in a function other than that for which it has been lexicalized within a given functional domain, special morphological and/or syntactic means must be used to code the function of that item. For example, nouns in Polish and Amharic (Ethio-Semitic) can be used as predicates if appropriate morphemes are added. One means of deriving verbs from nouns is to add so-called 'reflexive' markers:

(9) uśmiech 'smile' uśmiechać się 'to smile'
rumieniec 'blush' rumienić się 'to blush'
wstyd 'shame' wstydzić się 'be ashamed' (Polish)

(10) raqut 'nakedness' tä-raqqʷätä 'be naked'
REFL-be naked
šärik 'partner' (Arabic) tä-šärräkä 'become a partner'
REFL-be partner
(Amharic, Leslau 1995:469)

The model of lexicalization proposed below eliminates the need to postulate that a lexical category can represent the lexicalization of several functions, as proposed in Hengeveld (1992). The use of a lexical category in a functional domain for which it has not been lexicalized, e.g. the use of an adjective in a predicative function, does not necessarily indicate that the adjective has been lexicalized as both modifier and predicate, but rather that the role of the adjective in the predicative construction is identified by some other means.

3. Outline of the model of lexicalization

Lexicalization is the encoding in a lexical form of one or both of the following:

a. a function in some functional domain grammaticalized in the language. Typical functional domains include forming a proposition, modifying nouns,

coding modality, locative predication (cf. Chapter 10), equational predication, reference system, and many others;
b. a segment of the speaker's cognitive universe (as opposed to some part of the real world). This corresponds to traditional notions of reference.

If the domain (a) pertains to a function within a proposition, simultaneous lexicalization in the domains (a) and (b) results in the categories noun and verb. There are only two possible functions within a proposition, namely argument and predicate. The category 'noun' represents the lexicalization of the function of argument within a proposition (for a similar distinction, cf. Lazard 1999). The specific role of the argument in the proposition, i.e. its role with respect to the verb or to other arguments, is coded by grammatical means such as linear order, inflection, adpositions, agreement, serial verb constructions, and others. The category 'verb' represents the lexicalization of the function of predicate within a proposition. If a lexical item represents the lexicalization of the function of predicate, no other means is needed to code the function of predicate in a predicative construction (Frajzyngier 1986; Hengeveld 1992).

If the domain (a) pertains to modifying or narrowing the scope of a noun, simultaneous lexicalization in the domains (a) and (b) results in the category adjective. If the domain (a) pertains to the function of modifying the verb, simultaneous lexicalization in the domains (a) and (b) results in the category adverb. If the domain (a) pertains to the function of modifying a constituent of a proposition but is not specific as to the category being modified, it may be that the language has only one category of modifier. This is the case in a number of Chadic languages. In some languages the function of modifier may not have been lexicalized at all, in which case the language will have no adjectives or adverbs. In such a language one would expect to find syntactic constructions whose function is to code the modification of nouns and verbs.

Lexical items that encode the domain (a) but do not encode elements from the domain (b) belong to the closed set of free grammatical morphemes. Some languages have some adpositions that have no functions in domain (b), while other adpositions carry functions in both domains. These portmanteau morphemes, like the English prepositions *in*, *at*, *to* and *from*, code a locative function (domain (a)) as well as a certain spatial configuration (domain (b)). Mina (Central Chadic) is a language in which the locative function and the spatial configuration are coded by different markers. In the following example, the preposition *nə̀* codes the locative function of the complement and the form *mə̀* 'mouth' codes the spatial configuration:

(11) Yàɗírì ɮéɮé ɗáhà í ndí ɮə̀k á nə̀ mə̀ kúlmbòn-yíì.
millet long time ago exist 3PL HAB plant PRED PREP mouth black ant-PL
'A long time ago they used to plant millet around the black ants' nests.'

The fact that a language codes the functional domain of the proposition does not necessarily mean that the language has lexicalized the categories noun and verb. It is theoretically possible to have a language in which no propositional or modifying function has been encoded in lexical items. Words in such a language would encode only bundles of semantic properties; there would be no nouns, verbs, adjectives, or other lexical categories (cf. Gil 1994b). It is also possible to have a language where the category of a lexical item is coded by the form of the construction (Mandarin) or by the addition of derivational or inflectional morphemes. The Semitic verbal root is an example of the encoding of bundles of semantic features through such means. Through various morphological means, these roots can be made into either verbs or nouns. From a given root may be derived not only verb forms coding person, number, tense, aspect, mood, voice, and manner of the event, but also nouns describing the agent of the event, the type of action, and the instrument for the action. In some languages, derivational affixes to the verbal root may even code the place of the event. Thus, from the root *ngr* 'speak' in Amharic can be derived the following nominal forms, some by way of intermediary verbal forms:

(12) nägari 'speaker, announcer' (Cohen 1970: 193)
mängär 'the fact of speaking, announcing' (Cohen 1970: 194)
mängäriya 'what serves to say, announce' (Cohen 1970: 196)
annägagär 'the manner of speaking' (Cohen 1970: 232)

The use of the French suffix *-er* allows a verb to be derived from virtually any noun:

(13) Nous étions en train de **saucissoner**, et notre visiteur . . .
1PL be:1PL PREP PROG PREP sausage:V CONJ 1PL visitor
'We were having a meal of sausages, and our visitor . . .' (Gary 1980: 73)

In English, nouns, verbs, and adjectives are not phonologically marked for their categoriality. Consequently, adding morphological or syntactic marking characteristic of the category 'verb' to a noun allows the noun to be used freely as a predicate:

(14) to chair a meeting, to table an issue, to roof a house, to wall in the garden, to floor one's rival, to carpet the room, to drape the window, to room with a friend, to coffee with a friend.

By the same token, many English verbs can be used as nouns with the addition of the nominal plural suffix *-s*, e.g. '[many] drinks/breaks/falls/runs' and 'Good eats!' (sign on a restaurant in Estes Park, Colorado, observed in the early 1970s).

Even an adjective in English can be used as a predicate in a verbal clause, provided its categoriality is signaled by another element in the clause (here, the auxiliary 'could'):

(15) That guy couldn't **strong** his way out of a wet paper bag.
(Western U.S. colloquialism)

The coding of the categoriality of lexical items, as illustrated above for Polish, Amharic, and English, follows the requirements of the principle of functional transparency. The use of a lexical item without some means — inherent, syntactic or morphological — of coding its categoriality would leave the hearer in the dark as to what category the lexical item represented. If the inherent categoriality of the lexical item conflicts with the item's function in the clause, other syntactic or morphological coding means must be deployed to indicate the categoriality of the item in that clause. In Section 4 we show that the lexicalization of a function determines the forms of the constructions in which that lexical item occurs. In this way, we demonstrate the interaction of the lexicon with other coding means in the language.

4. Lexicalization of adjectives in Mupun

The purpose of the present section is to demonstrate that: (a) a lexical category displays its defining properties in the functions for which it has been lexicalized; (b) the lexicalization of a functional domain affects the forms of constructions serving that domain; and (c) the same inflectional morphology can code different functions when applied to different lexical categories. We also show that while two lexical categories may have the same formal properties in certain constructions, probably as a result of the historical process of lexicalization, this assignment of formal properties is unrelated to the functions of the two categories. Thus, morphological properties do not reliably indicate the categoriality of an item.

We base our discussion on the category adjective for two reasons: First, some linguistic theories claim adjectives as a major lexical category; and second, the characterization of this category has been controversial (Dixon 1977; Thompson 1988; Rijkhof 2002; Bhat 1994; Stassen 1997). We show that in Mupun (West Chadic), though the category adjective shares a number of formal characteristics with the category verb, the adjective is nevertheless a distinct lexical category. We also show that the defining properties of the category adjective are displayed when the adjective is used in the function for which it has been lexicalized, namely the modifying function. We show how these properties affect the forms of constructions in which adjectives occur, and we show how the functions of inflectional morphology differ when applied to the category adjective or to other lexical categories.

4.1. Similarities between adjectives and verbs

In Mupun, the category adjective shares with the category verb the property of serving as a predicate without any additional coding. When the subject of the clause is pronominal, the form of the pronoun preceding the adjective is the same as the form of the pronoun preceding a verb:

(16) a. n-ɓál 'I am strong.'
1SG-strong
n-ráp 'I am dirty.'
n-tə́p 'I am black.'
Cf.: b. n-saam 'I slept.'

Like verbs, adjectives follow the subject, take subject pronouns, and require no additional syntactic or morphological coding:

(17) Mu ɓal
1PL strong
'We are strong.'

In contrast, pronominal subjects in equational clauses with nominal predicates have a different, 'independent' form:

(18) An a siar dacya.
1SG COP friend Dacya
'I am a friend of Dacya.'

Like verbs, adjectives do not allow the use of the copula in the predicative construction (the ungrammatical example below uses the first-person independent pronoun *mun* that is required in an equational clause):

(19) *Mun **a** ɓal
1PL COP strong
for 'We are strong.'

In contrast, a noun in the predicative construction must be preceded by the copula *a*:

(20) Mun **a** nen kamkam.
1SG COP people teach
'We are teachers.'

(21) Wur **a** mis ɗə lee.
3M COP man REL little
'He is [considered] to be half a man.'

Like verbs, and unlike nouns, an adjective can be preceded by an auxiliary coding quantification:

(22) Lu wur **jar** kat.
place 3M be in excess small
'His place is very small.'

Wa **jar** seen.
3F be in excess wise
'She is very wise.'

Compare the use of the same auxiliary before a verb:

(23) Get n-**jar** n-siwa mwes.
PAST 1SG-in excess 1SG-drink beer
'I used to drink a lot in the past.'

Like verbs and unlike nouns, adjectives can be followed by quantifying adverbs and adverbs coding intensity:

(24) Wa seen **ɗes**.
3F wise very
'She is very wise.'

(25) Wa se dem sə **ɗɪal** **ɗak aŋ**.
3F depart go DEM wastefully like that
'She will go without progeny.'

Like verbs, adjectives can be reduplicated to derive adverbs. From the verb *siwal* 'to pain' may be derived the adverb *siwalsiwal* 'painfully', while from the adjective *bīs* 'bad' may be derived the adverb *bīsbīs* 'bad(ly)'; from the adjective *rét* 'nice' comes the adverb *rərét* 'well', from *lá* 'loud' the adverb *làlá* 'loudly', and from the adjective *zùum* 'be cold' the adverb *zumzuum* 'slowly':

(26) Mo muan **zumzuum**.
3PL walk slowly
'They walked slowly.'

The similarities between adjectives and verbs indicate that adjectives have been lexicalized like verbs when it comes to the predicative function. However, it is the modifying function, not the predicative function, that is the defining function of the category. By showing that adjectives and verbs behave differently in modifying constructions, we demonstrate below that adjectives form a lexical class distinct from verbs.

4.2. Adjectives in the modifying function

The modifying construction consists of a noun followed by the relative marker *də* or *de* and then by an adjective:

(27) nhək ɗe toon
stone REL heavy
'a heavy stone'

yoom ɗe ɓal
wood REL hard
'a hard wood'

fuan ɗə ɗes
rain REL big
'a heavy rain'

lusim ɗə ɓial
leopard REL dangerous
'a dangerous leopard'

zuul ɗə wuraŋ
mountain REL tall
'a tall mountain'

Yil ɗə get kə waa ji.
world REL past COMPL return come
'The world of the past has returned.'

Since *ɗə* is the relative marker, it might be supposed that the attributive construction with an adjective is a relative clause. If this were so, it would support the argument that adjectives are verbs. However, modifying constructions like those above are distinct from relative clauses in that modifying constructions with adjectives do not have subjects. Relative clauses, in contrast, must have subjects (the subject of the relative clause is in bold):

(28) Ba n-dem ngwe ɗe **wu** cii kàs.
NEG 1SG-like man REL 3M refuse NEG
'I do not like a man who refuses.'

N-dem ngwe ɗe **wu** cii.
1SG-like man REL 3M refuse
'I like a man who refuses.'

The modifying construction with an adjective is thus distinct from the relative clause involving a verb, and adjectives thus behave differently from verbs with respect to the modifying function. Since the defining criterion for adjectives is their behavior in the modifying function, adjectives constitute a lexical category distinct from verbs.

4.3. Same morphological process, different functions: the reduplication of verbs and adjectives

In this section we show that the same morphological process has different functions when applied to different lexical categories. These differences result from differences in the functional domains that have been lexicalized: in this instance, the propositional function for verbs and the modifying function for adjectives. This is evidence that morphological properties should not always be taken as indicators of the categoriality of a lexical item.

4.3.1. Reduplication of verbs

Most verbs in Mupun can be completely or partially reduplicated to derive nouns. A reduplicated verb can be followed by a possessive pronoun:

(29) Ba n-dem **sese** **wur** kas.
NEG 1SG-like eating 3SG NEG
'I don't like his eating.' (not 'I don't like eating him.')

In predicative constructions, the reduplicated verb behaves like a noun and must be preceded by the copula *a*:

(30) a. Mo **a** **popoor.**
3PL COP spread
'They are spread.' (*pōor* 'to spread')
b. Mo **a** **fifii.**
3PL COP dry
'They are dry.' (fíi 'to dry')

The reduplicated verb thus behaves like a noun in predicative and possessive constructions.

4.3.2. Reduplication of adjectives

Adjectives also can undergo complete or partial reduplication, but the function of reduplicated adjectives differs from that of reduplicated verbs in several respects. We have shown that reduplicated verbs differ from simple verbs in their propositional and predicative functions. Reduplicated adjectives, in contrast, retain their modifying function but differ from simple adjectives in the coding of number. Complete reduplication of the adjective encodes plurality of the modified noun:

(31)

Singular	*Plural*	
ɗík	ɗíkɗík	'different'
ɓál	ɓálɓál	'strong'
sìwál	sìwálsìwál	'long'
bís	bísbís	'bad'

(32) a. nen ɗə **ɓalɓal** mo
men REL strong PL
'strong men'

Cf. b. ngo ɗə **ɓal**
man REL strong
'a strong man'

In Mupun, reduplicating the first consonant of an adjective and inserting a schwa produces an intensive form of the adjective. Thus, the reduplicated form of the adjective X produces the meaning 'very X':

(33)	*Simple*	*Reduplicated*	*Gloss*
	tár	tə̀tár	'very mad'
	rét	rə̀rét	'good
	móol	mə̀móol	'thick'
	séen	sə̀séen	'clever, wise'

The complete reduplication of adjectives in Mupun is formally similar to the reduplication of verbs in Mupun and functionally similar to the reduplication of verbs in some other Chadic languages, though not in Mupun. In some languages the reduplicated verb codes plurality of the intransitive subject or the transitive object (Frajzyngier 1977, 1985b, 1997a; Newman 1990); in others it codes assertive focus (Mandara; cf. Frajzyngier to appear); and in others it codes perfective aspect (Hdi; Frajzyngier with Shay 2002). Reduplicated adjectives in Mupun also share with reduplicated verbs in some other Chadic languages the function of coding the frequentative manner and the plurality of the event (cf. Frajzyngier 1965, 1977; Newman 1990).

4.3.3. *Reduplicated adjectives in the predicative function*

Reduplicated adjectives in Mupun have an important syntactic property that sets them apart from the simple form: A clause with a reduplicated adjective in the predicative function must have the copula *a*, while a clause with a simple adjective in this function cannot have a copula. Thus, in the predicative function the reduplicated form of the adjective shares a nominal characteristic with the reduplicated form of the verb. However, unlike the reduplicated form of the verb, the reduplicated form of the adjective in the predicative function also must be preceded by the relative marker *ɗe*. Recall that the simple, i.e. non-reduplicated, adjective in the predicative function occurs without the relative marker.

Reduplicated form:

(34) a. Kam nə **a** **ɗə** məmool.
stick DEF COP REL thick
'The stick is very thick.'

Cf. the simple form:

b. Kam nə mool.
stick DEF thick
'The stick is thick.'

(35) a. War a ɗe səseen.
3F COP REL wise
'She is very wise.'

Cf. the simple form:

b. War seen
3F wise
'She is wise.'

Omitting the relative marker, the copula, or both results in an ungrammatical construction:

(36) a. *War a səseen.
3F COP wise
for 'She is very wise.'
b. *War səseen.
3F wise
for 'She is very wise.'
c. *War ɗe səseen.
3F REL wise
for 'She is very wise.'

The reduplicated form of the adjective does not behave syntactically like a noun because a noun cannot be preceded by the relative marker in the predicative function:

(37) a. *Wur a ɗə ngwa.
3M COP REL Hausa
for 'He is a Hausa man.'

Cf. b. Wur a ngwa.
3M COP Hausa
'He is a Hausa man.'

Reduplicated adjectives thus share some properties with reduplicated verbs, but not in the predicative function.

4.4. Conjunction of adjectives

The conjoined adjective construction in Mupun provides further evidence that the inherent properties of lexical items determine the forms of constructions coding a given function. Adjectives, like nouns, can be conjoined by the conjunction *kə̀*.

(38) Mò wùráŋ **kə́** ɓál.
3PL tall CONJ strong
'They are tall and strong.'

Compare conjoined nouns:

(39) Ám **kə̀** mwés.
water CONJ beer
'water and beer'

Except in rare instances, verbs cannot be conjoined by *kə́*:

(40) *Mò yól kə́ sèét.
3PL get up CONJ go
for 'They got up and went away.'

*mò táŋ kə́ rán
3PL read CONJ write
for 'They read and wrote something.'

Verbs may co-occur without a conjunction, forming a serial verb construction:

(41) Mò yól sèét.
3PL get up go
'They got up and went.'

A sequence of two adjectives without a conjunction is ungrammatical:

(42) *Mò wùráŋ ɓál.
3PL tall strong
for 'They are tall and strong.'

While two verbs in sequence represent sequential events, states, etc., two adjectives in sequence cannot represent sequential properties of the subject. Instead, the construction Adjective CONJ Adjective, like the construction NP CONJ NP, codes the conjoining of different elements of a set.

5. Relationship between nouns, verbs, and adjectives

We can now return to the problem of the relationships among the three lexical categories usually referred to as 'major'. The existence of such a relationship is implied by both formal and functional theories. In formal theories, this relationship is implied through the use of [N] and [V] feature notation. In functional theories, in particular in the studies of Givón (1984) and Thompson (1988), adjectives are said to share either semantic or discourse characteristics with nouns and verbs, and these characteristics are taken to determine the syntactic properties of the categories.

The present study has shown that nouns and verbs constitute a single group, in that both are products of lexicalization in the domain of the proposition, in which nouns have lexicalized the function of argument and verbs have lexicalized the function of predicate. Adjectives, on the other hand, are products of lexicalization in the domain of modification, where they have the attributive function. It is natural that the features lexicalized in adjectives include those of property concepts.

There remains the question of the relationships among the syntactic, semantic, and discourse functions of lexical categories. In the literature, the question has often been posed whether any of these categories is primary, i.e. determines most of the properties of the lexical item. Dixon (1977) argues for the primacy of semantic characteristics, as does Givón (1984), though the semantic characteristics proposed therein are different from those proposed by Dixon. Hopper and Thompson (1984, 1985) and Thompson (1988) argue for the primacy of discourse characteristics as determining factors for lexical categories. The discussion in this chapter has demonstrated that the lexicalization of a function within a larger construction is responsible for the existence of the lexical categories noun, verb, and adjective, as well as that of some conjunctions and perhaps other categories.

6. An illustration of lexical subcategorization

Any lexical category, as defined within the proposed approach, may have any number of subcategories. The category verb, for example, may contain subclasses of verbs representing specific types of events or states. A group of verbs represents a lexical subcategory if these verbs have common syntactic properties not shared by other verbs. Ditransitive verbs in English, such as 'give' and 'tell', represent such a subclass. Systems of nominal classification, including gender systems, represent another type of lexical subcategorization, one of whose functions is to enable the existence of a rich system of reference coding (see below).

In some languages, locative verbs and locative nouns represent lexical subclasses. The fact that the feature 'locative' may be lexicalized within the lexical category verb, within the category noun, or not lexicalized as a subcategory at all, is evidence against the argument that the coding of a fragment of reality imposes categoriality on a lexical item. Further evidence against this argument is provided by the fact that nouns having the same referent behave differently in different languages. The model of subcategorization is illustrated on Gidar (Central Chadic).

A locative predication consists of a predicate and a locative complement, which may be an argument or an adjunct. In English, all locative adjuncts of verbs of movement must be coded by a preposition such as 'to', 'from', etc. A handful of exceptions, including the noun 'home' and nouns referring to compass points such as 'east', 'north', 'west', 'south', can be used with a verb of movement and without a preposition, indicating that these nouns are inherently locative:

(43) He went **home** early.

In Gidar as in English, locative predication requires that the complement of the predication be either inherently locative or overtly marked by one or more locative markers. The feature 'inherently locative' is assigned by the language rather than by nature, much as masculine and feminine genders are assigned in German, Polish, or Russian. Place names in Gidar are inherently locative, as are the nouns *wálàŋlà* 'village' and *wrá* 'bush'. If a noun is [+locative], it is marked by a preposition alone when occurring in a locative predication. The preposition codes a specific spatial orientation:

(44) Và-skà ná ɗə́f tà-y á **wálàŋglà** ...
DEF-DEM COMP man PROG-3M:COP PREP village
'Once there was a man in a village ...'

(45) Mə̨̀lìy à-zə́-k á **wrá.**
chief 3M-get lost-PRF PREP bush
'The chief got lost in the bush.'

(46) À-dé-k sə́ **fígíl.**
3M-go:VENT-PRF from Figuil
'He came from Figuil.'

If a noun in a locative predication is not inherently locative it must be marked as a locative argument or adjunct by special markers. One marker that codes a complement as locative is the noun *zà* 'side'. A noun so marked may occur with a variety of locative prepositions:

(47) **Wín à-lə́-k á zà àfə́-ní ...**
child 3M-go-PRF PREP side father-3M
'The child went to his father ....'

(48) **Mə̧̀lìy à-hlə́nə̀-k á zà sómbò.**
chief 3M-send-PRF PREP side Sombo
'The chief sent to Sombo.'

(49) **Kà ə́smáɗ sə́ zà sómbò.**
PURP disappear surreptitiously PREP side Sombo
'In order to disappear from the sight of Sombo.'

(50) **À-l-k á zà mə̧̀lìy.**
3M-go PREP side chief
'He went to the chief.'

Whether a noun in Gidar is inherently locative or not cannot be predicted on the basis of knowledge of the external universe. For example, the noun *gènzék* 'shed', unlike 'village' and 'bush', is not inherently locative, as evidenced by the fact that it requires the marker *zà*:

(51) **À-l-k á zà gènzék.**
3M-go-PRF PREP side shed
'He went to a shed.'

Omitting the marker *zà* results in an ungrammatical expression:

(52) *À-l-k á gènzék.
3M-go-PRF PREP shed
for 'He went to a shed.'

Nouns that are [+human] are inherently non-locative. If the source or goal in a locative predication is a [+human] noun and the goal is the proper or permanent location of that noun, the locative complement is marked by the genitive preposition *ná* and the postposition *dà*:

(53) **À-mbàtə̀k á ná bàyná-n dà.**
3M-go PREP GEN friend-3M LOC
'He went to his friend's [place].'

A pronominal locative complement is coded by a possessive pronoun suffixed to the marker *ná*:

(54) À-dé-k **sə́ ná-w dà.**
3M-go:VENT-PRF from GEN-1SG LOC
'He came from me.'

If the noun representing the locative source of an object is inherently human, the source must be marked by the noun *và* 'hand':

(55) Kə̀zá tə̀-lbàh-ə́-k **sə́ và mə́lmù-kò.**
Kiza 3F-buy-3M-PRF from hand brother-2SG
'Kiza bought it from your brother.'

(56) Də́ lbà wàhlì sə́ và-w ɓà.
3M buy cow PREP hand-1SG NEG
'He did not buy a cow from me.'

The class of inherently locative nouns in Gidar is much larger than that in English, and the two classes do not necessarily overlap. This supports the contention that the lexicalization of a piece of reality does not determine the categorical status of a lexical item. Thus 'shed' and 'village', neither of which is inherently locative in English, belong to two different subclasses in Gidar. Because the proposed model of lexicalization is language-independent, it allows for the description of lexical subclasses independent of the characteristics of other categories or subcategories in the language.

7. Conclusions

In this chapter we have proposed a model providing for the language-independent characterization of lexical categories. The model allows each lexical category or subcategory to be characterized independently of all other lexical categories in the language. We have shown that the encoding of a given semantic feature, or the presence of a given morphological process, does not imply a particular lexical categorization. Discourse structure also has no bearing on the lexicalization of the categories noun, verb, or adjective. The proposed method provides the foundation for a typology based on functional similarities among lexical categories whose existence can be empirically established through an examination of the behavior of specific lexical items in specific constructions.

Lexical items interact with the grammatical system in the following way: If a certain bundle of semantic features has been lexicalized as a certain category, and if this bundle of features is to be used in some other function, some morphological or syntactic means must be deployed to mark this new function. This coding of different categoriality obeys the principle of functional transparency, in that a change in the inherent properties of a lexical item is overtly marked by morphological or syntactic means.

The grammatical system and the lexical items in a language complement each other. If a function has not been lexicalized it may be coded by the grammatical system, as is illustrated by the coding of locative predication in Gidar.

CHAPTER 3

Coding through linear order

1. Introduction

Linear order has been the subject of numerous functional and typological studies concerning the functions of linear order and the correlations between the orders of subject and object and the orders of other constituents. This is perhaps the oldest line of research in linguistic typology (Milewski 1950 and his other works from the 1950s, Greenberg's work on word order universals (Greenberg 1963), and works on the functions of word order and word order change (Li 1975). Contemporary studies of word order have been extended to other categories (Dryer 1992; Hawkins 1994; Siewierska 1998). In the generative tradition, linear order long served as the fundamental means of representing all types of linguistic structures and, more important, functions, specifically those of grammatical relations. The very notions of basic word order and free word order, as well as the functions of word order, have been the subject of numerous studies (cf. papers in Payne 1992, especially Mithun 1992 and Hale 1992, and papers in Downing and Noonan 1995). However, despite the great interest in linear order among proponents of virtually all theories of grammar, there have been no studies examining the prerequisites and implications of coding through linear order. The present chapter aims to fill this gap.

The term 'coding through linear order' means the coding of a function through the position of an element with respect to some reference point. The term linear order may refer to the order of morphemes within a construction, as in polysynthetic languages, or to the order of free morphemes. In the latter case, the term linear order partially overlaps with the most common usage of the term 'word order'.

In Frajzyngier, Krech and Mirzayan (2002), it is proposed that linear order is the simplest means of coding the relationship between two elements, as it involves nothing more than the position of one element with respect to another. This explicit claim may explain the largely intuitive assumptions about the importance of word order in traditional and contemporary linguistics. Coding through linear order has severe limitations. In order for linear order to be viable as a coding means, several conditions must be met. In this chapter, we discuss these conditions and address a number of empirical questions concerning coding by linear order. Our analyses also demonstrate that a language may have a default word order and that this notion accounts, to a certain degree, for the notion of a statistically 'dominant' word order.

We begin with a discussion of the prerequisites for linear order coding, including the criteria for a point of reference. We illustrate the constraints on linear order coding that follow from the position of the reference point. This is followed by a discussion of the implications for language structure of different types of reference points. Our analysis allows us to explain the link that other scholars have observed between different word orders and other linguistic phenomena. We then discuss the interaction between the coding through linear order and inflectional coding on the noun. Finally, we demonstrate that linear order is used to code a variety of functions, of which the grammatical relationship between verbs and arguments is but one.

2. Reference point for linear order

For linear order to be a viable coding means there must be a point of reference, and this point of reference must be available to the hearer. Potential points of reference could include initial or final position in an utterance or in a syntactic structure such as a sentence, clause, or phrase. However, utterance-initial or -final position is not a viable reference point because the structure of an utterance may differ greatly from speaker to speaker. Sentence- or clause-initial position is a potential reference point in languages in which such points are formally marked. Clause-structure rules, like the verb-second rule in Germanic languages, indirectly refer to such positions.

Clause-initial and clause-final positions are often used to code categories belonging to the domain of information structure, such as focus and topicalization (many Chadic languages), new information (clause-initial position in Polish and Russian), and modality (clause-final position in Chadic). The formal niche comprising clause-initial or clause-final position thus appears to be involved in the coding of at least two functional domains, viz. information structure and modality, where the latter includes the distinction between modal and non-modal adverbs.

There appear to be no languages in which the coding of grammatical roles is realized through the position of an argument with respect to clause-initial or clause-final position. Therefore, the coding of grammatical roles through linear order must rely on some other reference point, and this other reference point can only be another lexical item. In order for a lexical item to be a reference point, its categoriality must be readily identifiable to the hearer even if the hearer does not recognize the specific lexical item. Moreover, any construction in which linear order is to serve as the coding means must contain only one reference point, since with multiple points of reference the possibility of coding through linear order would be lost.

In a language in which linear order codes the relationship between the verb and noun phrases in a proposition, a noun may not serve as the reference point because there may be several nouns in one proposition. Therefore, in the functional domain of the relationship between verbs and noun phrases, only the verb is a potential reference point for coding through linear order.

For a verb to serve as the reference point, it must be recognized as such. It must have characteristics that distinguish it from all other lexical categories. These characteristics should preferably be phonologically realized, i.e. decodable in any utterance. Moreover, these characteristics should be few in number so that the pattern can be easily acquired. A simple knowledge of vocabulary or a listing of lexical items will not suffice, since it will not allow for the understanding of grammatical relations in novel utterances that contain new lexical items.

The distinctive characteristics of the reference point could be phonological, provided that different lexical classes have distinctly different phonological structures. In Hdi, a Central Chadic language, verbs may only begin with a consonant, while nouns can begin with a consonant or with a vowel. This is not a sufficient means of coding the verb, as there are both nouns and verbs that begin with a consonant. In Semitic languages, verbal roots have only consonants in their underlying structures, while nominal roots have both consonants and vowels. This too is not a sufficient distinction, because the verb in its phonetic realization will have both consonants and vowels and so will not be distinguishable from a noun on purely phonological grounds.

Morphological means also may be used to distinguish the reference point from other categories. Grammatical morphemes, whether inflectional or derivational, are excellent reference point markers, since these have a phonological realization and belong to a closed set of morphemes. When added to an otherwise unmarked lexical item, a grammatical morpheme marking person, number, gender, tense, aspect or some combination of these may serve as the indicator of categoriality. Verbs in Semitic languages, for example, are marked by a closed set of grammatical morphemes that code aspect, voice, mood, person, number, and gender. These markers make lexical categoriality recognizable to the hearer regardless of whether the hearer knows the meaning of the lexical item.

Once a reference point has been established, linear order can be used as a coding means. In Polish, the distinction between the nominative and the accusative case is neutralized for all plural nouns other than masculine human nouns. The verb codes the gender, number, and person of the subject by means of suffixes. This coding makes the verb available as a reference point, which in turn allows the linear order SVO to code the distinction between subject and object when case marking is neutralized (all examples from Sources):

(1) a. Musiały-by być to wielkie pieniądze, komendancie,
must:3PL:F-HYP be DEM big:3PL:F money:PL commandant:VOC
że-by przeważyły te pańskie inwestycje i
COMP-HYP tip scale:3PL:F DEM:PL:F 2:POL:POSS investments CONJ
projekty.
project:PL
'It would take big money, commandant, to outweigh your investments and projects.'

b. Wszystkie panie nosiły tylko kapelusze.
all:F ladies wear:3PL:F only hat:PL
'All ladies wore only hats.'

c. Synowe brały maszyny do szycia na
daughter-in law:PL take:PAST:3PL:F machine:PL for sewing on
bony PKO.
vouchers PKO
'Daughters-in-law acquired sewing machines with PKO [a bank] vouchers.'

Evidence that it is linear order coding rather than the semantic properties of lexical items that enables grammatical roles to be identified is provided by the fact that the meaning of an utterance may be opaque even when grammatical roles are transparent. We are not sure that our interpretation of the following sentence in Polish is correct, even though the grammatical roles of the constituents are evident from the linear order:

(2) Ruchy nabierały uroczystości.
movements acquire:IMPF:PAST:3PL:F ceremonies
'Movements were increasingly acquiring ceremonial nature.'? (Sources)

The need for a clear reference point allows us to explain a rather obscure phenomenon, the presence of third-person singular agreement in the English present tense.

3. Systems interaction in establishing the reference point in English

English codes the grammatical relations of subject and object through linear order with respect to the verb. However, there is no phonological distinction in English between nouns and verbs, so some other means must allow speakers of English to distinguish between nouns and verbs. These means must rely on the structural properties of English clauses rather than on the hearer's knowledge of individual lexical items; otherwise, readers would not be able to distinguish between nouns and verbs in nonsense works like 'Jabberwocky'. Non-specialists would not be able to distinguish arguments from predicates in scientific writings and in other types of discourse containing novel lexical items. Language acquisition would be more difficult because, in addition to learning the lexical meanings of individual items, the child would have to somehow discover the categoriality of each individual item. We propose that the categoriality of lexical items in English is coded by various morphological means whose other functions may include the coding of tense, aspect, number, and, in the case of nouns, various semantic classes. The evidence for the proposed hypothesis is that members of open-class lexical categories are coded by morphological markers. The only case in which an open-class lexical item is not marked by a morphological marker is when its categoriality can be computed from the categoriality of other items present in the utterance. Counter-evidence for this hypothesis would consist of utterances containing more than one open-class lexical item, none of which is marked for categoriality.

In the English past tense, every verb, with a few phonologically motivated exceptions, is coded by the suffix /-d/. Thus, verbs are identified as such by unique phonological means. A number of verbs, particularly those ending in an alveolar stop, e.g. 'fit', 'put', 'let', lack this suffix, but this clearly results from phonological constraints easily recoverable by native speakers. Another group of verbs codes the past tense through internal vocalic changes. Some of these also have a final alveolar stop, e.g. 'feed-fed', 'sit-sat'. These verbs are few enough in number to be easily acquired and recognized as verbs. If a new verb is introduced into English, its past tense is formed with the suffix /-d/:

1_1_0 <141 A> I'm ^not going to have my summers . **buggered** up in *this kind of !w\ay#*

1_1_0 <846 B> has ^been **be'devilled** 'long e"!n\ough#

In the progressive aspect, the verb is made identifiable as the reference point by the presence of the auxiliary verb 'be' and the suffix '-ing':

1_1_0 <848 B> ((he was ^talking)) about the :high literary !c\ontent#

1_1_0 <866 B> and they're ^even talking about
1_1_0 <867 A> *^[=m]#*
1_1_0 <866 (B> :setting a combined language and !l/\iterature (numbering as it occurs in the LLC corpus)

The interesting question, then, is how the reference point is established for the present tense. The presence of a subject pronoun may code the reference point, since subject pronouns belong to a closed set and are readily identifiable. The verb in a clause with a first- or second-person pronominal subject may have any phonological form and so need not be marked by any morphological means:

1_1_0 <897 B> and [@] . I ^mean there's :stuff like !Ch\urchill's#

1_1_0 <956 B> I've ^\also I :th/ink#

1_1_0 <1043 A> *^{\I get on} very :w\ell with him#*

It remains to be shown how the reference point is established in the present tense when the subject is a noun. If the noun is plural, it is usually marked with the suffix /-z/. A few easily memorized exceptions are marked lexically, e.g. 'cactus-cacti', 'child-children'. The presence of a plural subject noun enables the following constituent to be interpreted as the verb, i.e. the reference point for the clause:

1_1_0 <1071 A> and ^while those questions surv/ive# .
1_1_0 <1072 A> ex^aminers ."!bunch their m/arks . {^on [dhi] . /essay#} {((and)) ^compreh/ension#}#

When the noun is singular and therefore unmarked for its categoriality, the suffix on the verb in the third-person singular present tense establishes the verb as the reference point for linear order. The evidence is as follows.

Third-person singular agreement on the verb in English is a very curious phenomenon. It is a true agreement phenomenon in the traditional understanding of the term: It must occur in any clause with a singular nominal or pronominal subject in the clause and it cannot occur if there is no nominal singular subject in the clause. In many languages, so-called agreement phenomena are actually independent coding means in that they occur regardless of whether the argument that they code appears in the clause (cf. Frajzyngier 1986 and Chapter 6 in the present work). The fact that third-person singular subject agreement in English is obligatory, i.e. triggered by the presence of another constituent in the clause, makes it necessary to seek its function in some domain other than that of coding grammatical relations between the verb and its arguments.

The potential explanation that agreement is a retention from a previous stage in English when all persons were coded on the verb is correct, but it does not explain why third-person coding on the verb was retained while the coding of other persons was lost. Our explanation is as follows: The loss of agreement with first- and second-person subjects did not affect the identification of the reference point for linear order, since first- and second-person pronouns belong to a closed set and can themselves serve as markers of the reference point. In a clause with a nominal subject, however, both verb and noun belong to open classes of lexical items and cannot be distinguished by phonological means. Coding the third-person singular subject through the verbal suffix /-z/ marks the lexical categoriality of the verb, making it available as a reference point and enabling the hearer to parse the clause. This parsing may involve computing various possibilities, and it may take the native speaker considerable time to decide which constituent in a given written utterance is the verb. In the following newspaper headline, the only marker of the verb's categoriality is the third-person singular marker /-s/:

(3) Tough talk jets to race's end. (Daily Camera Oct. 28, 2000)

Deleting the agreement marker results in an uninterpretable sentence:

(4) *Tough talk jet to race's end

Adding a plural marker to the subject noun phrase makes the sentence interpretable again:

(5) Tough talks jet to race's end

A related example comes from the label on a jar of mango pickles:

(6) The art of pickling dates back hundreds of years

Omitting the third-person agreement marker from the predicate 'dates' renders this sentence uninterpretable:

(7) *The art of pickling date back hundreds of years

Adding the plural marker to the subject noun phrase makes the sentence interpretable again:

(8) The arts of pickling date back hundreds of years

Additional evidence for the proposed hypothesis is provided by the effects of suppressing the agreement marker in the examples below. This suppression results either in ungrammatical structures or in changes in meaning:

1_1_0 <26 B> ^but [@h] — I ^mean /\one#
1_1_0 <27 B> ^sets — - \one _question#

Omitting the suffix /-s/ after the verb 'set' completely changes the meaning, such that 'one' is interpreted as a numeral and 'set' is interpreted as a noun:

(9) but [@h] — I ^mean /\one# ^set — - \one _question#

Here is another example where omitting the third-person singular agreement marker completely alters the meaning of the clause:

1_1_0 <39 A> be^cause you see ((I)) — [@] ^some of our p\eople#
1_1_0 <40 A> (. clears throat) ((who)) are ^d\oing LEs# — -

Without the agreement marker, the word 'clear' could be viewed as an imperative form or perhaps as an adjective modifying 'throat':

(10) *be^cause you see ((I)) — [@] ^some of our p\eople#
(. clear throat) ((who)) are ^d\oing LEs# — -

Below, omitting the agreement marker simply produces an uninterpretable utterance:

1_1_0 <236 A> well ^that finishes th\at# .
1_1_0 <237 A> [@:m] . ((now)) ^what was the \other thing {I ^wanted to : =ask _you#}#

cf. the same sentence without the agreement marker:

(11) *well ^that finish th\at# .((now)) ^what was the \other thing {I ^wanted to :=ask _you#}# .

It could be argued that the presence of the agreement marker in a clause with a third-person singular pronominal (as opposed to nominal) subject contradicts our hypothesis, since we have claimed that the presence of a pronominal subject is sufficient to indicate that what follows is a verb and so there is no need to code the categoriality of the lexical item as a verb by means of the marker /-s/. It is true that the presence of the agreement marker along with a third-person subject pronoun cannot be said to be motivated by the need to set a reference point, but this does not constitute an argument against our hypothesis. This apparent redundancy results from a number of factors. Chief among them is the fact that a verb without the marker /-s/ in English explicitly codes non-third person. Using a third-person singular pronoun with a verb that inherently codes non-third person singular would constitute conflicting coding within the same domain. Recall that, although we claim that agreement does not exist, disagreement is not allowed.

There is no coding on the English verb when the subject is a conjoined noun phrase, because such a noun phrase is interpreted as plural. This allows the next constituent to be interpreted as the verb through the system of computation discussed earlier.

Verbal forms that follow auxiliaries coding tense, aspect, and mood also do not display any agreement coding, whether in the past or the present, and they are not marked for tense. Our hypothesis is that there is no need to mark such verbs as reference points, because auxiliaries, which form a closed set in English, are themselves reference points.

To sum up: third-person singular subject agreement in English is a coding means whose specific function is to set the reference point for coding by linear order. The evidence for the proposed hypothesis consists of an analysis of systems interaction wherein third-person agreement is in complementary distribution with first- and second-person pronouns, with past tense markers, and with the nominalized form of the verb. The following table illustrates the systems interaction in setting up the reference point for linear order in English:

Table 1. Setting the reference point for linear order in English

Past	Present (3SG)	Future	Aspect, modality
/-d/	/-z/ or subject pronouns	will, be going	can, must, etc.

The need to code the reference point for linear order obeys the principle of functional transparency in the following way. If linear order is used to code a function, determining the role of various elements within the linear arrangement crucially depends on the presence of a reference point. In the absence of a reference point, the roles of various elements in a construction that codes function through linear order would remain opaque.

4. The theoretical possibilities of linear order

The possibilities for exploiting position as a coding means are theoretically unlimited, since all positions and combinations could be used to encode specific functions. If we take the verb as the reference point and allow linear order coding to both the left and right of the verb, the following coding positions could be available (REF=reference point):

(12)

					V					
–5	–4	–3	–2	–1	REF	1	2	3	4	5

Theoretically, then, linear order alone could code an infinite number of relationships between a noun phrase and a verb. For example, in (12), position –1 could be agent, –2 could be patient, –3 benefactive, –4 locative, –5 instrumental, 1 associative, 2 adversative, and so on. However, having more than one constituent to the left or the right of the verb coded by position alone is not a viable coding means. In order for linear order alone to be viable as a coding means for, say, an argument in position –3, constituents –2 and –1 would have to be present in the clause. Omitting either of these would make it impossible for the hearer to know which position is actually filled and, consequently, what roles are being coded. In other words, a system that uses more than one position on either side of the verb as a coding means can function only if every noun phrase that the hearer expects to find with a given verb is present. In languages that allow omission of noun phrases, then, only positions –1 and 1, i.e. those immediately before and immediately after the verb, are viable coding means. There could be more than one constituent on one or both sides of the verb provided that: (a) the verb has fixed subcategorization characteristics; and (b) all of the categories with which the verb is expected to occur are present in the clause. Thus, positions –2 and 2 may be used only if –1 and 1 are filled and if the verb's subcategorization properties call for these positions to be filled. However, if the argument expected in the –1 slot were to be omitted for any reason, the –2 argument would be misinterpreted as the –1 argument.

5. Benefactive construction in English: Evidence for the constraints on linear order

The proposed analysis of linear order coding explains the behavior of the verb 'to give' and other ditransitive verbs in English. Such verbs can occur with two noun phrases marked by linear order alone. This is the way the verb 'give' usually appears in the London–Lund Corpus:

2_11_2 <198 A> ^I !gave ((them)) some m/oney#

2_12_0 <848 A> I ^gave him your 'home !n\umber#

2_13_0 <66 B> and in ^compens\ation# — .
2_13_0 <67 B> ^they [@m] — - they 'gave us . [m] :M\/ay Day#

3_2_2 <632 A> [@:] we ^p\ut up our n/umbers#
3_2_2 <633 A> which . ^gave us the nu!merical r\/ight#

5_4_0 <669 c> but ^G\od {^kn\ows#} {^what she'd !g\ive me#}#
5_4_0 <670 c> if I ^only gave her :three pound :ten a :w\eek# -

(13) but unfortunately the two guys who gave ((them)) the talk (LLC)

Reversing the order of noun phrases after the verb 'to give' requires the insertion of a preposition before the dative argument, i.e. requires the use of a coding means other than linear order alone:

3_3_0 <343 B> so ^I . !gave ^gave the . _title **to** the lib:r\/arian#

4_5_0 <720 a> *^gave* the 'wallet 'back **to** the \other 'chap# .

5_4_0 <685 h> at the "^/\end {of an ^\interview#}#
5_4_0 <686 h> which she ^gave **to** !\one re:p/orter# .

When the phonological form 'give' is used with only one argument after the verb, it represents the event from the point of view of the subject. In this usage, the verb has the meaning 'exude', 'produce' or 'present':

2_12_0 <592 A> it ^gave ((a lovely)) im":pr\/ession#
2_12_0 <592 A> that he was "^pr\obably#
2_12_0 <593 A> ^disap'pearing 'off to s\ee# .

7_3_11 <1182 A> he ^gave the :\aura#
7_3_11 <1183 A> of a ^man who'd :come into 'contact with . ":super'natural !f\orces#

11_4_0 <332 a3> I have nothing to add to the statement of Her Majesty's government's policy towards the Arab boycott of Israel which I gave on the fifth of May in reply to a question from my honourable friend (LLC)

4_4_0 <1511 A> but he ^drew himself /up#
4_4_0 <1512 A> and **gave** the :half sal/ute#

5_2_0 <253 F> for ^those who :**gave** their l/ives#
5_2_0 <254 F> in the ^w/ar# .

It is our hypothesis that the English construction with two nouns following the verb has the function of coding the first noun as beneficiary and the second noun as object. In other words, the only situation in English in which a verb can be followed by two arguments marked by linear order alone is when the first argument after the verb is the beneficiary of the object of the event and/or of the event itself and the second argument is the object being transferred. Evidence for the proposed hypothesis consists in showing that in all clauses with the structure V NP_1 NP_2, NP_1 is the beneficiary. Counterevidence for the proposed hypothesis would be cases in which the NP_1 is an adversely affected argument or an argument that cannot possibly benefit from the event. The notion of beneficiary subsumes the notion of recipient, in which the first argument following the verb receives the second argument:

1_8_0 <385 (A> *I'll ^write him* a 'little n/ote#

The evidence that the construction codes the beneficiary is provided by the fact that the construction cannot be used if the argument immediately after the verb is not the beneficiary of the object or the event. Example 14 is ungrammatical as a V NP NP construction because 'seminars' is not a potential beneficiary of the event 'write essays':

(14) * ^do they *write the s/eminar !\essays*

Compare the following, grammatical construction in which the argument 'seminars' is coded by the preposition 'for'.

1_9_0 <1072 A> ^do they *write !\essays* for the s/eminar#

It could be argued that the construction with two arguments after the verb is not a benefactive construction because it can be used with a meaning clearly detrimental to the first argument following the verb, i.e. the proposed benefactive:

6_4_1 <357 a> he ^gave **me** a tre!{m\endous} :t\alking-to#
6_4_1 <358 a> a^bout bad +l\anguage#+ .

10_1_0 <562 a> I should ^think that gave **his . :hand** a :v\ery _fair {^j\olt#}# – –

1_12_0 <61 a> well in my particular* case [dhi:] he gave **me** a dirty smile and said we'll send you to Farnborough asterisk.

2_4_1 <348 B> and I'm a^bout to 'write **the di'rector** a :nasty . ^nasty l\etter#

However, use of the V NP NP construction in the detrimental function may be explained by the metaphorical extension of the verb 'give', with the default meaning 'give something good', to the opposite meaning, 'give something bad'. The lexicalization of antonymic meanings, known in stylistics as 'antiphrasis', occurs across languages. Other examples include the English slang usage of 'bad' to mean 'good' and the use of Russian *dat'* and Polish *dać* 'give' to mean 'hit, do harm'.

It could also be argued that the semantic properties of the verb 'to give' require it to occur with two arguments and that this requirement is not a property of the coding system. The fallacy of the semantically based explanation is provided by the fact that semantically identical verbs behave quite differently in languages with different coding systems. In Polish, grammatical and semantic relations are coded by nominal inflection and inflection on the verb. The verb *dać* 'give', in the sense of 'transfer', can freely occur without any post-verbal noun phrase at all:

(15) Jak Pan Bóg nie **dał**, to jeszcze może dać.
like Lord God NEG give:PAST:3M COM still can give
'Even if Lord God did not give, he may still do so.' (Sources)

(16) Pan dyrektor z instytutu wyniósł za rewersem i
Mr. director from institute carry:PAST:3M:SG PREP receipt CONJ
do tej pory nie **oddał**.
till DEM:F time NEG give back:PAST:3M:SG
'Mr. Director carried it out from the institute, with a receipt, and has not given it back.' (Sources)

In Polish the verb 'to give' also may occur with only one noun phrase in addition to the subject. This noun phrase must be the object transferred. Below, the verb 'give' is used in two meanings. The first and last instances of 'give' involve the transfer of an object, while the second instance means 'to allow sexual intercourse' (from the point of view of the woman). Only the first occurrence of 'give' is followed by a noun phrase, in this case the object being transferred:

(17) Mówię sobie, **dawaj** **gnata**, to **dam**, a
say:1SG 1SG:REFL:DAT give:IMPER:PEJ bone[4]:ACC COM give:FUT:1SG CONJ

jak **dał** i się dobiera.
when give:PAST:3M:SG CONJ REFL grope
'I am saying: "Give me the gun!" If you do I will let you. And when he gave it to me and when he started groping …'

In (18) the verb 'give' also occurs with the subject and the object being transferred:

(18) Ktoś dał cieżarowe auto.
somebody give:PAST:3M:SG goods:ADJ:ACC car:ACC
'Somebody gave a truck.' (Sources)

If the object has not been mentioned before in discourse, and if several potential recipients have been mentioned in the discourse, the verb 'to give' may have two noun phrases in addition to the subject:

(19) Który choć bezładny dał **mi** jednak sporo
which although disorderly give:PAST:3M:SG 1SG:DAT nevertheless much
doświadczenia.
experience:GEN
'Which, although chaotic, nevertheless gave me much experience.' (Sources)

(20) Dałam **ci** przecież całkowitą **satysfakcję.**
give:PAST:1SG:F 2:DAT indeed complete:F:ACC satisfaction:ACC
'I gave you, didn't I, complete satisfaction.' (Sources)

In Polish natural discourse, three possible combinations using the verb 'give' are attested in the texts, viz. verb alone, verb with recipient and object of transfer, and verb with object only. The fourth possible combination, viz. verb with recipient only, is not attested in our data. This may be due to the fact that the recipient is the inherent object of the verb 'to give' in Polish. The differences between the combinations attested in Polish and those attested in English are due to the fact that the coding means of Polish, namely nominal and verbal inflection, are quite different from those of English. The requirement in English that two noun phrases occur after the verb 'to give' therefore is not a function of the meaning of the verb but rather of the coding system of the language.

6. Practical possibilities of coding through linear order

Given the constraints on linear order discussed in Section 4 of this chapter , there are only three possible linear orders for coding the role of a noun phrase by position alone, using the verb as the reference point:

(21) a. ___VERB
b. VERB ___
c. ___VERB ___

In other words, when a language codes the arguments of the verb through position alone, the maximum number of arguments that can be so coded is two. Moreover, if two arguments are to be encoded by position, the language must employ both the position before and the position after the verb. If only one of these positions is available, the maximum number of arguments that can be coded by position alone is one.

Following Dryer (1992) we refer to languages of the first type (21a) as 'left-branching' and those of the second type (21b) as 'right-branching'. The third type (21c) we refer to as 'dual-branching'.

We show here that the three linear order types are unequal with respect to their efficiency as coding means. In a left- or right-branching language, the default position (see below) is the only position available for coding by linear order alone. In left- and right-branching languages that use linear order to code relations between verb and noun phrases, linear order is never the only means to code such relations. In dual-branching languages, two arguments may be coded by position alone, and coding means other than linear order must be used to code additional arguments. The practical limitations of linear order as a coding means and the need to code the roles of more than one or two constituents are the motivation for the grammaticalization of adpositions, case marking, agreement, and possibly other coding means.

7. The default position in linear order coding

In an English clause with only one argument, this argument is coded by the linear order ___V and may not be coded by the linear order *V ___, except in very restricted instances (e.g., "Comes a horseman."). The position before the verb is thus the default position, i.e. the position that an argument must occupy if it is the only argument in the clause. Because of its obligatory nature, the default position by itself does not carry any specific semantic function such as agent, patient, etc. The evidence for this hypothesis is provided by the fact that the arguments in the default position may have a variety of semantic functions:

(22) **Another year** passes for Marino. (Daily Camera, Jan. 18, 1993)
'**It** worked all day for us', Thomas said. (Daily Camera, Jan. 18, 1993)
The presidential contest spanned the country with a week and a half left before the election. (Daily Camera, Oct. 28, 2000)

With some specific categories of verbs, such as transitive verbs, the default position may have a default semantic role. The language may then have special means to change the default role of the argument in the default position. This is the function of the formal means involved in passive constructions in English:

6_9_1 <671 b> it was ^evidently"![?]\/ordered# .
6_9_1 <672 b> ((as)) ^T H'T C tw\o#

Another piece of evidence that the default position does not code a specific semantic relation is the presence, in languages with default positions of coding means whose role is to indicate specific semantic relations between the predicate and the argument in the default position. In Hdi, a verb-initial language, a transitive verb with the vowel *a* codes the point of view of the goal (for the notion of point of view of goal, cf. Frajzyngier with Shay 2002). No information about the semantic role of the subject is carried by the default position after the verb:

(23) Dzà'á **phlá-phlá**-xən tá mndú kàbgà xáxəŋ tá **dzà**-tá
FUT kill.PL-kill.PL-3.PL OBJ man because 3PL COMP kill-REF
dá-ɗà ká gáwá.
father-1SG COMP Gawa
'"They will kill us, because it is they who killed my father," said Gawa.' (Frajzyngier with Shay 2002)

A verb with the vowel *u* codes the point of view of the subject. The subject may be controlling or non-controlling, affected or non-affected.

Non-controlling subject:

(24) Kà mt-**ú**-tá dá-nì.
SEQ die-SO-REF father-3SG
'And his father died.'

Non-controlling-affected subject:

(25) a. Dr-**ú**-drá xàsúù.
burn-SO-burn wood
'The wood burned.'
b. Bádz-**ú**-bádzá lgùt.
spoil-SO-spoil cloth
'The cloth spoiled.'

Controlling subject:

(26) S-**ù**-sà.
drink-SO-drink
'He drank everything.' (cf. Spanish: él se tomó)

An intransitive verb cannot code either the point of view of the object or the point of view of the subject:

(27) Kà zə́ ì kɗérí ndá zwàn-à-ní tá mghám.
SEQ live ASSC.PL Kderi ASSC children-GEN-3SG PREP well
'And Kderi and his children lived happily.'

Thus, the default position inherently codes no specific semantic relationship between the verb and the argument. A semantic relationship may be construed from the semantic properties of the verb and the noun phrase or it may be encoded through marking on the verb or through the presence of other elements in the clause.

Whether the default position in a language is before or after the verb depends on the language's paths of grammaticalization. We take the default position in a language to be given; i.e., we do not attempt to explain why a language's default position is to the right or left of the verb.

In a dual-branching language, the second position, i.e. the coding position that is not the default position, seems to have a narrower functional scope than the default position. However, with only two positions available for linear order coding, it is hardly to be expected that the second position will be limited to one specific semantic function. In English, for example, the position after the verb may be occupied by arguments having a variety of semantic functions, but it may not be occupied by an argument that is more controlling than the argument coded by the position preceding the verb. This constraint may well reflect a property characterizing many languages, that agents precede non-agents (Mallinson and Blake 1981).

8. Coding in dual-branching languages

8.1. Canonical coding in SVO languages

A dual-branching language offers two coding positions, one on each side of the verb. Putting both arguments before or after the verb, without any prepositions, results in an uninterpretable sentence:

6_9_1 <373 b> [@:m] . ^if we hit 'Send again :n\/ow#
* [@:m] . ^if we 'Send hit again :n\/ow#
* [@:m] . ^if 'Send we hit again :n\/ow#
etc.

It is possible to add a third noun phrase coded by linear order, as in the English ditransitive construction described above, but such a construction will be subject to strict semantic and structural constraints. Unless the construction V NP NP has been grammaticalized for a very specific function, as it is in English, adding a third noun phrase to a clause in a dual-branching language requires additional coding means. In English it requires the use of a preposition:

2_2_1 <821 A> un^less — you _you . put"!all your 'cards **on** the *:t\able#;-*;

2_2_1 <869 A> ^h\e 'merely#
2_2_1 <870 A> ^takes \on#
2_2_1 <871 A> ^Mr \Y#
2_2_1 <872 A> **as** a ^cl/ient# -
2_2_1 <873 A> ^and he _does his b/\est **for** him# .

This analysis of dual-branching languages allows us to define intransitive verbs in English as verbs for which the second position, i.e. the position after the verb, is not available as a coding means. For such verbs, the addition of any second noun phrase requires the use of a preposition:

1_1_0 <797 B> *((be^fore I'm f\inished **with** him# -

1_1_0 <814 A> he [@] ^sort of !l\ooks **at** _one#
1_1_0 <815 A> [so?] ^almost 'cross-\eyed#
1_1_0 <816 A> **with** ^those great "gl\asses ((of his#)) —
1_1_0 <817 A> and [@:m] — - it ^just strikes me **as** :\odd {^sort of th=ing#}#

The question of which preposition is chosen to code an additional argument is a lower-level problem, subject to the semantic properties of prepositions, the semantic properties of verbs, and idiosyncratic factors in grammaticalization.

8.2. Left-branching constructions in SVO languages

A language that uses SVO order as a coding means may have certain types of structures that are verb-final and so require additional coding means for indicating grammatical relations. Songhay, a Nilo-Saharan language spoken in Niger and Mali, has several dialects. In one dialect, Koyra Chiini, grammatical relations are coded by the linear order SVO alone:

(28) Yer o kar gi.
1pl.s impf hit 3pl.o
'We hit them.' (Heath 1999a: 128) (s-Subject, o-Object)

In the Koyraboro Senni dialect there are two types of transitive clauses: those with underived, i.e. prototypical, transitive verbs, and those with verbs involving less transitivity. Clauses with prototypical transitive verbs have the direct object preceding the verb. However, the object is not coded by linear order alone but by other means. If there is an auxiliary, the object occurs after the auxiliary in the structure S AUX O V:

(29) Ay **ši** i bey.
1sg.s impf.neg 3pl.o know
'I didn't know.' (Heath 1999b: 195)

If there is no auxiliary, a transitive marker *na* precedes the object in the structure S *na* O V (Heath 1999b: 159):

(30) Ay **na** ni kar.
1sg.s tr 2sg.o hit
'I hit you.'

(31) Woy-oo na ar-oo wii.
woman-DEF.SG TR man-DEF.SG kill
'The woman killed the man.' (Heath 1999b: 212)

Thus, in a verb-final construction in this SVO language, the noun phrase is marked as object either by the position after an auxiliary or by a special morpheme whose specific function in this dialect appears to be to code direct objects.

An excellent piece of evidence for the proposed constraints on linear order coding in a left-branching construction is provided by Mina (Central Chadic), an SVO language. In the pragmatically neutral clause, the distinction between subject and object is coded through linear order alone:

(32) À wə̀r góŋg sk-á.
3SG want truth NEG-Q
'He wants the truth, doesn't he?'

(33) Hà kə́ r hìdì-yíì zà.
2SG INF insult man-PL AUX
'You have insulted people.'

Focus on the object is coded by placing the object noun phrase in the position preceding the verb and following the subject. This constitutes a disruption of the SVO order, and so the object noun phrase is marked by a preposition:

(34) Á **n** **kə̀ɗə́m** ngə̀n ɓə̀t.
3SG PREP calabash 3SG take
'She took her calabash.'

(35) Báy **nə̀** **kə̀ɗə́m** ngə̀n ɓə̀t déɓ á déɓ ká á ìdá.
chief PREP calabash 3SG take carry 3SG carry AFF PREP home
'The chief$_i$ took his$_j$ calabash and carried it home.'

Thus, disrupting the SVO order by placing the object between the subject and the verb requires the use of additional coding means to code the role of the object.

9. Coding in right-branching languages

In a right-branching language there is only one position available for coding through linear order, namely the position to the right of the reference point.

In such a language, any argument other than the first must be coded by means other than linear order. The second argument could be coded by nominal inflection, verbal inflection, adpositions or other means, depending on what means are available in the language. Addition of arguments beyond the second argument may require the use of several coding means at the same time. In what follows, we discuss two types of coding whose existence is motivated by the position of the point of reference in a right-branching or verb-initial language: coding on the verb and coding through prepositions.

9.1. Coding on the verb in right-branching languages

Evidence for the interaction between linear order and head coding is provided by Hona, which is verb-medial in the imperfective aspect and verb-initial in the perfective. In agreement with our hypothesis, the language uses different means to code arguments in the imperfective and perfective aspects.

In the imperfective aspect, grammatical roles are coded through the linear order SVO (all data from field notes by Frajzyngier and by Laurie Jordan; for some data, tones were not recorded):

(36) Bə̀ní-fà kí sə̀ghdírá wà.
man-INDEF eat vultures NEG
'One does not eat vultures.'

An object marker may occur on the verb, not to code grammatical relations, but to code definiteness of the object:

(37) Nà nú-nà à tsáɓ-**àŋ** lú-nnà-ɗ́.
IMPF wife-1SG FUT wash-OBJ shirt-1SG-ALL
'My wife will wash my shirt.'

The perfective clause is verb-initial. A verb followed by all of the nouns allowed by its argument structure is not marked by any affixes, since all arguments are present. This is consistent with our hypothesis that multiple arguments to the right or left of the verb may be coded by position provided that all expected arguments are present in the clause:

(38) Fí nú-nà ɬú-wà.
bake wife-1SG meat-INDEF
'My wife baked meat.'

In the perfective clause, as in the imperfective, definiteness of the object is coded by an object suffix on the verb:

(39) ɬe-**n** Ali hur-ghen.
slaughter-OBJ Ali neck-3SG
'Ali slaughtered it.' (lit. 'Ali cut its neck')

If there is only one argument following the verb, linear order alone (i.e., without any additional coding means) indicates that this argument is the subject:

(40) Ngwálà ɬú-wà.
finish meat-INDEF
'The meat finished.'

A pronominal subject is suffixed to the verb:

(41) ɗáɗ-**ì**.
run:PRF-1SG
'I ran away.'

ɗán-**nà**.
run:PRF-2SG
'You ran away.'

Pə̀ r-**ɗá** háy.
jump-3SG down
'He jumped down.'

If there is only one noun phrase following the verb and there is a subject marker on the verb, the noun phrase after the verb is interpreted as object. If the object is definite, it too is marked on the verb:

(42) a. Ky-**án-ɗ**ɬú-dì pát.
eat-OBJ-3SG meat-DEF all
'He ate all the meat.'

b. S-**án-ɗ**ám-dì pát.
drink-OBJ-3SG water-DEF all
'He drank all the water.'

c. Ngwálà-**ŋ-ɗì** ɬú-dì.
finish-OBJ-1SG meat-DEF
'I finished the meat.'

If the neutral linear order in the perfective aspect is disturbed, e.g. if an argument is moved into clause-initial position for focusing or topicalization, some additional coding means must be used to identify the role of the fronted argument. If the subject is fronted, its role may be computed from the presence of a subject marker on the verb:

(43) a. Wá-nà fan-ɗ́.
child-1sg wash-3sg
'My child washed.'

Cf. the neutral order:

b. Fàn wá-nà.
wash child-1sg
'My child washed.'

(44) a. Pàshí-nà péreɗ wí-**ndà**.
friend-1sg all leave-3pl
'All my friends left.'

Cf. the neutral order:

b. Wí pashí-nà.
leave friend-1sg
'All my friends left.'

If the verb has both a subject marker and an object suffix, the fronted argument is interpreted as subject:

(45) Ali ɬe-**n**-**ɗə**.
Ali slaughter-obj-3sg
'Ali slaughtered it.'

An object may be moved into the position immediately before the verb for topicalization or to allow it to serve as the head of a relative clause. In this case, the role of the noun phrase before the verb is coded by the presence of an object suffix on the verb:

(46) Mbe-nè **iya-ɗí** fwo-né-**n**.
enjoy-1sg food-def cook-1sg.dat-3sg.obj
'I liked the food that she cooked for me.'

9.2. Coding arguments through prepositions in verb-initial languages

Arguments in left-branching or right-branching languages also may be coded through prepositions or postpositions. In Hdi, a Central Chadic language, the position after the verb codes the subject. The object is marked by the preposition *tá*:

(47) Tsghà-dá-f xáxən **tá** sánì.
put up-all-UP 3PL OBJ one
'They sent up one [bag]'

(48) Lá-mà zíngá dà tùghwázàk kà hlà-ná-ghá-tá-tsí **tá**
go-IN Zinga PREP hibiscus SEQ find-DEM-D.PVG-REF-3SG OBJ
pákáwá ghúvì kà ks-ú-tá-tsí.
hyena SEQ touch-SO-REF-3SG
'When Zinga entered the hibiscus, he found Hyena and devoured him.'

The object is marked by the preposition *tá* even if the subject is moved into preverbal position. The identity of the fronted argument could not otherwise be computed, since Hdi is not an SVO language and the position before the verb is not a means of coding a grammatical role. Retention of the preposition codes the post-verbal argument as object and, by process of elimination, allows the argument preceding the verb to be properly interpreted as subject:

(49) a. Pghíntà nà sà **tá** ímì wà.
Phinta DEM drink OBJ water NEG
'As for Phinta, she did not drink water.'

Cf. the neutral order:

(49) b. Sà-á-sà pghíntà **tá** ímì.
drink-PART-drink Phinta OBJ water
'Phinta drank some water.'

An object in the position preceding the verb is not marked by the preposition *tá*. However, its identity as object is revealed through computation. The argument following the verb is not preceded by a preposition, so it must be the subject. Therefore, the argument that precedes the verb must be the object:

(50) Mbízà z-ú-zà pghìntà.
bean dish eat-so-eat Phinta
'The bean dish, Phinta ate it.'

Hdi also has a referential marker *tá*, which is not followed by a subject marker. When the referential marker occurs, the object marker *tá* is not used. This co-occurrence constraint may have to do with the probable derivation of the referential marker *tá* from the object marker *tá*, or from haplology, or from both at the same time:

(51) a. Mbàɗ ká pákáwá ghúvì kà klà-á-**tá** vàrà.
then COMP hyena SEQ take-PART-REF beans
'Hyena took some beans.'

b. Dghàɗ-áy-tàn dghàɗ-áy-tàn mbàɗ ká krì kà klà-gá-f-**tá**
chew-PO-3PL chew-PO-3PL then COMP dog SEQ take-INN-UP-REF
ìr-á zwáŋ-á pákáwá ghúvì.
eye-GEN child-GEN hyena
'While they were chewing it, Dog picked up an eye of a child of Hyena.' (Frajzyngier with Shay 2002)

In Hdi, then, we see the interaction between linear order and prepositional coding. The subject is coded through linear order by the position directly after the verb and the object is coded by a preposition. The role of a fronted argument is computed from the way in which the other argument is marked.

10. Coding in left-branching languages

A left-branching language has only one position available for coding through linear order. In such a language, the position immediately before the verb is the default position. If a language has the categories subject and object and the neutral word order is SOV, the language can code the object through linear order alone. We predict that a verb-final language uses SOV order as a coding means if and only if the following conditions are fulfilled: (1) all of the arguments required by the minimal argument structure are present; (2) the clause is pragmatically neutral: and (3) there is no additional material between the arguments and the reference point. If any of these conditions is not met, a left-branching language uses adpositions, verbal inflection or other means to code grammatical relations.

Old Japanese (about AD 700), like contemporary Japanese, was a verb-final language. Like its contemporary counterpart, Old Japanese had a postposition *o* that could be used with the object. However, the object did not have to be marked by this postposition. Miyagama (1989: 205) gives the following example from Old Japanese (___ indicates where the object marker *o* would occur if the object were overtly marked):

(52) Ware wa imo ___ omou.
1SG TOP wife think
'I think of my wife.'

Miyagama (1989) provides ample evidence that the marker *o* in Old Japanese was not an obligatory marker of object but rather an emphatic marker that could mark many types of arguments or could even be used to mark a clause. The role of the noun phrase occurring in the default position thus was computed from the fact that it occurred in default position. If the default position did not code the role of object, the above sentence could be interpreted as 'My wife thinks of me'.

For further discussion of Japanese postpositions, see Kuno (1974) and Shibatani (1990).

10.1. Interaction of verbal inflection, linear order, and case marking

In a left-branching language, coding the subject on the verb is a sufficient means of coding grammatical relations on condition that (a) the canonical set of complements of a given predicate is present in the utterance; and (b) these arguments occur in the neutral word order. The canonical set of complements is the number of arguments that the hearer expects with a given verb. If either of these conditions is not met, the language must use some other means to code grammatical relations. If a transitive verb occurs with only one argument X, subject coding on the verb is a sufficient means to code the role of X provided that the subject features coded on the verb (e.g. gender, number, or other characteristics) have different values from the corresponding features of argument X. Consider Amharic, in which the verb codes the gender, person, and number of the subject. The default position, i.e. the position before the verb, is occupied by the subject in the intransitive clause:

(53) Ləğ-u wäddäqä.
child-DEF fall:3MSG.PRF
'The child fell.' (Leslau 1968: 68; glosses ours)

With transitive verbs, the default position is occupied by the object of the clause. Thus, the structure NP NP V (without argument markers on the noun phrases) codes the first noun as subject and the second noun as object. The verb codes the person, gender and number of the subject:

(54) Wəšša-w ləğ näkkäsä.
dog-DEF child bit:3MSG.PRF
'The dog bit a child.' (Leslau 1968: 68)

If the object is the only argument and it is definite, i.e. is marked by the definite suffix *-u*, the object noun phrase must be marked by the suffix *-n*:

(55) Bärr-u-**n** käffätä.
door-DEF-OBJ open:3MSG.PRF
'He opened the door.' (Leslau 1968: 68)

The object may have the object-marking suffix *-n* even if it precedes the verb in a transitive clause with an overt subject. This coding may have the function of focusing the object noun phrase, as is implied by some translations in Cohen (1970):

(55) a. Waldä maryam amätä səllasye-**n** agäbbä.
Walde Maryam Amete Sellasye-OBJ marry:3MSG.PRF
'Walde Maryam married Amete Sellasye.' (Cohen 1970: 340)
b. Abbat-ye ba-tkəlt wust gommä-**n** zärra.
father-1SG PREP-garden in cabbage-OBJ plant
'My father planted cabbage [not other vegetables] in the garden.'

Placing the object before the subject in order to code some pragmatic function constitutes a disruption of the SOV coding system. The fronted object must be marked by a determiner and the object noun phrase must be marked by the object suffix *-n*:

(56) Ləğ-**u-n** wəššaw-w näkkäsä.
child-DEF-OBJ dog-DEF bite:3MSG.PRF
'The dog bit the child.' (Leslau 1968: 68)

Omitting the object marker from the first noun in the above clause yields the meaning 'the child bit the dog':

(57) Ləğ-**u** wəššaw-w näkkäsä.
child-DEF dog-DEF bite:3MSG.PRF
'The child bit the dog.'

Descriptive grammars of Amharic state that a definite object must be marked by the suffix *-n*. However, there is evidence that the marker *-n* serves as the object marker regardless of whether the object is definite. If the noun is modified by the unspecified marker *and* 'one', this marker takes the object marker-*n* to code the role of the noun phrase:

(58) Andə-**n** ləğ wəššaw-w näkkäsä.
one-OBJ child dog-DEF bite:3MSG.PRF
'The dog bit a child.'

The object also is marked by the suffix *-n* when another constituent in the clause, such as a prepositional phrase, intervenes between the object and the verb, resulting in the order S O PP V:

(59) Abbat-ye gommän-**u-n** ba-tkəlt bota zärra.
father-1SG cabbage-DEF-OBJ PREP-garden place plant
'My father planted the cabbage in the vegetable garden [rather than somewhere else].' (Cohen 1970: 341)

The object marker *-n* in Amharic thus has the function of coding focus on the object when the object is in the default position and coding the grammatical role of a noun as object when the neutral word order is disrupted or other canonical conditions are not met.

10.2. SVO constructions in left-branching languages

Dahalo (East or South Cushitic, depending on the classification one accepts), presents yet another strategy for coding arguments in a verb-final language. The subject precedes the object when both arguments are present (morphemic division, glosses and translations as in the original):

(60) Múnta+da guho b'urú-i[e] líimamummi.
farm-LOC people maize-HAB work-3P
'They cultivate maize on the farm.' (Tosco 1991: 85)

Because the subject is coded on the verb, a single argument before the verb is interpreted as object if it differs in person from the argument marked on the verb:

(61) Nat'á+t[o] 'ini te lúbuto.
woman+that-F FOC AFF beat:2s
'You are going to beat the woman.' (Tosco 1991: 86)

Arguments other than subject and object are marked by adpositions:

(62) ‘Ani+j[e] ali+nto háasoobo.
1SG+HAB Ali+ASSC speak:1SG
‘I converse habitually with Ali.’ (Tosco 1991:85)

When the object is moved into clause-initial position for topicalization, resumptive pronouns referring to the object are suffixed to the subject:

(63) Gwíttsa ‘úku ‘ini gaano-**ku** lúbbi.
child that FOC man-that hit-3M
‘The child, the man beats him.’ (Tosco 1991:85)

The object may follow the verb in a focus construction. In this case, the object is marked by the postposition *kabe*:

(64) ‘Áata ‘életo **dawa kabé?**
you know-2s Dawa ACC
‘Do you know Dawa?’ (Tosco 1991:88)

A pronominal object in a focus construction is marked twice, once as a suffix to the verb and again as an independent pronoun followed by *kabé*:

(65) ‘Áata ‘életo+’**i** **’án kabé?**
you know-2s-1SG 1SG ACC
‘Do you know me?’ (Tosco 1991:88)

The importance of the Dahalo data is that the neutral order is SOV. Because the SVO order is derived and the position after the verb is not a coding means, an object in that position must be overtly marked as such.

11. Linear order and compensatory means

To test our hypothesis that verb-final languages use compensatory coding means when the SOV linear order is disrupted, we have examined the coding means available in a variety of verb-final languages. The following table is based on Mallinson and Blake (1981). The column labeled ‘Position before the verb’ shows which argument, if any, may be encoded solely by being placed in that position. In Amharic, as we have seen, the object in an SOV clause need not be marked by inflectional means but is coded as object solely by its position before the verb. Therefore, ‘object’ appears in the ‘Position before the verb’ column.

'Nominal inflection' refers to markers on the noun, e.g. case markers, that encode its relationship to the verb. 'Coding on verb' refers to the coding of the person (P), gender (G) or number (N) of some argument of the proposition. We use the terms subject and object for the arguments of nominative-accusative languages and the terms ergative and absolutive for the arguments of ergative languages. Table 2 confirms that the default position in a left-branching language is the position before the verb and that if this position codes an argument, that argument is the object.

12. Linear order coding and the subject-object dichotomy

When English replaced Latin as the language on which the agenda for linguistic research and the model of representation of functions and structures were based, the case system of Latin was replaced by the subject-object dichotomy as the central means of describing clause structure (cf. Gil 1999 for similar views). Ever since then, linguists within the generative tradition have been searching for better ways to define and characterize the two grammatical relations.

We propose that this dichotomy in linguistic theory is an artifact of taking one specific type of language to be a paragon of language structure. The subject-object dichotomy results from the fact that this is the distinction coded by linear order in dual-branching languages. We have shown that the first argument in such a language is coded by the default position while the second argument is coded by the second position available. Adding any other noun phrase to the clause must involve a preposition. The fact that this occurs in dual-branching languages gave rise to the assumption that arguments coded by prepositions universally carry functions different from those of arguments coded by linear order.

The subject-object dichotomy does not have to exist in a language that codes the relations between verb and noun phrases through adpositions and/or case inflection, provided there are more than two cases and or adpositions to code grammatical relations. Some languages, such as Lezgian, code a one-to-many opposition wherein the absolutive (unmarked) case is opposed to all other cases, which are built by adding additional case markers to the ergative case (cf. Haspelmath 1993). In Hdi, the subject, which is coded by linear order, is opposed to all other relations, which are coded through prepositions.

Table 2. Coding means in verb-final languages[5]

Language	Adpositions	Nominal inflection	Coding on verb	Position before the verb
Amharic (Semitic)		Object only	Subject (P,G,N)	Object (inflection optional
Ometo (Cushitic)		Subject only	Subject (P, G(3p), N)	
Dahalo (Cushitic)	Object (chiefly when object does not occur in pre-verbal slot)		Subject (P,G,N) and other arguments	Object
Kanuri (Saharan)	Subject and object (when order is other than SOV)		Subject	Object (subject in pre-verbal slot must be marked)
Masalit (Maban)		Object only	Subject (P)	Object marked
Nubian (Chari-Nile)		Object only	Subject (P,G,N)	
Uzbek (Altaic)		All arguments except subject, which is unmarked	Subject (P,N)	
Korean	All arguments, except when object is in pre-verbal slot			Object
Japanese	All arguments, except when object is in pre-verbal slot			Object
Basque		Ergative	Absolutive and ergative	
Tibetan (Classical)		Ergative		
Enga (Papuan)		All marked except for absolutive	Agent (P)	
Siroi (Papuan)			Subject, Object[a]	
Kūi (Dravidian)		All except object	Subject, Object (1p or 2p)	
Other Dravidian		All arguments		
Warlpiri	All except absolutive			
Yaqui (Uto-Aztecan)	All except subject[b]			
Quechua		All except subject	Subject	

[a]In Siroi, classes of verbs differ in the arguments that can be encoded on them.
[b]In Yaqui, the plural object is unmarked.

13. Conclusions

Linear order is the simplest coding means. For linear order to be a viable coding means there must be one and only one reference point in a given construction. The reference point must be phonologically marked as such, either by having a limited set of morphological markers or by having a specific phonological structure.

The number of functions that can be coded through linear order is limited. In a language in which the point of reference occurs in clause-initial or clause-final position, there is only one position available for coding by linear order. Because this position is the default position, it cannot be used as a coding means when only one argument is present in the clause. Therefore, languages in which the reference point is at the beginning or end of the clause have grammaticalized other means to code the relationship between the verb and its arguments. These means include adpositions, nominal inflection, coding on the verb through a system of subject and object markers, and a combination of these means. Even a language whose reference point is in clause-internal position must have some other means of coding grammatical relationships when the number of noun phrases in the clause exceeds two.

Linear order can be used to code all kinds of functions outside the domain of argument structure. It can code information structure, including topicalization and focus; modification (Frajzyngier, Krech and Mirzayan 2002); and a number of other functions. The presence of inflectional coding in a language allows greater flexibility of linear order and so allows linear order to code a greater number of functions.

CHAPTER 4

Coding through nominal inflection

1. Introduction

This chapter shows not only that inflection is complementary with other coding means but that it enables the coding of a larger number of functions than can be coded by linear order alone. Moreover, we show that the presence of nominal inflection increases the number of linear orders available in a language and thereby the number of functions that may be coded by linear order. The focus of the present chapter is coding by case, but we also touch on other types of nominal inflection. We demonstrate that nominal inflection of any kind, including case marking, is an independent coding means in that the inflection of nouns, adjectives, and pronouns is not assigned by any other overt or covert category.

There is a vast literature dealing with the semantics of case marking and with the general and semantic functions of individual cases, e.g. Jakobson (1963); Kuryłowicz (1964); Agud (1980); Wierzbicka (1980); Blake (1995); Dąbrowska (1997). Due to the volume of the literature, we do not attempt to summarize or undertake discussion of the various claims that have been made about the semantic roles of individual cases. We concentrate instead on a few systematic properties of case coding (Sections 2–4) and on the functional interactions among various cases (Sections 5–7). Specifically, we discuss properties of the nominative and absolutive cases, properties of the accusative case, and coding through the genitive case. We concentrate on the interaction of cases in Polish and on the implications of the absence of case coding in English.

The syntactic consequences of inflectional coding are many, but we focus here on only two. The first, which also pertains to the inherent properties of lexical items, has to do with the subcategorization of verbs (Section 8), while the second has to do with the problem of word order (Section 9). Steele (1978) has studied the relationship among free word order, case inflection, and verb agreement. Steele's findings support our hypothesis about the interaction and complementarity of various coding means: Although Steele found that not all languages with so-called free word order have nominal inflection, she has nevertheless observed that all such languages in her sample have argument coding on the verb.

Like any other coding means, case marking can be used for a variety of functions. In the present chapter we concentrate on functions in the domain of the relationship between the verb and the noun phrases in a construction. We conclude the chapter with a discussion of the implications of the availability of nominal inflection for the forms of discourse, an issue touched upon in the introductory chapter (Section 10). In Chapter 11, we describe the use in Russian of case marking in the domain of reference.

2. Evidence for the independent nature of case marking

Case marking is an independent coding means. This implies that case marking is not assigned by the verb, a preposition, or any other component of the clause. Evidence that case is an independent coding means is provided by the fact that the same noun — not just the same lexical category but the same lexical item — can have different case marking in the same syntactic environment and after the same verb (cf. also Moravcsik 1978: 261 on accusative and partitive in Hungarian). As evidence, we first demonstrate the use of different cases in the same syntactic environment. We then discuss those environments that have usually been taken by traditional grammar and modern case theories to represent instances of case assignment by some element in the clause.

The question of what categories are coded by case inflection must be answered for each language individually. In some languages case may code grammatical relations, such as subject or object. In other languages it may code semantic relations. Our approach differs from that found in many studies in Aikhenvald et al. (2001), where it is assumed that a single grammatical relation, such as object, may be coded by more than one case in a given language.

In what follows, we demonstrate the contrast between two different case markings in Polish, a language with a relatively rich case marking system. Each of the following (a) examples is taken from natural, mainly written, discourse. Each (b) example represents the same utterance with different case marking on one lexical item. The relevant nouns or noun phrases are bolded:

Genitive vs. accusative case:

(1) a. Kupiłem **cukier**.
buy:PAST:1SG sugar:ACC
'I've bought (the) sugar.'

Cf. b. Kupiłem **cukru**.
buy:PAST:1SG sugar:GEN
'I've bought some sugar.' (Bacz 1989)

Vocative vs. nominative case:

(2) a. **Obywatelu kapitanie**, pobędzie u nas obywatel trochę
citizen:VOC captain:VOC be:PRF:FUT PREP 1PL citizen:NOM a bit
dłużej, to się obywatel przekona.
longer COM REFL citizen:NOM convince:FUT:3SG
'Citizen captain! If you stay with us a bit longer, you will become convinced.' (Sources)

Cf. b. **Obywatel kapitan** pobędzie u nas trochę dłużej,
citizen:NOM captain:NOM be:PRF:FUT:3SG PREP 1PL a bit longer
to się obywatel przekona.
COM REFL citizen:NOM convince:FUT:3SG
'If citizen captain will stay with us a bit longer, you will become convinced.'

Accusative vs. dative case:

(3) a. Później należałoby dać **sylwetkę** jakiego starego
later ought:PAST:HYP give profile:ACC some:GEN old:GEN
działacza.
activist:GEN
'Later one would need to give a profile of an old activist.' (Sources)

b. Później należałoby dać **sylwetce** jakiego starego
later ought:PAST:HYP give profile:DAT some:GEN old:GEN
działacza dziarski wygląd.
activist:GEN brave image
'Later one would need to give the profile of an old activist a brave image.'

In the examples above, it is clear that the verb cannot have assigned surface case to the arguments in bold, since there are no variations in the verb form that would account for the variations in case marking. This is further illustrated in (4)–(6), where nouns having different case marking are used with the same verb form:

Nominative, dative, and instrumental:

(4) a. Uciek-ł **Jan.**
run away-PAST:3M.SG Jan:NOM
'Jan ran away.'

b. Uciek-ł **Janowi.**
run away-3M.SG Jan:DAT
'He ran away from Jan.'

c. Uciek-ł **rankiem.**
run away-3M.SG morning:INSTR
'He ran away in the morning.'

Accusative and instrumental:

(5) a. Złapa-ł **obcęgi.**
catch-3M.PRF pliers:ACC
'He grabbed a pair of pliers.'

b. Złapa-ł **obcęgami.**
catch-3M.PRF pliers:INSTR
'He grabbed [it] with pair of pliers.'

c. Rzuca-ł kamienie.
throw-3M.IMPRF stone:PL:ACC
'He was throwing stones.'

d. Rzuca-ł kamieniami.
throw-3M.IMPRF stone:PL:INSTR
'He was throwing stones.' (The difference between c and d remains to be investigated.)

Dative, instrumental, nominative, and vocative:

(6) a. Wyłgał się **śmierci.**
lie:PRF:PAST:3MSG REFL death:DAT
'He escaped death by lying.'

b. Wyłgał się **śmiercią.**
lie:PRF:PAST:3MSG REFL death:INSTR
'He lied, claiming death.'

c. Wyłgał się **Piotr.**
lie:PRF:PAST:3MSG REFL Peter:NOM
'Peter got out by lying [and other people did not].'

d. Wyłgał się, **Piotrze!**
lie:PRF:IMPER:SG REFL Peter:VOC
'He got out through a lie, Peter!'

3. Prepositions and case marking

It is well known that in inflectional languages, such as German, the same preposition may be followed by nouns with different case marking. Because the preposition cannot be said to assign case, case is an independent coding means. The functions of the various case markers used after prepositions are unpredictable from one language to the next. In Polish, different cases code the difference between a stative and a directional locative complement. The prepositions *na* 'on', *w* 'in', and *z* 'from, with' can be followed by nouns marked for different cases. Accusative case marking codes the noun as a directional complement, while the instrumental case codes a stative complement:

(7) a. Upał ci padł na **mózg.**
heat 2SG:DAT fall:PAST:3M on brain:ACC
'The heat must have affected your brain.' (Sources)

b. To spotkamy się na **Nowym Świecie.**
COM meet:FUT:1PL REFL on Nowy:INST Świat:LOC
'So we will meet on Nowy Świat [a street in Warsaw].'

After the preposition *w*, accusative case marking on the noun codes the direction of movement while the locative case codes a stative locative complement:

(8) a. Skręcam **w prawo** na boczną drogę.
turn:1SG PREP right:ACC on side:ACC road:ACC
'I am turning right, into the side road.'

b. Chłopiec urodził się **we wsi** rybaki
boy give birth:PAST:SG:M REFL PREP village:LOC Rybaki
dwa tygodnie wcześniej, niż to podano w jego
two week:PL earlier than DEM give:UNSP:PAST in 3M:GEN
papierach.
papers
'The boy was born in the village of Rybaki, two weeks earlier than stated in his papers.' (Sources)

Potential counterevidence to the proposed independence of inflectional coding would be the existence of a language in which case marking is always predictable from some other element in the utterance or in which an inflectional marker must always be present in a very specific syntactic environment and must be absent when this specific syntactic environment is not present. In such a case, and only in such a case, could we say that inflectional coding is assigned by some other element in the utterance.

4. The richness of inflectional case marking

A language with as few as three case markers already has a richer coding system than that offered by linear order alone. This is because the number of linear order positions available in a given construction is limited to two, the position before and the position after the point of reference (the verb, in a clause). Viewed from another angle, since the potential number of inflectional markers in a language is far greater than the potential number of coding positions, the functional range of each inflectional marker is predictably much narrower than the functional range of each coding position. As a result, inflectional markers are capable of conveying finer grammatical or semantic distinctions than those conveyed by position alone. Since the functional range of inflectional markers in a given language need not overlap at all with the functional range of linear order, the coding potential of a combination of linear order and inflectional coding is very rich indeed.

To use an old illustrative device, let's assume an inflectional system with four cases. The range of functions of each case is considerably narrower than the range of functions of each linear order position. Compare the distinctions marked by 1 and 2 in Figure 1, a language with linear order coding only, with the distinctions marked by 1 and 2 in Figure 2, a language with four cases. Thus, a language with four cases may code both more and finer functional distinctions than a language that employs linear order coding alone. Of course, there are languages that have six, seven and more inflectional cases, each coding a different function. Because the type of coding means, and so the number of potential distinctions, varies from language to language, one cannot expect a function coded by linear order in one language to have a one-to-one correspondence with a function coded by case or by adposition in another language. However, if a language has an unmarked case (discussed below), this case may

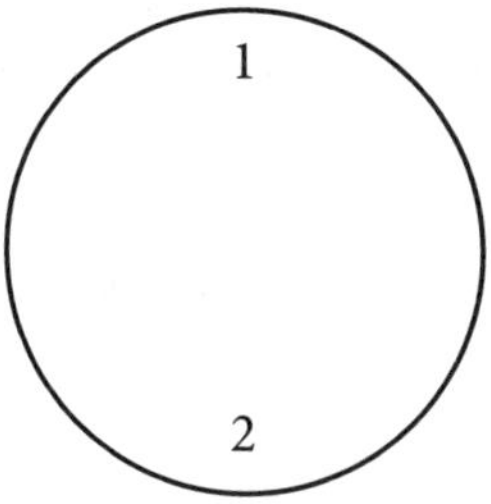

Figure 1.

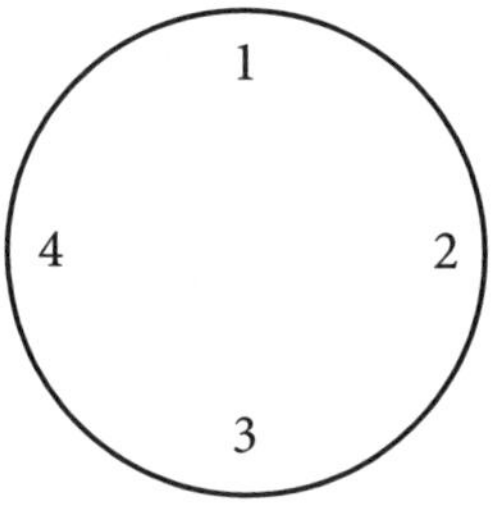

Figure 2.

correspond functionally to the unmarked position in linear order coding. This would account for functional similarities, discussed later in the present chapter, between the category subject as coded by case and the category subject as coded by linear order.

In this chapter we discuss one of the functional implications of having a rich case system, namely the possibility of coding the semantic categories of affected and non-affected object. In Chapter 9 we discuss the category of indirectly affected subject or object.

5. Unmarked and marked cases: Nominative and absolutive

It is possible to have a case system in which each case has a specific semantic function, e.g. that of coding a noun phrase for the role of agent, patient, etc. This is the situation in some Amerindian languages (cf. Mithun 1991). Many case systems, however, present a different picture. In many languages a single case — nominative in some languages and absolutive in others — is used in a variety of apparently unrelated functions, while other cases in the same languages have much narrower functions. We propose that the nominative or absolutive case in such a language is the default form and that its function is similar to that of the default position in coding by linear order. This similarity lies in the fact that neither the default case nor the default position codes a specific semantic role. In many nominative-accusative languages (e.g. Slavic), and in ergative systems (e.g. Lezgian), the nominative or absolutive case also is morphologically unmarked in comparison to other cases (Haspelmath 1993).

Evidence that the nominative case is semantically unmarked is that noun phrases marked by the nominative may have a number of semantic roles. In

Polish or Russian, a noun phrase marked by the nominative case may occur as the subject of an intransitive verb, stative verb, or verb of movement; as a controlling or non-controlling subject; as the predicate of an equational clause; or as the affected subject of a passive clause. Compare the following examples from Polish:

Controlling subject:

(9) Niech **Pan** zgasi to światło i kładzie się spać jest
let Sir:NOM turn off DEM light and lie REFL sleep be:3SG
Pan przecież poważnym człowiekiem.
Sir:NOM after all serious:INSTR man:INSTR
'You'd better turn off this light and go to sleep. You are, after all, a serious person.' (Sources)

Non-controlling subject:

(10) Co **Pan kolega** zaczyna rozumieć?
what Sir:NOM colleague:NOM begin:3SG understand
'So, colleague, what do you begin to understand? (Sources)

Subject of a passive sentence:

(11) **Ośrodki** mowy w mózgu nie zostały
center:PL:NOM speech:GEN in brain:GEN NEG become:3PL:F
zniszczone, jedynie zablokowane.
destroy:PASS:PL only block:PASS:PL
'The speech centers in the brain were not destroyed, they were just blocked.' (Sources)

Subject in a clause representing point of view of subject, as coded by the reflexive pronoun:

(12) **Słabe światło**. Psuje się przy silniejszej burzy.
weak light. spoil:PRES:3SG REFL at stronger storm
'Weak light. It gets interrupted with any stronger storm.' (Sources)

In (9)–(12), any semantic role attributed to the noun phrase marked by the nominative case is not inherent to the case but results from the computation of information provided by the form of the verb and other noun phrases present in the clause.

6. Functions of the accusative case

Theories that postulate the universality of grammatical relations such as subject and object (e.g. Lexical-Functional Grammar) imply that the function of a noun marked for the accusative case has a one-to-one correspondence with the function of a noun marked as object by linear order. A similar assumption probably was the basis for the Case Theory proposal that the object position is assigned accusative case. However, as illustrated above, it does not make sense from a theoretical perspective to assume that a language with case marking codes the same number and types of distinctions as a language in which grammatical roles are coded by linear order. Moreover, to assume so is to miss an important insight into the semantic properties of case marking, which may differ from language to language. Moreover, the same case may have different functions within the same language depending on the semantic properties of verbs and the availability of other coding means.

Hopper and Thompson (1980: 262) claim that the accusative case marks 'totally affected Object'. That this generalization is too broad is evidenced by the fact that the accusative case codes complements of verbs of perception and of cognitive verbs, i.e. complements that cannot be affected in any sense of the word:

(13) Dziś rano widziałem niedźwiedzia.
today morning see:PAST:1SG:M bear:ACC
'I saw a bear this morning.'

(14) Znałem kiedyś rachunek różniczkowy.
know:PAST:1SG:M once calculus differential
'I once knew differential calculus.'

In what follows we propose an analysis of the function of the accusative case that more accurately accounts for the data. Our analysis also explains the coding options available in languages with rich case systems.

Our hypothesis is that the accusative case is the default case for marking the second argument. With verbs that allow affectedness, the argument marked by the accusative is completely affected:

(15) To ja zjadłem **kiełbasę** w wielki piątek dnia piętnastego
DEM 1SG eat:PAST:1SG sausage:ACC on Good Friday day fifteenth
kwietnia tysiąc dziewięćset dwudziestego szóstego roku.
April thousand nine hundred twenty six year
'It was I who ate the sausage on Good Friday, April 15th, 1926.' (Sources)

The evidence that the accusative case with such verbs codes complete affectedness is provided by the fact that the genitive case cannot be used with the verb in the perfective aspect and with the subject in focus:

(16) *To ja zjadłem **kiełbasy** w Wielki Piątek dnia piętnastego
dem 1SG eat:PAST:1SG sausage:GEN on Good Friday day fifteenth
kwietnia tysiąc dziewięćset dwudziestego szóstego roku.
April thousand nine hundred twenty six year
for 'It was I who ate some sausage on Good Friday, April 15th, 1926.'

With verbs that do not imply affectedness, the argument marked by the accusative case does not bear any specific relationship to the predicate apart from the fact that it is not a controlling argument.

The genitive case in Polish codes a non-affected object or partially affected object (see below). The genitive must be used in negative clauses, i.e. clauses in which the object cannot be affected:

(17) Nie mogłem **jej** zatrzymać.
NEG be able:1SG:PAST 3F:GEN retain
'I could not stop her.' (Sources)

Cf.:

(18) Mogłem **ją** zatrzymać.
be able:1SG:PAST 3F:ACC retain
'I could have stopped her.'

An argument marked by the accusative case cannot be used in a clause representing the point of view of the subject. In Frajzyngier (1999), it was claimed that the role of the so-called reflexive marker *się* in Polish is to code the point of view of the subject. Whether or not the second argument is affected is not coded in the clause. This argument can be coded by the instrumental or the genitive case, depending on yet-to-be-identified properties of the verb, but not by the accusative case:

(19) Kto by się przejmował **Termopilami.**
who HYP REFL worry Thermopylae:INSTR
'Who would worry about Thermopylae?' (Sources)

(20) Bałem się **ludzi,** ich **opinii.**
fear REFL people:GEN 3PL:POSS:GEN opinion:GEN
'I feared people, their opinion.'

Compare the use of the accusative case in a clause that does not code point of view of the subject:

(21) Kto zdobył **Termopile.**
who capture Thermopylae:ACC
'Who captured Thermopylae?'

In the following clause coding point of view of the subject by means of the reflexive marker, the second argument is coded by the instrumental case:

(22) Czy kadra też posługuje się tą **nazwą.**
Q cadre also use REFL DEM:INSTR name:INSTR
'Does the cadre also use this name?' (Sources)

In a clause that does not code the point of view of the subject, the second argument is marked by the accusative case:

(23) Kadra też zna tę **nazwę.**
cadre also know DEM:ACC name:ACC
'The cadre also knows this name.'

The accusative is the default case of the second argument in an affirmative clause not marked for point of view. The accusative case does not by itself code affectecness, since it can occur in clauses where the second argument cannot possibly be affected. The accusative case cannot be used when the clause represents point of view of the subject or when the clause is negative.

7. Coding the non-affectedness of an argument: the genitive case

A number of studies have shown an association between genitive case marking and the negative clause (Pisarkowa 1959; Timberlake 1975; Hopper and Thompson 1980: 262). Our hypothesis about the function of the accusative case allows us to explain the function of the genitive case in the domain of coding relationships between the verb and noun phrases. In a language in which the accusative case marks affected object, an object that is not affected must be marked by some other means, whether inflectional or adpositional. In Polish, the non-affected object is coded by the genitive case.

The evidence for this hypothesis is provided by the fact that the genitive case must code the second argument of a negative clause:

(24) a. Niech **jej** Pan nie drażni.
let 3F:GEN Sir:NOM NEG tease
'Don't tease her, Sir.' (Sources)

b. Nie będziecie mieli komu złożyć **prośby** o pola.
NEG be:FUT:PL have:3PL:M who:DAT submit petition:GEN about field:PL
'You will not have anybody to whom to submit the petition for the fields.'

c. Przecież ja **tego** nie znam.
but 1SG DEM:GEN NEG know:PRES:1SG
'But I do not know that.' (Sources)

Compare the affirmative clause, in which the second argument is marked by the accusative:

(25) Przecież ja **to** znam.
but 1SG DEM:ACC know:PRES:1SG
'But I do know that.'

The genitive case also codes the second argument of inherently negative verbs, i.e. verbs that indicate that the event should not or will not happen, e.g. *zakazać* 'forbid' and *zaniechać* 'give up', *odmówić* 'deny'. These verbs, like the negative clause, imply non-affectedness of the object:

(26) Pan wczoraj fotografował dziewczęta w kąpieli chociaż wyraźnie zakazałem **jakichkolwiek zdjęć** transportu.
Sir yesterday photograph:PAST:3M girl:PL:ACC in bath although clearly forbid:PAST:1SG any:GEN picture:PL:GEN transport:GEN
'Yesterday you were taking pictures of girls in the bath, although I have clearly forbidden taking any pictures of the transport.' (Sources)

Finally, the genitive case may be used to code the second argument in a clause coding point of view of subject (repeated from 15b):

(27) Bałem się **ludzi**, ich **opinii**.
fear REFL people:GEN 3PL:POSS:GEN opinion:GEN
'I feared people, their opinion.' (Sources)

Thus, three pieces of evidence support the hypothesis that the genitive case in Polish marks non-affectedness of the second argument: (1) the second argument in a negative clause is always coded by the genitive case; (2) the genitive case marks the second argument in affirmative clauses containing verbs that cannot affect the object; and (3) the genitive case is used to code the second argument in a clause representing the event from the point of view of the subject. This analysis also supports the argument that the accusative case marks affectedness of the object, since the accusative is used in those circumstances in which the genitive does not occur.

We want to stress that we have not postulated any sort of universal semantic values for various inflectional cases. Our analysis does allow us to explain why cases have overlapping functions in some languages but different functions in other languages. In Agul (a Lezgian language; Magometov 1970), Lezgian (Haspelmath 1993), and As'wali (closely related to Avar; Magomedbekova 1967), all of which are ergative languages, neither the genitive nor any other case is used to code an argument as non-affected. The absolutive, which is the unmarked case, codes both the patient of a transitive verb and the subject of an intransitive verb. These languages have no inflectional means of marking an argument as affected, and it is possible that affectedness is simply not a domain that is coded in those languages.

8. Inflectional coding and linear order: An unexpected advantage

A second and related consequence of the presence of inflectional coding on the noun is that linear order is free to perform functions other than that of coding relationships between verb and noun phrases. Past concentration on the coding of grammatical relations and on English as the language from which the agenda for syntactic research was drawn has led to a typology in which languages are labeled as either configurational or non-configurational. In this view, configurational languages are those that code grammatical relations through linear order, like English, and non-configurational languages are those that code grammatical relations through other means. However, when one carefully examines the roles of inflection and linear order within various grammatical systems, it becomes apparent that there are many more possibilities for linear order coding in languages with inflection than in languages without inflection. Recall Jakobson's (1963) example of a clause in Russian:

(28) Lenin citiruyet Marksa.
Lenin cite:PRES:3SG Marx:ACC
'Lenin cites Marx.' (Jakobson 1963: 268)

This clause can have five other linear orders and still maintain the same truth-value with respect to the relationships between the verb and the arguments. By contrast, any changes in the linear order of the English translation result in either a changed relationship between the verb and the noun phrases or in an ungrammatical expression. In Russian and in Polish, increasing the number of elements in a clause further increases the number of linear orders, hence the number of functions that can be coded. Consider the following clause:

(29) Twardą ma pan skóre.
hard:F have:3SG Sir skin
'You have a hard skin.' (focus on 'skin') (Sources)

The constituents of this clause may have 23 other linear orders, each of them coding a different function yet retaining the same relationship between the verb and its arguments. The functions coded by various linear orders have not yet been described for Polish and certainly cannot be discovered by considering the linear orders outside of a natural discourse context. These functions have to do with information structure, referentiality, relationships between the speaker and the hearer, and possibly other domains. The important fact is that the possible linear orders are attested in natural discourse. Here we provide several different linear orders involving the verb *mieć* 'have' in the present tense, mainly with third-person singular subjects. These examples do not involve the use of the verb as an auxiliary. All examples are from Sources:

Subject before the verb (SV order):

(30) We śnie nic nie ma znaczenia.
in dream nothing NEG have significance
'In the dream nothing is significant.'

(31) Ja mam nie tracić zimnej krwi kiedy okazuje się, że
1SG have:1SG NEG lose cold blood:GEN when turn out REFL COMP
mnie nie ma.
1SG:ACC NEG have
'Am I supposed to keep my cool when it turns out that I do not exist?'

VO order; no subject noun or pronoun (second clause):

(32) A cóż ona tam robi?
CONJ what:FOC 3F there do
'And what is she doing there?'

Ma tam jakieś zajęcie.
have there some employment
'She has some business there.'

VOS order:

(33) Przecież dziś ma dyżur Marian.
but today have duty Marian
'But today Marian is on duty.'

OSV followed by prepositional phrase:

(34) Jakie on ma na to dowody.
what 3M have PREP DEM proof:PL
'What evidence does he have for that?'

Verb alone, without a pronominal or nominal subject or object:

(35) Nie, nie ma, wyjechał.
no NEG have depart:PAST:3SG:M
'No, he is not here. He has left.'

OV order, no subject noun or pronoun:

(36) Forsy ma jak lodu.
moolah have like ice:GEN
'He has money like ice.' (a figure of speech) (Sources)

OVS order:

(37) a. Pietra ma Pan teraz.
fear:ACC have Sir now
'Now you are afraid.'

b. mnie czasem interesuje inne pytanie
1SG:ACC sometimes interest:PRES:3SG different question: NOM
gdzie ona ich ma.
where 3F:NOM 3PL:ACC have
'Sometimes I am interested in a different question: Where does she have them?'

Question word followed by SOV order:

(38) No, jakie ona ma imię ta, co tu spała?
so what 3SG:F have name DEM:F:SG what here sleep:PAST:3F
'So what's her name, the one who slept here?'

Modifier of the object preceding the verb, with subject and object following the verb:

(39) Ładne ma Pan samoloty.
nice:PL have Sir airplane:PL:ACC
'You do have nice airplanes.'

The important fact about languages with nominal inflection is that the possibility of different word orders exists precisely because grammatical relations are coded by means other than linear order. Languages with rich systems of verbal inflection, such as many Bantu languages, also offer many possibilities for coding through linear order. Since linear order in such languages does not code grammatical relations, it is available to code functions in other domains. One of these domains is information structure as traditionally understood, viz. topicalization and focus. However, given the multitude of possible linear orders in such languages, there are certainly many other possible functions. One possible function is that of multiple focusing and multiple topicalizations within a single utterance, as in the following example, repeated from Chapter 1:

(40) Ty mnie, na polskiej ziemi, polskiego słowa zabronisz.
2SG 1SG:ACC on Polish soil Polish:GEN word:GEN forbid:FUT:2SG
'You are going to forbid me the use of a Polish word on Polish soil?'
(Sources)

The question could be posed whether there is a default linear order in a language in which linear order is not used to code grammatical relations. In the past, statistical data have been used to establish basic word orders for various languages, especially with respect to the orders of major constituents (subject, verb, and object). Indeed, it is very likely that there is a default word order for such languages. This 'neutral' order would not add anything to the meaning of a clause beyond what is coded by adpositions or by inflectional coding on nouns and verbs. Discovering the default word order in a given language would involve determining the functional domains coded by inflection, adpositions, and phonology, then determining the functional domains coded by word order. If there is a word order that does not code a function in any domain, this could be considered the default word order for that language.

9. Discourse implications of case coding

Accepting the hypothesis about the independence of inflectional case marking allows us to explain certain facts about language that have been rather neglected in theoretical studies, namely the effects of grammatical systems on discourse structure. Before we address that issue, a little background is necessary. In studies of discourse structure, in particular those attempting to connect the structure of discourse with grammatical structure, some linguists have taken the approach that the requirements of discourse structure determine the form of grammar. The studies of DuBois regarding ergativity and Hopper and Thompson's studies of lexical categories make some of the most explicit claims in this regard. There are a number of open issues here, one of which is the non-trivial question of the distinction between discourse and the rest of the grammar. But if we take the question of what a speaker decides to include or not to include in a clause to be a question about discourse rather than about grammar, the Systems Interaction approach provides evidence that the form of the grammar can determine the shape of discourse.

The evidence for this proposal is that expressions having the same discourse function have different forms across languages and that these forms are determined by the grammatical systems of those languages. Counterevidence would consist in showing that the same discourse function is coded by the same form in languages having different grammatical structures

We have shown in Chapter 1 that in a language where modifiers code the gender, number, and person of the head noun, the modifier alone, i.e. without the head, may function as an argument. Polish is such a language. This fact has discourse implications in the domain of argument of a proposition, as evidenced by comparing the Polish sentences and their English translations below:

(41) Gdyby **moją** **starą** wzięli na spytki.
when:HYP 1SG:POSS:F:ACC old:F:ACC take:3PL on investigation
'If they were to take my old [lady] for investigation.' (Sources)

(42) Znasz tę **starą**, Karol?
know:2SG DEM:F:ACC old:F:ACC Charles
'Do you know that old [woman], Charles?'

Znam, porządna babina.
know:1SG decent:F old woman:DIMIN
'I know [her]. A decent little old [lady] she is.' (Sources)

It is common in Polish to use adjectives like *gruby* 'fat', *chudy* 'slim', *stary* 'old', *łysy* 'bold', *mały* 'small', as terms of reference for people and entities. The contemporary Polish political lexicon has such terms as *czerwony* 'red (sg)' as a cover term for communists and *czarny* 'black (sg)' as a cover term for the clergy. The latter term represents an interesting twist, since, as recently as at the beginning of 20th century, the same term was used in a number of dialects to designate the devil. Any color term that carries number and gender coding can be used without a noun, even if this usage has not already been conventionalized:

(43) Ja lubię niebieski kolor.
1SG like:PRES:1SG blue color.
'I like the blue color.'

Najbardziej lubię niebieski.
most like:PRES:1SG blue
'Blue [color] I like the most.' (Sources)

English adjectives can be used alone if they have been lexicalized as proper names, e.g., 'Reds', 'Whites'. But apart from a few exceptions of this kind, English adjectives can be used only if they accompany the head they modify. The use of an adjective alone as the head of a clause results in an ungrammatical sentence:

(44) *If they were to take my old for investigation.
*Do you know this old, Carol?

Thus, the differences between the form of the clause in English and the form of the clause in Polish are determined by the grammatical characteristics of the two languages.

The presence or absence of coding of noun features on the modifier also has implications for the coding of possession. Because possessive pronouns in Polish code gender, number, and person, a possessive pronoun alone is a sufficient means of coding. As a result, the language does not have a distinction between dependent and independent possessive pronouns. English, however, does not code the gender and number of the possessor, so the possessive pronoun alone is not a sufficient coding means. English has accordingly grammaticalized a distinction between independent possessive pronouns, e.g. 'mine' and 'yours', which may occur without their heads, and dependent possessive pronouns, e.g. 'my' and 'your', which may not. Compare the Polish examples below, which use a single set of possessive pronouns, with the two types of possessive pronouns in the English translations:

(45) To twoja wina.
DEM 2SG:POSS:F fault
'That is your fault.'

Moja?
1SG:POSS:F
'Mine?' '***My?'**

Naturalnie, że twoja.
naturally COMP 2SG:POSS:F
'Naturally, **yours**.' *'Naturally **your**.'

Thus, the range of functions coded in English through two series of pronouns is coded in Polish through nominal inflection.

This is not to claim, however, that every language with rich adjectival morphology allows adjectives to stand alone in an utterance or that every language in which adjectives can stand alone has rich adjectival morphology. Gil (1994a) reports that in a number of languages with little adjectival morphology, including Hungarian, Estonian, Peranakan, Malay, and Tagalog, adjectives can stand alone. We have examined data for several of the languages that Gil mentions in his study. The results of our investigation indicate that (a) if a language has inflectional morphology, this morphology is applied when the adjective stands alone; and (b) if the language does not have inflectional morphology, it uses some other means to code the adjective as having the function of an argument.

Edith Moravcsik informs us that adjectives in Hungarian do not show any kind of agreement with the head noun. However, adjectives used headlessly are inflected for number and case just as nouns are. For example *nagy kalap* 'big hat' and *nagy* 'big one':

	Singular		Plural	
	Adj.+Noun	Adj. alone	Adj.+Noun	Adj. alone
Nom.	nagy kalap	nagy	nagy kalap-ok	nagy-ok
Acc.	nagy kalap-ot	nagy-o	nagy kalap-ok-at	nagy-ok-at

In Hungarian, therefore, inflection on the adjective (or, in the case of the nominative singular, the absence of inflection in contrast with the presence of inflection) codes the number and case of the potential head.

In Tagalog there is indeed no inflectional morphology on adjectives, and adjectives can occur without a noun. However, adjectives in Tagalog, like nouns in the language, are marked as arguments by prepositions. The preposition is therefore the marker of the nominal function of the inherent adjective in the clause. Here are a few examples of adjectives in different semantic roles:

(46) Nakita ko ang azul.
see 1SG PREP blue
'I saw the blue one.'

Nakita ko si kulot.
see 1SG PREP curly
'I saw the curly one.'

Nakita ko si taba.
see 1SG PREP fat
'I saw the fat one.'

Nakita ko si matanda.
see 1SG PREP old
'I saw the old one.'

(47) Nakita ako ni kulot.
see 1SG PREP curly
'The curly one saw me.'

Nakita ako ni taba.
see 1SG PREP fat
'Thee fat one saw me.'

Nakita ako ni payat.
see 1SG PREP slim
'The slim one saw me.' (All data from Mrs. Flor de Lys Houston, courtesy Alanna Van Antwerp)

Interestingly, the adjective 'young' cannot be used without a head noun in any semantic role:

(48) *Nakita ko si bata.
see 1SG PREP young
'I saw the young one.'

*Nakita ako ni bata.
see 1SG PREP young
'The young one saw me.'

The use of adjectives in Tagalog illustrates the principle of systems interaction across languages. Although the language does not have inflectional morphology, the presence of prepositions that code the roles of nominal constituents is sufficient to code an inherent adjective as having the role of an argument.

In Malay, adjectives do not have inflectional morphology. Adjectives can be used alone, but like any other noun in the language an adjective must be preceded by a classifier whose role is to code the type of entity that the adjective modifies:

(49) Si chantik datang.
CLAS beautiful came
'A beautiful one came.'

Si kurusk datang.
CLAS thin came
'A thin one came.'

Compare the use of nouns as arguments:

(50) Si adik datang.
CLAS younger sister came
'A younger sister came.'

Se ekor anjing datang.
one CLAS dog came
'A dog came.' (Faridah Hudson, p.c.)

Consider now discourse involving questions and answers. In English, questions about the subject or object usually are answered with the help of a predicate. This could be the same predicate used in the question or one of the auxiliaries 'do', 'have', 'be', etc. In the first hundred pages of the London Lund Corpus we counted twenty specific (wh-) questions about the human or non-human subject or object of the clause. Eight of these were not answered or were answered indirectly. Eleven of the remaining twelve answers contained a predicate:

1_2_1 <597 A> ^what ex:isting arrangements *:**are** _they#*
1_2_1 <598 B> ^well you see they'**re** ((the)) ar:rangements for ex/ample with !M\ace#

1_3_0 <322 A> ^what would you !l\ook at# — - -
1_3_0 <323 A> [@m] . ^g\ive us# .
1_3_0 <324 A> ^one th\ing#

1_3_0 <325 A> that ^you would l\ook at# .
1_3_0 <326 A> well ^I **would look** at illuminated m\anuscripts# -

1_3_0 <736 A> and ^I !s/aid# — -
1_3_0 <737 A> ^what particular needs did you have in !m\ind# *- -*
1_3_0 <738 A> and ^she s=aid#
1_3_0 <739 A> [@m] — oh I ^don't **mean** their
1_3_0 <740 b,c> *(— - laugh)*
1_3_0 <741 (A> physio:l\ogical _needs# *.*
1_3_0 <742 A> which ^I thought was m\arvellous#

In a larger sample of conversation, we found several examples in which the answer to a specific question was a bare noun. Many of these occurred in an interview environment in which the applicant obviously was not at ease. All of the bare nouns as answers were produced by the applicant and not by the interviewer:

3_1_3 <1169 a> yes . [@m] what was the last book you read for pleasure —
3_1_3 <1170 A> **for "^pl\easure#**
3_1_3 <1171 a> [m] —
3_1_3 <1172 A> ^\oh#
3_1_3 <1173 A> (. giggles) **The ^C\astle#**
3_1_3 <1174 A> **^K\afka#**

Even in this conversation, the applicant often replied with predicate:

3_1_3 <1194 a> what living English novelists do you like — -
3_1_3 <1195 A> what "^l\iving 'English +' [nov]+
3_1_3 <1196 a> +[m]+
3_1_3 <1195 (A> . [@:m] . I **^like /Eliot#** .

For comparison, we examined 100 pages of Polish natural discourse. Our query was limited to questions about human participants as subject or object of the clause. In the sample we found 27 questions about human subjects or objects. Nine questions went unanswered. Of those that were answered, 18 had a bare noun phrase for an answer and only one answer included the noun phrase with a predicate. Thus, in Polish, bare noun-phrase answers far outnumber answers with a predicate, while the opposite is true for English.

Answers to questions about the subject in Polish have the noun in the nominative case, a coding means that enables the hearer to recognize the role of the noun:

(51) Czy oni mają pragnienie?
Q 3PL have:3PL thirst
'Are they thirsty?'

Kto? Kaci czy **katowani.**
who henchman:PL or tortured:PL
'Who? The henchmen or the tortured?' (Sources)

(52) Kto ciebie tego nauczył?
who 2SG:ACC DEM:GEN teach:PAST:3M:SG
'Who taught you this?'

On.
3M
'He did.' (Sources)

(53) Kto po tym gościu dziedziczył?
who after DEM:INSTR fellow:LOC inherit:PAST:3M
'Who inherited after that fellow?'

Rozumie się, że **żona.**
understand REFL COMP wife:NOM
'[The] wife did, of course.'

Answers to questions about the object have the noun in the accusative case:

(54) Co Pani widziała?
what Lady see:PAST:F:SG
'Madame, what did you see?'

Wszystko cholera.
everything:ACC [Curse]
'Bloody everything!' (Sources)

The differences between English and Polish can be explained by the fact that a noun in Polish is marked by inflection for its role in the clause while a noun in English is not. Adding a predicate or auxiliary in English allows the role of the noun to be coded through linear order.

A potential counterargument against the proposed functional motivation for the forms of answers in Polish and English is that the hearer does not need to code the role of the noun phrase in his/her answer because its role is already coded in the question, which is still in the memory of the person who asked the question. Thus one could, in English, provide an answer consisting of the noun alone and rely on hearer's memory to infer its function. But this is not the way answers are usually formulated, as evidenced by the natural language data. Language production in English apparently does not rely on memory, even if the time between the question and the answer is very short.

Another piece of evidence for the proposed hypothesis is the absence of auxiliaries and predicates when the question is about an adjunct. Most adjuncts in English are marked by prepositions, and prepositions are also used in answers to questions about adjuncts. Hence, there is no need to use auxiliaries or other verbs:

1_2_2 <892 B> ((but ^which [bo:])) ^where did it come !\up ((then))#
1_2_2 <893 A> ((**at**)) the ^academic c\ouncil#

1_3_0 <648 A> ^where do you want me to s\it# -
1_3_0 <649 A> ((and)) ^she s/aid#
1_3_0 <650 b> (. laughs)
1_3_0 <651 (A> ^**on** my . right h\and#

Answers to specific questions in English and Polish illustrate how systems interaction in the coding of grammatical relations affects the forms of discourse. In Polish, where arguments are coded by case, there is no need to use predicates to code the roles of arguments in the answer; a bare noun phrase marked by the appropriate case carries all the information needed about its role. In English, where there is no case marking for nouns, a predicate or an auxiliary is used to code the role of the noun phrase. If the question is about an adjunct in English, the answer contains the appropriate preposition and no auxiliary or predicate need be used.

10. Conclusions

It has been demonstrated that case marking on nouns is an independent coding means. Case is not assigned by any other component of the clause. The presence of a rich system of inflectional coding in a language allows for the coding of both more and finer functions than may be coded by linear order alone. Within a system of inflectional coding on nouns there may be one case, the default case, that does not carry any specific semantic relationship with the verb.

Inflectional coding on nouns has important implications for discourse structure. In languages with inflectional coding, modifiers without heads can occur as arguments. Moreover, answers to specific (wh-) questions in languages with inflectional coding on nouns may have a different form from answers in languages without inflectional coding. The explanation for this lies in the principle of functional transparency. The domain of the relationship between predicates and arguments has been grammaticalized in both Polish and English. In answers to specific questions, Polish can deploy a noun alone because case marking codes the role of the noun in the functional domain of the relationship between predicate and noun phrase. In English, these relations are not coded by inflection but rather by position with respect to some reference point. The noun alone cannot be used in an answer to a specific question and so some other means, usually an auxiliary verb, must be used to code the role of the noun.

CHAPTER 5

Interaction of phonology with other coding means

1. Introduction

This chapter deals with the problem of the relationship between phonology and other coding means, specifically linear order and morphology. It is well known that prosodic means alone can code a variety of functions, such as lexical distinctions and modalities (interrogative, imperative, dubitative) and a variety of functions involved in turn-taking in conversations (Local et al. 1986). We take these functions for granted. Miller et al. (1997) and Zwicky and Pullum (1986) discuss whether syntactic rules as understood in the generative tradition, i.e. rules of forming phrasal structures, are sensitive to phonological structures. De Jong (1990), papers in Inkelas and Zec, and Xu (1992) discuss whether phonological rules are sensitive to syntactic structures. With respect to the first question, Miller et al. argue on the basis of selected problems in French that rules of syntax are not sensitive to phonology. They also claim, without providing evidence, that the rules of syntax are not sensitive to morphology. In the present chapter we go beyond the traditional issues pertaining to the syntax-phonology interface and discuss the role of phonology in encoding the internal structure of the utterance.

Our approach posits the following means for coding the functional domains of a given language: lexicon, linear order, inflectional and derivational morphology, and segmental and prosodic phonology. While we take it for granted that phonology is one of the means of conveying lexical distinctions, the present chapter focuses on the interaction of phonology with two other means, linear order and morphology, in the coding of non-lexical domains. Within this approach, part of the task of studying the phonology of a language is to determine what functional domains and specific functions are coded by phonological means in that language. We propose that one function of the phonological component of some languages is to code the internal structure of the utterance. Another function of phonology is to code the functional domain within which a given constituent should be interpreted by the hearer. The determination of functional domain is the prerequisite for applying the principle of functional transparency and a prerequisite for the semantic interpretation of the utterance.

In a language in which phonological means code constituent boundaries, a study of the phonological properties of morphemes will reveal what types of phrasal categories exist in that language. This approach contrasts with assuming *a priori* the existence of a closed universal set of phrasal categories. We may well find that different languages have different phrasal categories, though some categories probably occur more frequently than others. The existence of various categories in individual languages and their relative frequency across languages should be topics for typological research.

Just as one cannot predict the types of phrasal categories to be found in a language, one cannot predict the internal organization of a sequence of morphemes in a language. We show below that phonological means can be used to code contrasting internal organizations of the same sequence of morphemes. We explore the role of phonology in coding the internal structure of the utterance in Mina (Central Chadic) and Polish and examine the role of phonology in the coding of several functional domains in East Dangla (East Chadic) and Welsh. In all instances, phonology interacts with other means of coding the relevant functional domains.

2. Coding the internal structure of a sequence of morphemes

A problem for all types of linguistic analysis is that a given sequence of components may have several different internal structures. The sequence ABC thus may have at least four different internal structures, viz. [ABC], [AB][C], [A][BC], and [A][B][C], where square brackets represent the boundaries of some constituent. If we accept the notion that different structures have specific functions, it remains to be explained how the hearer knows which structures, and consequently which functions, are represented in a given sequence of components.

It appears that languages have means of indicating the internal structure of a sequence of components when more than one internal structure is possible. In what follows, we describe in detail the use of phonological means to code the internal structure of a sequence of lexical items in Mina and Polish.

3. Coding internal structure of an utterance through vowel reduction and vowel retention

Descriptive grammars of many Chadic languages postulate the existence of two types of contexts that affect the phonological form of a lexical item. These contexts are usually described as free, or pre-pausal, and non-free, or non-pausal. Such formulations in effect postulate that some constituent structure determines the phonological form of a word. Hoffmann (1963: 37) set the pattern of description for many Chadicists when he postulated that

> [I]n Margi and its related languages it is necessary to differentiate between the final and the non-final forms of a word. The final form is used at the end, i.e. when the word takes the last place in a sentence or word-group — also when it is followed by a short pause, before the speaker continues — or when the word is used in isolation, as mere word without a surrounding context. The non-final form is used when the word is followed by a suffix or by another word in close connexion, as e.g. a noun by its attributes, a verb by its objects, &c.... The difference may be a difference of the final vowel or a difference of its tone.

This approach has been followed by other linguists whenever similar phenomena have been encountered. Jarvis (1989), for example, postulates that all nouns in Podoko (Central Chadic), with the exception of one class, change their high tone to low if they occur after a pause, i.e. at the beginning of a sentence; after certain prepositions; and when the noun is a focused object (Jarvis 1989: 53).

For Mafa (Central Chadic), Barreteau and Le Bleis (1990) postulate a vowel laxing rule in non-pausal position, as illustrated by the following examples (Barreteau and Le Bleis 1990: 21):

	Pre-pausal	Non-pausal	Gloss
a → ə	mávár	mávər	'guinea-corn mush'
e → i	ɮe	ɮi	'cow' (ɮ = voiced lateral continuant)
o → u	ndó	ndú	'man'

These descriptions and many others imply that it is linear order that determines the phonological shape of a word. The fallacy of this approach is demonstrated by instances in which lexical and grammatical morphemes may have different shapes even though they occur in the same linear order:

(1) Sə̀-lím-é **gwáɮá** mùmbùrkó.
3SG-see-GO elephant yesterday
'I saw an elephant just yesterday.'

(2) Sə̀-lím-é **gwáɮ** mùmbùrkó.
3SG-see-GO elephant yesterday
'I saw an elephant yesterday.' (Mina)

In contrast to traditional approaches, we propose that the phonological form of a word may signal the internal structure of the utterance. We show that in some languages it is the phonological form of the word or morpheme that codes phrasal boundaries and thus enables the hearer to decode the internal organization of the utterance and to interpret it properly.

4. Phrase-final and phrase-internal forms

In Mina, lexical categories including nouns, verbs, and pronouns have two phonological forms. An analysis of these forms as pre-pausal and non-pausal would be inaccurate, since the forms with non-reduced vowels may occur even when not followed by a pause.

Our hypothesis is that the function of the form with the underlying final vowel is to mark a phrasal boundary, while the function of the form with the reduced vowel codes phrase-internal position. The evidence for the hypothesis is that, in all instances, the lexical item following the item with the reduced vowel belongs to the same constituent as the preceding element. Counter-evidence to this hypothesis would consist of clauses in which the element following the item undergoing vowel reduction does not belong to the same constituent as the preceding element.

Vowel reduction is accompanied by vocalic changes, tonal changes, and consonantal and vocalic changes combined, as described below. If the deletion of a phrase-final vowel would result in a disallowed syllable structure or consonant cluster, an epenthetic schwa is inserted. Consider the underlying form *ìdá* 'home, compound'. When the noun is followed by a possessive pronoun, the final vowel of the noun is deleted and a schwa is inserted to prevent the disallowed sequence consisting of two alveolar stops with different voicing values [dt]. The tone of the deleted vowel is realized on the epenthetic vowel. It is important to realize that the final vowel reduction is not merely vowel shortening, because the deletion of one vowel is followed by the insertion of another:

(3) á ìdə̀ tkóŋ
PREP house 2SG
'at your compound'

The word *trá* 'month, moon' becomes [tr] after deletion of the last vowel. If a three-consonant cluster would emerge as the result of deletion, a schwa is inserted between the first and the second consonant to create the syllable [tə́r]:

(4) trá láy → tŕ láy → [tə́r láy]
month time vowel deletion schwa insertion
'time'

(5) Tə́r láy tə́ mìtə́š.
month time GEN hunger
'The year of the hunger.'

The rule of final vowel deletion also operates within words, where word-final vowels are deleted before suffixes are added. Consider the addition of the plural suffix *yíì*:

(6) *Singular* *Plural*
ɮà 'cow' ɮ-yíì
wùlá 'neck' wùl-yíì
wútá 'house' wùt-yíì [note the tone change in the stem]

Vowels that function as derivational or inflectional markers are never deleted, either phrase-internally or before a suffix. Thus, the distal marker *á*, which may be added to a verb, is never deleted. Similarly, the noun *ɮì* 'meat', probably a derived form of ɮ*à* 'cow', never loses its final vowel:

(7) ɮì tə́ gə̀ldàm → [ɮì tə́ gə̀ldàm]
meat GEN pig
'pork'

5. Forms of pronouns as evidence for the function of alternations

It could be claimed that the phrase-final forms described above result from simple deletion and that there is no function associated with either the full or the reduced form of the word. Evidence against this claim is provided by the behavior of pronominal, anaphoric, and deictic forms in Mina. All of these have two variants, one occurring in phrase-internal position and the other in phrase-final position. Neither form necessarily represents the underlying form of the morpheme. The phrase-final forms are derived, resulting from the addition of the suffix *ŋ* to the underlying form. Adding this suffix results in various phonological changes in accordance with the phonological rules of Mina, including the lowering of high vowels. The phrase-internal forms also are derived, through the reduction of the final vowel. The vowel *a* is reduced to schwa. The table of pronouns below includes only singular and plural forms; the first-person dual form *námù* is not included:

Singular		*Plural*	
Phrase-internal	*Phrase-final*	*Phrase-internal*	*Phrase-final*
1 sə̀	sáŋ	nìnì	nénèŋ (EXCL)
		nòk	nòkòŋ (INCL)
2 hú	hó-n	hìnì	hìnèŋ
3 tə̀	táŋ	tə̀tə̀	tə̀táŋ

The anaphors and deictic forms are:

	Phrase-internal	*Phrase-final*
Anaphor	mbí	mbíŋ or mbə́ŋ
Deictic	wà	wàcíŋ and wàhíŋ

The phrase-final form of the pronoun may be discovered by examining the pronoun in sentence-final position. A pronoun in this position always occurs with the suffix *ŋ*:

(8) À-l zá kái à sì dáì kə̀ **sáŋ**.
3SG-say COMP INTERJ 3SG run surpass PREP 1SG
'He said, "Hey, he runs faster than me."'

The phrase-internal form has the final vowel reduced. An epenthetic schwa is inserted for syllabification:

(9) əngə məna hoŋ sə nkə zana lai a tiki.
if REL 2SG 1SG FUT find field PREP where
'If it were not for you, where would I have my field?'

The second-person singular phrase-final form is *hoŋ*, probably derived by adding the suffix *ŋ* to the underlying form *hu*:

(10) Diiga rukut ɗal tə nə məŋ fuu ha-gər kə ɗal vaŋai sei **hoŋ**.
from? clothes money GEN PREP LOC all 2SG-want INF do how so 2SG
'The cloth, and the money in the cloth, what you want to do with it is up to you.'

The third-person plural pronoun *tə̀ tà* has the form *tə̀ tə̀* in phrase-internal position:

(11) Hìd-yíì wà í **tətə̀** máàkáɗ.
man-PL DEM 3PL 3PL three
'There were three men.'

In phrase-final position the form has the suffixŋ:

(12) Kə́ ɓə̀t sì zà gómbòk-yíì wìhíŋ ábə̀ dúwə̀ŋ fə̀ɗá **tə̀táŋ**.
INF take run AUX frog-PL DEM ASSC after wake-up 3PL
'It (hyena) took flight, and these frogs woke up after it.'

The anaphor *mbí* occurs in phrase-internal position without the suffix *n*:

(13) Mə́ sə̀ yə̀m ábə̀ **mbí** táŋ.
REL drink water ASSC 3SG.ANAPH DEM
'He should drink water with that.'

The suffix ŋ is added in sentence-final position:

(14) Hídì míndíŋ à-nkə́ bə̀hl də̀vər gə́gə́ rə̀ súlúɗ ábə̀ **mbə̀ŋ**.
man other 3SG-FUT make hoe twenty ASSC 3SG
'Another person will make twenty hoes with that.'

The proposed rule of lexical reduction in phrase-internal position allows us to explain the source of the genitive marker *tə́*, which is obtained through reduction of the demonstrative *ta* in phrase-internal position (cf. Frajzyngier, Johnston with Edwards Ms.):

(15) a. Wə́l tə́ ɮ-íì.
COW GEN COW-PL
'necks of cows'
b. ɮə̀ tə́ bítsì.
COW GEN Bitsi
'Bitsi's cow'

Evidence that the word-final nasal in pronouns, anaphors, and deictic forms is a suffix is provided by two facts: (1) the nasal occurs with only one class of morphemes and in only one position, viz. phrase-final; and (2) other lexical items that end in a nasal consonant retain this consonant in phrase-internal position:

(16) də́wə́ŋ mə̀bíŋ
back door
'back of the door'

6. Functions coded by phrase-final forms

6.1. Topicalization

The coding of a phrasal boundary is the principal means of indicating that a noun phrase is topicalized: A topicalized subject occurs in phrase-final form while a non-topicalized subject occurs in phrase-internal form. The phrase-final forms of lexical items also serve to distinguish between topic and focus constructions, in that discourse and sentential topics form a phrase separate from the material that follows. Evidence that the topic constitutes a separate phrase lies in the retention of the final vowel, as illustrated by the following elicited examples (natural examples follow):

Topicalized object (our English translations, though unacceptable in most dialects, are intended to render the notion of topicalization):

(17) Wùdá zə̀m-ù.
food eat-ANAPH
'The food, eat it!'

(18) Wùdá kə́ zə̀m zá.
food INF eat AUX
'The food, he ate it.'

The underlying form also occurs in phrase-final and clause-final position:

(19) Zə̀m wùdá.
'Eat food!'

The non-topicalized object, when not phrase-final, has a reduced vowel:

(20) Zə̀m wùdə́ zà.
eat food AUX
'Eat the food!'

The topicalization of a pronominal subject is coded by the use of the phrase-final form of the pronoun:

(21) Halləm waciŋ a za saŋ kə ɓəgam abə hoŋ gəlbə tə jip.
daughter DEM 3SG COMP 1SG INF speak ASSC 2SG better GEN hole
'That girl said, "Me, talking with you; a grave is better than that."'

Similarly, topicalization of the pronominal object is coded by the phrase-final form of the pronoun:

(22) Dók zá hà kúl kə̀ dzə́m ábə̀ mbí skù **sáŋ** à nkə̀
horse COMP 2SG able INF wrestle ASSC 3SG NEG 1SG 3SG FUT
kwár-á-k kwár kwár kə̀ s kúl kə̀ ɗál-á-ŋ skə̀ŋ skù.
drive-OBJ-1SG drive drive AFF 1SG able INF do-OBJ-3SG thing NEG
'The horse said, "You cannot fight against him. Me, he made me run and run; I cannot do anything."'

Compare the phrase-final form of the first-person singular pronoun:

(23) Ha-waŋ abə **saŋ**.
2SG-sleep ASSC 1SG
'You have to sleep with me.'

When the subject pronoun is not topicalized, the pronoun *sà* is reduced to *s* and an epenthetic schwa is inserted for the purpose of syllabification and tone realization:

(24) Sə̀ tsú nàŋ.
1SG went 1SG(ICP)
'I went away.'

6.2. Phrase-final form of the noun as marker of the predicative function

Final vowel reduction serves to distinguish between the predicative construction and the modifying construction when the predicate and the modifier are either nouns or adjectives. Subjects in the nominal predicative construction retain their final vowel. The noun *ɮà* 'cow' retains its vowel when it serves as the subject of a predicative construction:

(25) ɮà féš.
cow small
'The cow is small.'

When the noun *ɮà* is modified by a determiner, the vowel *a* is deleted and a schwa is inserted to allow proper syllabification:

(26) ɮə̀ wá féš.
cow DEM small
'This cow is small.'

The noun *ńkwá* 'goat' retains its vowel when it serves as the subject of a predicative construction:

(27) Ńkwá féš.
goat small
'The goat is small.'

When the noun *ńkwá* occurs in phrase-internal position, its vowel is deleted and the segment [w] is realized as the vowel *u*. This indicates that the sequence Noun-Modifier is a modifying rather than a predicative construction:

(28) ńkù báétə
goat large
'a large goat'

(29) ɮə́ ntá ábə̀ ńkù ntá
cow one ASSC goat one
'one cow and one goat'

6.3. Marking a phrasal boundary

A device that marks phrasal boundaries allows the hearer to properly interpret the assignment of arguments within a clause. The marking of phrasal boundaries does not result from the presence of a pause, because quite often no pause is present. Instead, the marking of phrasal boundary is an independent coding means. As noted earlier in this work, final vowel retention on the element preceding the adverb of time codes this adverb as being a separate phrase, and therefore in focus:

(30) Sə̀-lím-é **gwáɮá** mùmbùrkó.
3SG-see-GO elephant yesterday
'I saw an elephant **yesterday**.'

The non-focused adverb has the preceding vowel deleted:

(31) Sə̀-lím-é **gwáɮ** mùmbùrkó.
3SG-see-GO elephant yesterday
'I saw an elephant yesterday.'

In the following example the noun *ɮà* 'cow' retains its final vowel, marking it as the end of the affirmative clause. The noun *ńkwa* 'goat' is reduced to *ńkù*, allowing this noun to be properly interpreted as belonging to the next phrase:

(32) À-skə́m-á **ɮà** **ńkù** skù.
3SG-buy-GO cow goat NEG
'It is a cow that he bought, not a goat.'

The progressive marker *rà* retains its vowel to code the boundary between two clauses:

(33) Á nd **rà** á-ldr kàt.
3SG walk PROG 3SG-slip just
'He walked and slipped.'

In phrase-internal position the final vowel of the progressive marker is deleted:

(34) Á ndə̀ **r** rə́ cíŋ.
3SG go PROG PREP his father
'He is going to his father.'

Similarly, the end-of-episode marker *za* retains its vowel to code phrase-final position:

(35) Kə́ bér-á ńkù **zá** kə́ skə́m-á rə̀kút **zà**.
INF sell-GO goat AUX INF buy-GO dress AUX
'She sold a goat and bought a dress.'

7. Functions coded by the absence of phrasal boundaries

7.1. The direct object is part of the verb phrase

The underlying form of the verb 'to gather' is *ɗá*, as illustrated in the next example:

(36) **ɗá ɗá** á ɗə̀ wàné. (Ful)
fetch fetch 3SG pour a lot
'It rained a lot.'

The object following the verb is part of the phrase to which the verb belongs, as evidenced by the deletion of the final vowel of the verb, followed by insertion of the tone-bearing schwa:

(37) Kə́ ɗə́ tìpíɗ tsáy zà.
INF gather termites finish AUX
'She has finished looking for termites.'

The final vowel on the progressive marker *rá* is retained to mark phrase-final position:

(38) Í nd-**rá** í-nd-**rá** váŋ wáp kə́ ɗá.
3PL walk-PROG 3PL-walk-PROG rain fall INF gather
'They walked, walked, and the rain started to fall.'

7.2. The auxiliary is part of the preceding verb phrase

Some auxiliaries, e.g. the end-of-event marker *zà*, occur after the object of a transitive verb or after an intransitive verb. The auxiliary belongs to the phrase consisting of the verb or verb plus object, as evidenced by the fact that the final vowel of the verb or object is deleted before the auxiliary. Thus the noun *mávù* 'homemade beer' is reduced to *máv* before the auxiliary *za*:

(39) Sə̀ kə́ gr-á **máv** zà.
1SG INF want-GO beer AUX
'I used to like beer.'

(40) Há-nkə́ də́ **wúdə́** zà.
2SG-INF cook food AUX
'You prepared food.'

Cf. the noun with the final vowel:

(41) Zə̀m **wùdá.**
eat food
'Eat!'

7.3. The negative marker is part of the preceding phrase

The negative marker *skù* in Mina occurs in clause-final position. This marker belongs to the preceding phrase, as evidenced by the fact that the preceding element undergoes final vowel deletion:

(42) Á sə̀ **máv** skù.
3SG drink beer NEG
'It is not beer that he drinks.'

Cf.:

(43) Á sə̀ **mávù.**
3SG drink beer
'It is beer that he drinks.'

7.4. The associative phrase is not part of the verb phrase

The associative construction is a separate phrasal category in Mina, i.e. it is not part of the verb phrase. The evidence for this claim is that the final vowel is not deleted before the associative phrase. The noun *lúmù* 'market' retains its final vowel before the associative phrase:

(44) Tsú n-**lúmù** ábə mbí.
go PREP-market ASSC 3SG
'He went to the market with her.'

8. Marking phrasal boundary through tonal changes

If the underlying form of a lexical item does not end in a vowel, the phrasal boundary is coded by tonal changes. The third-person possessive pronoun *ngə̀n* cannot be phonologically reduced. Instead, in sentence-internal, phrase-final position it has high tone:

(45) Kə́ vl-á-h wə̀də̀ zá à-ɗál-á-h ɗámà tsú kə̀ də̀bə̀l **ngə́n**.
INF give-OBJ food COMP 3SG-do-OBJ-2SG good left INF leave home 3SG
'If she gives you food, she does you good, and if she leaves her home …'

(46) Wál wà á ndí tàl **ngə́n** dàp á ndí tàl **ngə́n** dàp á dámù.
wife DEM 3SG HAB walk 3SG only 3SG HAB walk 3SG still PREP bush
'The wife would still take walks in the bush.'

Compare low tone on the same pronoun in phrase-internal position:

(47) Ábə̀ nd-á **ngə̀n** wùtá.
ASSC go-GO 3SG village
'Then she returned to her village.'

Other Chadic languages have grammaticalized other means of coding phrasal boundaries. Barreteau (1988) postulates that in Mofu-Gudur (Central Chadic) every word and every morpheme has two forms, one contextual and the other non-contextual. The contextual form is characterized by the change of the vowel in a closed syllable from *a* or *e* to schwa. This change takes place only when a word is followed by another word or morpheme:

(48) Vèr é → və̀ré.
room DEF
'the room' (Barreteau 1988: 465)

9. Prepositional forms of pronouns in Polish

It is well known that the isolated forms of third-person pronouns in Polish (and Russian) are different from the forms that follow a preposition. The forms in isolation have an initial palatal glide (all examples from Sources):

(49) Albo jest dyktatura proletariatu, albo **jej** nie ma.
either is dictatorship proletariat:GEN either 3F NEG have
'Either there is a dictatorship of the proletariat or there is not.'

Ile **jej** zawdzięczamy.
how much 3F owe:PRES:1PL
'How much do we owe her.'

Zawsze ci mówiłam, żebyś się **jej** trzymał.
always 2SG say:PAST:1SG:F COMP:SUBJ:2SG REFL 3F hold:M
'I was always telling you to stick with her.'

Po czym wmówił dozorcy **jej** osobowość.
after what:INSTR persuade:PAST:3M janitor 3F personality
'Afterwards he instilled in the janitor an image of her personality.'

In some constructions, third-person pronouns following a preposition begin with a palatal nasal. All pronouns begininng with the nasal consonant are clitics. This is again illustrated on the third-person singular feminine form:

(50) Nie darmo chyba **o niej** mówią.
NEG free probably about 3F talk:3PL
'It is not for nothing that they talk about her.'

Zaraz może się **od niej** wynieść.
immediately can:PRES:3SG REFL from 3F take out
'He can leave her immediately.'

Dobrać **do niej** trzeba chłopaków.
take to 3F need boys:GEN
'One should add a few boys to her.'

Może pewne cechy **w niej** przetrwały.
maybe some features in 3F survive:PAST:3PL:F
'Maybe some features have survived in her.'

Dostrzegałby te cechy **po niej** odziedziczone
notice:HYP:3SG:M DEM:3PL features after 3F inherit:PASS:PART
'He would have kept noticing those features that were inherited from her.'

Niespodzianka **dla niej**, kiedyś ją uśpili chloroformem.
surprise for 3F once 3F sleep:3M.PL:PAST chloroform:INSTR
'A surprise for her. She was once put to sleep with chloroform.'

The occurrence of the nasal cannot be explained by any current phonological rule prohibiting a palatal glide after a preposition, since a preposition may be followed by a noun beginning with a palatal glide:

(51) jeżeli chodzi **o jabłka**
if go:3SG about apples
'as far as apples are concerned'

Było trochę placka **z jabłkami.**
be a bit pie with apples:INSTR
'There was some apple pie.'

(52) na jagnię — o jagnię
'on a lamb' — 'about a lamb'

przed jagnię — z jagnięciem
'before a lamb' — 'with a lamb'

The nasal form of the pronoun has the instrumental function even when not preceded by a preposition, as illustrated in the answer to the following question:

(53) To po co ci taka piłka?
DEM PREP what 2SG such ball
'So what do you need such a ball for?'

Żeby **nią** rzucali tacy duzi chłopcy.
COMP:SUBJ 3F:INSTR throw:3PL:M such:M:PL big:M:PL boys
'So that she would be tossed around by such big boys.'

Our hypothesis is that the nasal variant codes the pronoun as belonging to the same phrase as the preceding word, while the palatal variant indicates that the pronoun does not belong to the preceding phrase and so should be interpreted as belonging to a separate phrase. If a preposition is followed by a pronoun that is a modifier rather than the head of the noun phrase, the pronoun is not cliticized and does not begin with the nasal:

(54) Wyznaczyłem dwa tysiące nagrody za **jej** zwrot.
establish:PAST:1SG:M two thousand reward:GEN for 3F return
'I have established a reward of two thousand for her return.'

Jeżeli ona nie rozumie, że w **jej** wieku …
if 3F NEG understand COMP in 3F age
'If she does not understand that at her age …'

Wzięłabym na **jej** miejscu, będąc, innego chłopa.
take:HYP:1SG:F on 3F place be:ACT:PTCPL another man:ACC
'If I were her, I would have taken in another man.' (ACT:PTCPL = active participle)

Więc on mówi, że to wszystko, co po **jej** mężu
so 3M say COMP DEM all what after 3F husband
nieboszczyku w kotle na Hanamecie znaleźli.
deceased in pot on Hanamet find:3PL
'So he says that is all they found of her dead husband in the boiler on the Hanamet.'

To bardzo ładnie z **jej** strony.
DEM very nice from 3F side
'It is very nice of her.'

I tak wciąż się coś wali na **jej** głowę.
CONJ so always REFL something collapse on 3F head
'And so something always comes up for her.'

Nie w **jej** guście …
NEG in 3F taste
'Not to her taste …'

The function of the palatal glide at the beginning of the pronoun, then, is to code the pronoun as belonging to a phrase that does not include the preceding element. The isolated form of the third-person pronoun thus codes a phrasal boundary, while the form with the nasal onset codes continuation of the same phrase. Whether the pronoun begins with a nasal consonant or a palatal glide is crucially important for the interpretation of the pronoun as a modifier of the possessive construction (the form with the palatal glide) or as the head of a noun phrase (the form with the nasal consonant). In the behavior of pronouns we see the principle of functional transparency at work: The domains coded in Polish are specific to this language and are not linked with any elements of a language-independent reality.

10. Vowel assimilation in East Dangla

In East Dangla (East Chadic), vocalic changes in the forms of demonstrative pronouns have a syntactic function. The language has several series of demonstratives, including the proximate demonstratives *ὲka* or *ìka* (masculine singular), *ὲta* or *ìta*; (feminine singular), and *àku* (plural). The vowel preceding the demonstrative pronoun and the first vowel of the pronoun may undergo phonological assimilation for the features [round] and [ATR]. The assimilation may proceed from left to right or from right to left. In the following example, the temporal preposition *báa* assimilates to the demonstrative *ὲka*. The preposition also undergoes vowel shortening, in accordance with the phonological rules of the language:

(55) **Bέ-ὲk** ŋàa-kí bákárdà tʸàŋkò.
TEMP-DEM COP-2M strong but
'If so, you must be very strong!'

In other utterances, the first vowel of the demonstrative after the preposition *báa* remains unchanged:

(56) Báa **ὲk** às-tí ŋàs ŋaa ób-ín-tí, tʸà
TEMP DEM come.PRF-3F.IO 3M.COMP 3M.IRR marry-INF-3F.POSS 3F
pootʸ-ga.
refuse.PRF-3M.O
'When one (man) came wanting to marry her, she refused him.'

The demonstrative *ὲka* sometimes assimilates to the third-person masculine object marker *gà*:

(57) Géedè mín tal-tí-gà-**àk** tʸàs 'àwyá!'.
Geede PREP see.PRF-3F-3M.O-DEM 3F.COMP INTERJ
'Geede, as soon as she saw him, said, "Look!"'

In other utterances, the demonstrative does not assimilate to the object marker *ga* (tone on this marker codes aspect):

(58) Tʸàs 'tál-di ŋùu ɗúu tin-ga **ɛ̀ka**.'
3F.COMP see.SUBJ-only 3PL NEG bury.PRF-3M.O DEM
'She said, "Just look, they buried it right here."'

Since the first vowel of the pronoun may or may not interact with the preceding vowel in exactly the same environment, the question arises whether assimilation carries a functional load. The possibility that it is an idiosyncratic characteristic of individual speakers has to be ruled out, since both forms of the demonstratives occur in the speech of the same speaker.

There is, in fact, a functional distinction between the retention of the underlying vowel and assimilation. Assimilation between the demonstrative and the preceding syllable indicates that the demonstrative is part of the preceding syntactic unit, while retention of the underlying vowel indicates that the demonstrative belongs to a separate syntactic unit. We illustrate below some of the functions of vowel changes in demonstrative forms in East Dangla. We also show the interaction between these functions and the functions coded by phrase-internal and phrase-final vowel deletion.

10.1. Functions of the demonstrative with underlying first vowel

The demonstrative with the underlying first vowel may function as the only constituent of a locative phrase or the only constituent of noun phrase. In East Dangla as in Mina, final vowel retention marks phrase-internal position, while final vowel deletion codes phrase-final position:

Locative phrase:

(59) Tʸàs 'ŋàa ŋúu **ɛ̀ka**.'
3F.COMP 3M NEG DEM
'She said, "There he is."'

Noun phrase:

(60) Wer-ìk **ɛ̀ka** nʸèsá **ɛ̀k** sá nʸèsá.
place-DEM DEM pull.IMPF DEM also pull.IMPF
'Then the one (man) pulled, and the other (man) pulled, too.'

In a verbless clause, it is not always possible to tell whether the demonstrative functions as a noun or a locative phrase:

(61) Ŋàa kó **ɛ̀ka**.
3M already DEM
'It's right there.' or 'It's that one.'

The demonstrative with underlying first vowel also occurs as the initial morpheme of a number of fixed expressions, e.g. *ɛ̀k dúu* 'then', *ɛ̀k sá* 'still, even so':

(63) **ɛ̀k** ɗúu kɛ́k! kɛ́k! kɛ́k! daɗ-dʸi-t dindìl tát.
DEM NEG IDEO cut.PRF-3M-PRF club large
'Then, chop! chop! chop! he cut a large club.'

(63) **ɛ̀k** sá báa no tòmiɗ bɛ tʸà bòr sooɗ di kíi tálé
DEM still TEMP 1SG finish.PRF CONJ 3F dry.PRF little only 2M.IRR see.VN
daan di noo mín-ín-tí.
now only 1SG.IRR fill.VN-INF-3F.POSS
'Even so, I will finish and it will dry a little, and then you will see; I will fill it.'

10.2. Functions of the assimilated demonstrative

Assimilation between the demonstrative and the preceding vowel indicates that the demonstrative has some function within the preceding syntactic unit, but it does not specify the nature of that function or its functional domain. Functions of assimilated demonstratives including coding a preceding clause as dependent, coding spatial deixis, and coding an argument as previously mentioned. The masculine demonstrative *ɛ̀ka*, when it interacts with the preceding vowel, may have any of these functions. Feminine and plural demonstratives function only in the domain of modifying a noun or noun phrase. In the following example, the assimilated plural demonstrative *òku* (underlying form *àku*) codes previous mention of the noun phrase *gam-tʸò-òku* 'their things':

(64) Kúŋ kòkìráarà dʸàlak kó andè-èka, ŋà nʸáam
COLL chickens.DIMIN prepare.IMPF already mush-DEM, 3M give.IMPF
bi-y eenè tʸuy tʸuy ak gam-tʸò-**òku**.
mouth-3M.POSS here IDEO PREP things-3PL.POSS-DEM.PL
'While the chickens were preparing the mush, he kept sticking his nose like this into the middle of what they were doing.'

In the next example, the first bolded masculine demonstrative *ɛ̀ka* assimilates to the preceding syllable, indicating that the demonstrative belongs to the preceding syntactic unit. Here the function of the demonstrative is to code the temporal clause beginning with *báa* as a dependent clause. The masculine demonstrative *ìka* after the noun 'snake' codes previous mention of this noun. The form *ìka* is identical with one variant of the underlying form. Evidence that *ìka* here is the product of assimilation is that the underlying form of the oblique suffix is *rì* and that the form **àalo-l-ɛ̀ka* (snake-OBL-DEM) would not be possible:

(65) ɛ̀k-ɗúu dʸamin ɾákkí tʸàs 'báa kú élél
DEM-NEG old woman one 3F.COMP TEMP 2PL want.IMPF
ìml-ín-tí ka **Géedè-èka**, kú-dʸì gìne
bring out.VN-INF-3M.POSS DEM Géedé-DEM 2PL.IRR-3M.IO make.VN
rayin ku àalo-l-**ìka**.'
trick DEM snake-OBL-DEM
'Then one old woman said," If you want Geede's freedom, you have to play a trick on the snake."'

Evidence that the assimilated demonstrative *èka* in the preceding example codes the end of a clause as opposed to the end of the genitive phrase 'Geede's freedom' is that *Géedé* is a feminine proper name while the demonstrative *ɛ̀ka* is masculine. Compare the use of the feminine demonstrative *ɛ̀ta*, in the assimilated form *èt*, in the genitive phrase 'Geede's navel':

(66) Mín ɗebèr-dʸi-tè, às-dʸi-t ób ɗìpk-ít ta
PREP close.PRF-3M-PRF come.PRF-3M-PRF catch.SEQ navel-DEM DEM
Géedè-èt ŋàs ŋà wáaɗ-gì-tʸ kó.
Géedé-DEM 3M.COMP 3M nurse.IMPF-IMPF-3F.O already
'As soon as he had closed the door, he grabbed Geede's navel and started nursing it.'

In the following example, the first instance of the demonstrative is identical with one variant of the underlying form but in fact reflects assimilation to the preceding high vowel. Evidence for the presence of assimilation here is that the potential variant *kát-dʸi-ɛ̀k* is not acceptable. The assimilation of the demonstrative to the pronoun *dʸi* indicates that the two elements belong to the same clause. The precise function of the demonstrative is to mark the clause as dependent (see below). In the second instance, the masculine demonstrative assimilates to the [+ATR] vowel of *bàrre* 'basket' and therefore belongs to the same syntactic unit. Because the noun *bàrre* is feminine, the masculine demonstrative cannot belong to the noun phrase; therefore, the demonstrative again codes a dependent clause. The third instance of the demonstrative marks the end of the ideophone, which is treated here (and elsewhere) as a fragment of direct speech. The final instance of the demonstrative marks the end of the prepositional phrase *iŋ bàrre-èta*. Assimilation indicates that the demonstrative belongs to the preceding syntactic unit, while the use of the feminine demonstrative indicates a modifying function within the domain of the noun phrase:

(67) Kát-d^{y}i-**ìk** Gàllàam bɛ ìt^{y} kó bàrre-**èk** ŋà
go.IMPF-3M-DEM Gallaama CONJ take.PRF already basket-DEM 3M
t^{y}ɔ̀tɔtɔ! t^{y}ɔ̀tɔɔ!-**ɛ̀ka**, ŋàs ŋàar bɛ bug iŋ bàrre-**èta**.
IDEO-DEM 3M.COMP 3M CONJ fill trough.IMPF ASSC basket-DEM
'As he was going there, Gallaama had taken up the basket again and was letting the water go plink! plink!, as if he were watering with the basket.'

10.3. Interaction between vowel harmony and other coding devices

Evidence that vowel harmony in demonstrative pronouns is an independent coding device in East Dangla is provided by the interaction between this and other coding devices, namely phrase-internal vowel deletion and coding through linear order.

10.3.1. Vowel harmony and phrase-internal final vowel deletion

In East Dangla, as in Mina, words in phrase-internal position undergo final vowel deletion. The presence of the final vowel of a morpheme that can undergo final vowel deletion codes a syntactic boundary:

Phrase-internal form:

(68) Tyàs 'gín **máakít** goy tar bɛ, ǐ-dù ɓaaka.
3F.COMP make.IMPF thing be.IMPF DEM CONJ put in.IMPF-1SG.IO fear
'There was an animal there, and I was afraid.'

Phrase-final form:

(69) Haa-à, gín-núu **máakítí**.
no make-NEG thing
'No, there's nothing.'

We have argued that a demonstrative pronoun that undergoes assimilation with the preceding syllable is thereby coded as belonging to the preceding syntactic unit. This is distinct from coding the end of that syntactic unit, since a morpheme can belong to the preceding syntactic unit without being at the end of that unit. The presence or absence of the final vowel of a demonstrative form indicates whether the demonstrative occurs within a phrase or at a phrasal boundary. Thus, either the assimilated or the unchanged form of the masculine proximate demonstrative may occur with or without the final vowel *a*.

Recall that the unassimilated form of the masculine demonstrative may mark the end of a fragment of direct speech. The demonstrative does not assimilate to because it is not part of the preceding syntactic unit, i.e. the speech fragment. The presence or absence of the final vowel of the demonstrative indicates whether the fragment of speech is itself part of a larger syntactic unit. In the following, deletion of the final vowel of the demonstrative indicates that the sequence "*ɓùyúus*"-*ìk* is part of a larger syntactic unit:

(70) Sókíríy ŋàs 'yǎllà báa gìn-in-tè "ɓùyúus"-**ìk** kán
squirrel 3M.COMP INTERJ TEMP make.PRF-1SG.O-PRF IDEO-DEM 2F
giy ríyáaw.'
TOP sing.SUBJ.PL
'The squirrel said, "Now, whenever I go 'snip', you start singing." '

In the next example, the presence of the final vowel of *ὲka* codes a phrasal boundary, in this case the end of the protasis clause marked by *báa*. Therefore, the demonstrative is the final element of the larger syntactic unit containing the demonstrative and the fragment of speech:

(71) ŋàs 'báa ròŋ-kè bɛ an-kè ŋùs "iyà
3M.COMP TEMP children-2F.POSS CONJ say.PRF-2F.IO 3PL.COMP mama
seese, seese"-**ὲka**, buw-kè aa gìne ɗúutú.'
hello hello-DEM milk-2 F.POSS IRR make.VN bitter
'He said, "If your children say to you, 'Hello, mama, hello,' your milk will turn bitter."'

10.3.2. Vowel harmony and linear order

We have shown that one of the functions of the assimilated masculine demonstrative is to mark the preceding clause as dependent. One type of dependent clause that may be so marked is the temporal/conditional protasis clause (example 63, repeated here):

(72) Báa kú élél ìml-ín-tí ka **Géedè-èka,**
TEMP 2PL want.IMPF bring out.VN-INF-3M.POSS DEM Géedé-DEM

kú-dʸì gìne rayin ku àalo-l-ìka.
2PL.IRR-3M.IO make.VN trick DEM snake-OBL-DEM
'If you want Geede's freedom, you have to play a trick on the snake.'

The protasis clause is marked by the assimilated demonstrative if and only if the apodosis clause is not overtly marked as a separate clause. Marking of the apodosis may take one of several forms, one of which is linear order. The linear order SVO in East Dangla occurs only in the independent clause. If the apodosis clause in a temporal construction has SVO order, the protasis is not marked as dependent by the assimilated demonstrative or by any other means. Since subject and object pronoun forms are distinct, it is not possible to interpret the pronominal subject of the apodosis clause (bolded) as belonging to the protasis:

(73) Ŋàs báa ŋà ròóp-gu **ŋaa gìn-inʸ-tʸò**
3M.COMP TEMP 3M meet.PRF-3PL.O 3M.IRR make.VN-INF-3PL.POSS
raɗa.
difficulty
'He says that when he meets them he will make trouble for them.'

The construction consisting of the *irrealis* marker *aa* followed by a subject clitic occurs in dependent clauses but always occurs in clause-initial position. If the apodosis in a temporal construction begins with the sequence *aa*+subject, the protasis clause is not marked by the assimilated demonstrative (apodosis bolded):

(74) Báa ŋù bèr-du-tʸa giy **a-n-dʸìŋ bèr-ín-tí**
TEMP 3PL give.PRF-1SG.IO-3F.O TOP IRR-1SG-2M.IO give.VN-INF-3F.POSS
di.
only
'When they give it to me, I will just give it to you.'

If the apodosis clause has verb-initial order, a characteristic confined to dependent clauses, the protasis clause must be marked by the assimilated form of the demonstrative *ɛ̀ka*:

(75) Báa tʸà saa kó-**òka,** ɗàwaɗ gáaɗʸ-tí.
TEMP 3F drink.IMPF already-DEM hit.SUBJ neck-3F.POSS
'While she is drinking, hit her neck.'

(76) Báa mín tòmoɗ-tí-t té-n-tí-**ìk**
TEMP PREP finish.PRF-3F-PRF eat.VN-INF-3F.POSS-DEM
hádʸám-gì-dʸi wáaɗʸ-ín-tí.
begin.IMPF-IMPF-3M nurse.VN-INF-3F.POSS
'Always, after she had finished eating, he started nursing her.'

Regardless of the form of the apodosis clause, the protasis is marked by *ɛ̀ka* if the protasis (bolded) lacks overt arguments:

(77) Héytàra, **báa kís-ìk** noon élél-lúuɗé.
INTERJ TEMP like-DEM 1SG want.IMPF-NEG
'If that's the way it is, I don't want it.'

An implication of the fact that the assimilated form of *ɛ̀k(a)* codes what precedes it as a dependent clause is that the protasis may consist solely of grammatical morphemes, e.g. the temporal protasis marker *báa* or the preposition *mín* (Arabic). Without the assimilated demonstrative, such markers would be interpreted as belonging to the following clause:

(78) **Bɛ́-ɛ̀k** dàa-tènʸ-tʸà kó èéɗ di.
TEMP-DEM finish-1PL.INCL-3F.O already here only
'If so, we'll finish it right here.'

(79) **Mín-ìk** táty-tyò tùulay-dyi-t kalàk.
PREP-DEM father-3PL.POSS continue.PRF-3M-PRF immediately
'At that, his father kept right on going.'

In East Dangla, phonological interaction between the first vowel of the proximate demonstrative and the preceding vowel indicates that the two constituents belong to the same phrase. The absence of such interaction indicates that they belong to different phrases. Retention or deletion of the final vowel of the demonstrative codes phrase-final or phrase-internal position, as it does in Mina. As is the case in Polish, the functional domain coded by phonological properties in East Dangla is that of coding the syntactic organization of the utterance rather than some segment of extralinguistic reality.

11. Consonant mutation in Welsh

This section concerns the functions of consonant alternations in Welsh. Welsh has three types of consonant alternations referred to as mutations, viz. soft, nasal, and aspirate. The initial consonant of any lexical category may undergo mutation under certain conditions. The following chart illustrates soft mutation, the focus of our discussion:

Basic sounds (radicals):	p	t	c	b	d	g	m	ll	rh
Soft mutation:	b	d	g	f	dd	∅	f	l	r

Descriptive grammars of Welsh and theoretical studies using Welsh as a source of data assume that consonant mutation is triggered by some component of a clause, specifically by the preceding constituent (Borsley and Roberts 1996: 46; Williams 1980; Zwicky 1984; Harlow 1989). This assumption requires scholars to postulate that if soft mutation is present but the trigger is absent, there is some underlying structure in which the trigger directly precedes the element undergoing mutation. Zwicky considers soft mutation to be a manifestation of Case triggered by the verb, an assumption that requires him to account for the presence of mutation when the trigger and the target are not adjacent. Sproat (1985) posits an underlying SVO structure for Welsh whereby soft mutation takes place in the underlying structure and movement of the verb to clause-initial position yields VSO order with a mutated object. Harlow (1989) proposes that soft mutation is triggered by phrasal categories rather than by the verb.

A crucial fact for the understanding of mutation in Welsh is that mutation is not limited to nouns in the object function but may occur with any lexical category, including verbs and determiners, provided the underlying phonological structure includes a consonant that can undergo mutation. Scholars of Welsh agree that consonant mutations had their origin in phonological changes triggered by preceding lexical items. Nasal mutation still appears to be triggered largely by the phonological structure of the immediately preceding constituent. However, contrary to other descriptions of Welsh, we propose that soft and aspirate consonant mutation in Welsh is an independent coding means, i.e., that mutation is not triggered by any constituent present in the utterance.

Mutation as a coding means does not code a specific semantic or discourse function; instead, the presence of soft or aspirate mutation instructs the hearer to interpret the component that has undergone mutation **not** in connection with the immediately preceding component but in connection with something else. That 'something else' could be another component in the same clause, phrase, or utterance. Mutation can also instruct the hearer to interpret the mutated constituent as a marked member of some functional domain such as gender, number, modality or type of predication. In any case, a mutated constituent is to be interpreted with reference to something other than the immediately preceding constituent.

The following analysis is based on examples from the literature and data kindly provided by Trefor Roberts, Gareth Roberts and their Welsh-speaking friends. Without these data, which often were accompanied by very thorough commentary, we would not have been able to conduct the analysis. All Welsh examples below that are not accompanied by a citation have come to us from native speakers of Welsh, courtesy of Trefor Roberts. Needless to say, our conclusions are not necessarily shared by Mr. Roberts or by other Welsh speakers.

In what follows, we provide evidence for the proposed functions of consonant mutation by examining the conditions under which various constituents do or do not undergo mutation.

11.1. The domain of gender and number

Welsh has a possessive construction consisting of a possessive pronoun followed by a noun. The noun may in turn be followed by another pronoun coding the person, gender and number of the possessor. This pronoun is optional in some dialects and obligatory in others. The form Possessive pronoun Noun Pronoun is considered the full, formal form, but one or both pronouns may be omitted provided that meaning can be preserved through consonant mutation. If the noun cannot undergo mutation, both pronoun forms must be used. Thus, the form *tad* 'father', which undergoes mutation, need not be accompanied by either pronoun, since mutation is sufficient to code the presence and nature of the possessor. The full form *fy nhad i* (Possessive pronoun-Noun-Pronoun) is seldom heard and is considered redundant (Trefor Roberts, p.c.):

tad	nhad	fy	nhad i
'father'	'[my] father'	1SG.POSS	father 1SG
		'my father' (full form)	

The noun *stafell* 'room' does not undergo mutation, so both pronoun forms must be used to code possession:

stafell	ei	stafel e	ei	stafell hi
room	3SG.POSS	room 3M	3SG.POSS	room 3F
'room'	'his room'		'her room'	

The third-person singular possessive pronoun *ei* is not marked for gender, so the construction *ei* Noun codes possession without coding gender. The domain of gender in Welsh thus constitutes a different domain from that of possession. The domain of gender, and sometimes of number, is coded by mutation. Soft mutation on the possessum codes a masculine possessor while aspirate mutation codes a feminine possessor:

(80) ei gath
3SG cat
'his cat' (cath 'cat')

(81) ei chath
3SG cat
'her cat'

(82)	car	'car'		
	ei char (hi)	'her car'	ei gar (e)	'his car'
	plant	'children'		
	ei phlant (hi)	'her children'	ei blant (e)	'his children'
	teulu	'family'		
	ei theulu (hi)	'her family'	ei deulu (e)	'his family'

In the South Glamorgan dialect, the third-person plural possessive pronoun is identical with the third-person singular pronoun. The possessum after the plural pronoun does not undergo mutation. Therefore, the presence or absence of mutation codes number while the type of mutation codes gender:

(83)	[ka:θ]	[i ga:θ]	
	cat	'his cat'	
	[i ka:θ]	[i xa:θ]	
	'their cat'	'her cat'	(Thomas 1984:209)

According to the grammatical descriptions, the definite article *y*, *yr*, or *'r* does not trigger soft mutation in masculine nouns but does trigger soft mutation in feminine nouns (Williams 1980:7). We propose instead that soft mutation after the article is the marker of the feminine gender of the noun (data from Williams 1980; translations by the authors of the present work). The domain of definiteness is coded by the definite article and the domain of gender is coded by the presence or absence of mutation. The feminine noun undergoes mutation while the masculine noun does not; thus, the feminine is the marked category within the domain of gender:

(84) pon 'bridge' y bont 'the bridge'
torth 'loaf' y dorth 'the loaf'
cyllell 'knife' y gyllell 'the knife'
buwch 'cow' y fuwch 'the cow'
dafad 'sheep' y ddafad 'the sheep'
gardd 'garden' yr ardd 'the garden'

(85) Gwelais y bont.
see:1SG DEF bridge
'I saw the bridge.'

(86) Gwelais y fuwch.
see:1SG DEF COW
'I saw the cow.'

Additional evidence that soft mutation after the definite article codes the gender of the noun is provided by nouns that can be either masculine or feminine. Again, soft mutation codes the feminine gender while the presence of the radical (i.e. absence of mutation) codes the masculine gender:

(87) y dyn
'the man'
y ddyn
'the woman' (archaic; Williams 1980:20)

(88) y priod
'the spouse' (m.)
y briod
'the spouse' (f.) (rare)

These examples demonstrate that it is not the nature of the noun that triggers the mutation but rather mutation that codes the properties of nouns. The reason masculine nouns do not undergo soft mutation after the definite article, even in the object function, is that such mutation would constitute a conflicting coding of features belonging to the same domain, in this case the domain of gender:

(89) Gwelodd y ci.
see:3SG DEF dog
'He/she saw the dog.'

(90) Gwelais y ci.
see:1SG DEF dog
'I saw the dog.' (Awbery 1976:7)

11.2. Grammatical relations

11.2.1. Mutation of the subject

Within the domain of grammatical relations in Welsh, the category subject is unmarked and the category object is marked. In pragmatically neutral clauses, the subject occupies the position after the verb. When the subject follows the verb, the first consonant of the subject is not mutated. If the subject is separated from the verb by any other element for any reason, the subject undergoes soft mutation. The absence of soft mutation when the subject follows the verb, and the presence of mutation when the subject is separated from the verb, indicates that soft mutation is not triggered by the preceding element. Here as elsewhere, soft mutation on a lexical item indicates that the item should not be interpreted in connection with what immediately precedes it but rather in connection with some other element. When the lexical item undergoing mutation is an argument, the element in connection with which the argument should be interpreted is the verb.

The evidence for the proposed hypothesis begins with an examination of existential clauses. When the subject follows the verb there is no mutation:

(91) Mae **caws.**
exist-3M cheese
'There is cheese.' (caws 'cheese')

Mae **caws** gen i.
exist-3M cheese with:1SG 1SG
'I have cheese.'

When the subject is separated from the verb it undergoes soft mutation:

(92) Mae gen i **gaws.**
be PREP 1SG cheese
'I have cheese.'

Unmarked word order:

(93) Mae **cath** yno.
be cat there
'There is a cat.' (cath 'cat')

Marked word order, emphasizing *yno*:

(94) Mae yno **gath**.
be there cat
'**There** is a cat.'

11.2.2. Mutation of the object

The function of soft mutation on the object in the VSO clause is to direct the hearer to interpret the mutated noun in connection with the verb. This is the same as the function of soft mutation on the subject in clauses where the subject does not occur immediately after the verb.

In modifying constructions, neither the head nor the modifier undergoes any mutation. The underlying initial consonant of a noun can thus be identified through the modifying construction:

(95) **ci** plentyn
dog child
' (a) dog (of a) child' (ci 'dog')

In a pragmatically neutral clause, the object follows the subject in the order VSO and is always coded by soft mutation:

(96) Gwelodd y dyn **gi**.
see:3SG DEF man dog
'The man saw (a) dog.'

Soft mutation is also present when the object immediately follows a verb whose subject is marked by inflection:

(97) Gwelais **gi**.
see:1SG dog
'I saw (a) dog.'

The only case in which the object does not undergo soft mutation is when the object is in clause-initial position. In this case the object cannot be interpreted in connection with the preceding verb because there is no preceding verb. Nor can the object be interpreted within any domain outside of the discourse, since the functional domain of a noun phrase in clause-initial position cannot be determined:

(98) **Ci** welais i.
dog saw.1SG 1SG
'A dog, I saw.'

(99) Y **ci** welodd e.
DEF dog saw.3SG 3M
'The dog, he saw.'

(100) **Pont** mae'r dyn wedi gweld.
bridge exist.DEF man after see
'A bridge, the man has seen.'

In the domain of grammatical relations, consonant mutation interacts with linear order in a rather complex way. The object is always coded by mutation when it follows the verb, whether immediately or after some other constituent(s). In the neutral order VSO, the object is distinguished from the subject because only the object undergoes mutation. The same is true of the linear order SVO, in which only the object mutates. In the linear order OVS neither argument undergoes mutation, allowing this linear order to be distinguished from the subject-initial linear order.

In the literature, attention has been drawn to cases in which the object follows the verb and does not undergo soft mutation. This appears to occur only when the verb is nominalized, producing a construction that is not a verbal clause but rather a modifying construction having the structure Verbal noun Noun. As already observed, in modifying constructions neither the head nor the modifier undergoes soft mutation:

(101) Mae'r dyn wedi gweld ci. (not *gi).
is.3SG-DEF man PRF.PTCL see(VN) dog
'The man has seen a dog.' (Sproat 1985: 179) (VN-verbal noun; PTCL: presumably 'particle', though Sproat does not expand this abbreviation)

11.3. Polarity

Within the functional domain of polarity in Welsh (as in many other languages), affirmative modality is the unmarked value and negative modality is the marked value. Negative polarity in the past tense is marked by aspirate mutation. Mutation in this case directs the hearer to interpret the mutated constituent in connection with some functional domain in the language, in this case the domain of polarity:

(102) [kləuas ɪ] [xləuas ɪðɪm]
'I heard.' 'I didn't hear.'

[təulɔn nʊ] [θ əulɔn nʊ ðɪm]
'They threw.' 'They did not throw.'
(South Glamorgan dialect; Thomas 1984: 219)

clywed 'to hear' chlywes i neb 'I heard no one.'
talu 'to pay' thalodd e ddim 'he did not pay.'
para 'to last' phariff e ddim 'it will not last.'

11.4. Types of predication

In the domain of types of predication, verbal predication is unmarked. A verbal predicate may be preceded by the form *yn*, which appears to have a function similar to that of a copula. When the form *yn* precedes a verb there is no soft mutation. Nominal, adjectival, and adverbial predicates must be preceded by *yn*, and nouns, adjectives, and adverbs in the predicative function undergo soft mutation. This soft mutation is not triggered by *yn*, since a verb after *yn* does not undergo soft mutation. Therefore, soft mutation is an independent coding means.

In verbal and adjectival predications derived from the same root, the verbal predication does not undergo mutation:

(103) Mae Tom yn gwella.
exist:3SG Tom COP improve (V)
'Tom is getting better.'

In the adjectival predication, the predicate undergoes soft mutation:

(104) Mae Tom yn well.
exist:3SG Tom COP better (ADJ)
'Tom is better.' (gwell 'better')

Other adjectival predications (examples from Williams 1980):

(105) Mae ef yn dda.
exist:3SG 3M COP good
'He/it is good.' (da 'good')

(106) Cysgod yn drwm.
sleep COP heavy
'He/she slept heavily.' (trwm 'heavy')

Nominal predication:

(107) Mae ef yn feddyg.
exist 3M COP doctor
'He is a doctor.' (meddyg 'doctor')

(108) (Mae'r) Canu'n glir.
exist:DEF singing:COP clear
'The singing is clear.' (clir 'clear')

(109) Gyrrwch yn ofalus.
drive COP careful
'Drive carefully.' (gofalus 'careful')

Soft mutation after *yn* in the copular function indicates that the predicative expression is non-verbal, regardless of the source of the lexical item coding the predication. Even if the lexical item is underlyingly verb, soft mutation instructs the hearer to interpret the predication as nominal.

11.5. Prepositions

According to the literature, 'soft mutation follows all prepositions except *er* [for/since/though], *rhag* [before/against/from], *rhwng* [between, among], which take the radical [i.e. the underlying form], and *yn*, which can take soft or nasal mutation or the radical according to its function' (Williams 1980: 127). The list of prepositions after which soft mutation occurs includes: *am* 'about', *ar* 'on', *at* 'to', *dros* 'over', *drwy* 'through', *gan* 'with/by', *i* 'to/for', *wrth* 'by', *o* 'of/from)', *hyd* 'until', *heb* 'without', *dan* 'under'.

Mutation, when it occurs, takes place only when the preposition immediately precedes the noun. It does not occur if some element intervenes between the preposition and the noun:

(110) am blant
'about children' (soft mutation)

am ei phlant hi
about 3F children 3F
'about her children' (no mutation)

am gar
'about a car' (soft mutation)

am y car
about DEF car
'about the car' (no mutation)

Soft mutation after prepositions is subject to several possible interpretations. The traditional view is that prepositions trigger soft mutation. This interpretation is suspect on two accounts: (1) there are many instances of soft mutation that are unrelated to prepositions; and (2) after some prepositions there is never any mutation. Hence, categoriality of the lexical item as preposition does not trigger soft mutation. Moreover, since the prepositions that are followed by mutated nouns end in many different segments, it cannot be said that soft mutation is triggered by phonological properties of the prepositions.

The second possible interpretation is that soft mutation after prepositions is a syntactic variant of nouns, i.e. a lexical variant occurring in a specific environment. This hypothesis cannot be sustained because the mutated form does not occur after all prepositions. Alternatively, one could assume some kind of leveling process whereby the phonological product of contact between a certain preposition and the following noun was extended to all situations in which a noun follows a preposition. Again this notion cannot be sustained, because nouns are never mutated after certain prepositions.

Another possibility would be to view soft mutation as a coding means that tells the hearer to interpret the noun after the preposition in connection with some element preceding the preposition, such as a verb or perhaps another noun. If a certain preposition is never followed by mutation, this would indicate that the noun is to be interpreted only in connection with the preposition. Since explanations invoking triggering, leveling and lexical variation cannot be supported, we incline towards this last possibility. Additional evidence for this hypothesis is that the three prepositions after which there is no soft mutation, viz. *er* 'for/since/though', *rhag* 'before/against/from', and *rhwng* 'between/among', do not relate the following noun to a preceding one but have only the succeeding noun(s) in their scope. The preposition *yn* 'in, at, into', which is the only preposition followed by nasal mutation, is discussed below.

11.6. Domain of modification

The modifying construction in Welsh usually has the order Head Modifier. Recall that neither the head nor the modifier undergoes mutation. We take such a construction to be the unmarked modifying construction. However, if the modifier precedes the head, the head undergoes soft mutation. The function of soft mutation is to indicate that, contrary to the norm, the modifier precedes rather than follows the head. In other words, soft mutation enables the hearer to recognize which element in the sequence is the head and which is the modifier. *Hen* 'old' is one adjective that always precedes the noun, which in turn undergoes soft mutation:

(111) am hen gar
about old car
'about an old car'

am yr hen gar
about DEF old car
'about the old car'

Possessive pronouns also precede the noun, which may be followed by a second pronoun referring to the possessor. These constructions have the order Modifier Head, and the possessum noun undergoes mutation as follows: soft mutation in the second-person singular and third-person masculine; aspirate mutation in the third-person feminine; and nasal mutation in the first-person singular. There is no mutation in the third-person plural:

	Possessor	*Possessum*	*Possessor*
1SG	*fy* (my)	noun (+nasal mutation)	i
2SG	*dy* (your)	noun (+soft mutation)	di
3SG(M.)	ei (his)	noun (+soft mutation)	e (S. Wales)
3SG(M.)	ei (his)	noun (+soft mutation)	o (N. Wales)
3SG(F.)	ei (her)	noun (+aspirate mutation)	hi
1PL	*ein* (our)	noun (NO mutation)	ni
2PL	*eich* (your)	noun (NO mutation)	chi
3PL	*eu* (their)	noun (NO mutation)	nhw

(courtesy of Trefor Roberts)

We cannot yet explain the function of aspirate mutation after the numerals *tri* 'three' and *chew* 'six' and the absence of mutation after other numerals.

11.7. Nasal mutation

Nasal mutation occurs in only two instances: after the preposition *yn* (which also marks verbal nouns) and after the first-person possessive pronoun *fy*. In the former case, at least, nasal mutation appears to be a phonological phenomenon without an independent coding function. The following chart shows the products of nasal mutation:

Basic sounds (radicals):	b	c	d	g	p	t
Nasal mutation:	m	ngh	n	ng	mh	nh

(112) yng ngwaith y bardd
in work DEF bard
'in the work of the bard' (gwaith 'work')

(113) ym Methel
'in Bethel' (place name)

(114) yng nghochliw'r machlud
PREP red color:DEF set
'in the red sunset' (coch 'red'; lliw 'color') (Williams 1980)

(115) yn nhywydd teg Mehefin
in weather fair June
'during the fair weather of June' (tywydd 'weather')

Given its limited distribution, nasal mutation appears to be conditioned by the phonological environment. As such, it may be a synchronic piece of evidence for how consonant mutations in general came to be. Mutations probably started as products of phonological changes and eventually acquired a grammatical function of their own that allowed them to occur even in the absence of the appropriate phonological environment.

12. Conclusions

Phonological devices, in addition to providing the means for conveying lexical, grammatical and semantic distinctions, have an independent coding function in some languages. As such, phonological devices are in complementary distribution with other coding means discussed in the present work. In some languages, phonological means code the boundaries of constituents within a sequence of morphemes. In languages of this kind, the study of phonological means may provide the basis for a typological study of the types and frequency of syntactic constituents. In other languages, phonological means direct the hearer to interpret a given constituent in connection with some other previously mentioned constituent. If no such constituent is available, the hearer is directed to interpret a given element as a marked member of some functional domain coded in the language.

The phonological coding in languages discussed in this chapter belongs to the functional domain of signalling the syntactic organization of the utterance. The scope of the principle of functional transparency is the formal characteristics of the utterance rather than some part of extralinguistic reality. At the same time, understanding the syntactic structure of the utterance is what enables the hearer to understand the meaning of the utterance.

CHAPTER 6

Agreement, or coding on other constituents

1. Introduction

The phenomena we deal with in the present chapter are usually referred to as 'agreement', or 'head coding' (Van Valin 1985; Nichols 1986). Matthews (1997) gives the following definition: 'Syntactic relationship between words and phrases which are compatible, in a given construction, by virtue of inflections carried by at least one of them.' In the present work we use the term 'agreement' rather than 'head coding' because of inherent difficulties in determining the category 'head'. The Bloomfieldian criteria for the definition of 'head' would have us exclude prepositions. Moreover, agreement phenomena apply equally to heads and to dependents, e.g. adjectives in modifying constructions. As observed in Corbett (1991), adverbs, numerals, and even conjunctions and complementizers may show agreement.

We take agreement to be the coding on category X of some characteristic(s) of category Y, whether or not category Y is present in the construction. The coding on category X may reflect specific features of category Y, such as gender, person, and number, or may simply represent the category Y without specifying any of its features. We reiterate that the presence of the same feature on two different lexical items does not prove that the presence of the feature on one item is caused by the presence of that feature on another item.

In what follows we briefly review some of the most important approaches to agreement, concentrating on the issues rather than on the history of these approaches. We then outline briefly a typology of agreement systems. Our own analyses focus on coding on the verb, the issue most frequently discussed in contemporary literature on agreement.

2. Approaches to agreement

The traditional approach to agreement treats agreement as an automatically controlled phenomenon that can be summarized as follows: The presence in a construction of an element Z with features Y triggers a corresponding feature Y on another element X in the construction. Agreement so conceived may involve case, gender, number, and person. In this view, the presence of a noun in a clause can trigger the presence of some features of this noun on the verb. This approach to agreement can be found in many dictionaries of linguistics and in functional studies (Marouzeau 1951; Moravcsik 1978; Dik 1989; Van Valin 1993: 72–4; Lehmann 1982, 1988; Seiler 1986; Steele 1990). The discussion of agreement has also been intricately linked with the discussion of anaphors as documented in Bosch (1983). Many contemporary formal theories have focused on the representation of agreement (Elliot 1981; Lapointe 1985 (written in 1980); Davies 1986; Bok-Bennema 1991). In the Minimalist program (Chomsky 1995, 1992) there are two types of AGRPs (agreement phrases). An agreement phrase is 'a collection of features (gender, number, person); these are common to the systems of subject and object agreement, though AGRs and AGRo may of course be different selections, just as two verbs or NPs may differ' (Chomsky 1992: 10).

A refreshingly different approach to agreement is presented in Nichols (1986). The author proposes a typology of languages wherein some languages are head-marking and others are dependent-marking, where marking refers to a broad range of relationships that hold between the head and dependent constituent of a construction.

Frajzyngier (1985b), analyzing phenomena often referred to as 'number agreement', proposes that in many languages what is usually called number agreement is an independent coding means. Thus, number coding on the verb is not triggered by the number (singular or plural) of arguments in the clause but rather serves to indicate whether such arguments are singular or plural. In some languages in which there is number coding on both nouns and verbs, number may be coded on either the noun or the verb of a given clause, but not both. For another analysis that does not treat agreement as an automatically controlled phenomenon, see Barlow (1992).

3. Evidence against the mechanistic operation of agreement: toward a typology of agreement mechanisms

Evidence that agreement markers are not the result of an operation whereby the presence of a noun phrase in the clause triggers the presence of some marker(s) on the verb is provided by two types of phenomena. In the first, the same noun may have different agreement markers in different clauses. If agreement were the automatic result of the presence of the noun, then only one agreement marker should be possible with that noun. Consider object coding in Gidar (Central Chadic). Some animate nouns may be accompanied by either masculine or feminine agreement markers. The noun *wín* 'baby, child' may have the accompanying agreement marker *n* 'third-person masculine singular' or the agreement marker *ta* 'third-person feminine singular'. The role of these markers is to code the gender of the baby:

(1) a. Mà wín tà-t ə́-zgə̀lə́-**n**.
mother child PRES-F INF-feed-3M
'Mother is feeding the baby (M).'

b. Mà wín tà-t ə́-zgə̀lə́-**tà**.
mother child PRES-F INF-feed-3F
'Mother is feeding the baby (F).'

Now consider agreement with the first-person singular subject in Russian. The first-person singular pronoun *ja* does not code gender. In the past tense, the verb always codes the gender, number and person of the subject. The first-person singular pronoun *ja* may occur with a verb coding either masculine or feminine gender:

(2) Odin raz ja dazhe zatormozíl ego u Fanderflita.
One time 1SG even stop:PAST:M:SG 3M PREP Fanderflit:GEN
'Once, I even stopped it [train] at Fanderflit' (Russian sources).

(3) Ja ran'she ne znala, chto jest' takoe nazvanie serpantin.
1SG before NEG know:PAST:SG:F COMP exist such name serpantin
'I never knew before that there was such a name as "serpantin".' (Russian sources)

This type of agreement is evidence that coding on the verb is an independent coding means rather than an automatically triggered phenomenon.

The other type of evidence against the automatically controlled operation of agreement is provided by those languages in which 'agreement' markers are present but the noun phrase with which the verb 'agrees' is not. Slavic languages, Latin, Italian, Spanish, and Bantu languages are just a few examples.

The past tense of the Polish verb codes the person, gender, and number of the default argument, i.e. the subject, as well aspect. This coding is shown on the verb *jeść* 'eat':

	Masculine	Feminine
First	*jadł-e-m*	*jadł-a-m*
Second	*jadł-e-sń*	*jadł-a-ś*
Third	*jadł*	*jadł-a*
Plural		
First	*jedl-i-śmy*	*jadł-y-śmy*
Second	*jedl-i-ście*	*jadł-y-ście*
Third	*jedl-i*	*jadł-y*

This agreement coding on the verb is not triggered by the presence of another element in the clause because the overt nominal argument does not have to occur in the clause, as shown below. The first-person singular independent pronoun in Polish is *ja*. It does not distinguish gender. The first-person subject is marked on the verb even if *ja* is not present in the clause. In either case the marking on the verb is an independent coding means, since it codes gender of the speaker, the category not coded by the first person pronoun:

(4) Jak to dobrze, że jednak ciebie **znalazłam.**
how DEM good COMP nevertheless 2SG:ACC find:PAST1SG:F
'How good that, despite everything, I [F] have found you.' (Sources)

(5) Więc nie dlatego **znalazłem** śmiech u mojej
therefore NEG because of this find:PAST:1SG:M laughter at 1SG:POSS:F
córki.
daughter:GEN
'So it is not because of this that I [M] found laughter in my daughter.' (Sources)

Similar systems of coding on the verb not triggered by any component of the clause are attested in Lango (Western Nilotic; Noonan 1992), Arabic (Jelinek 1993), Cayuga (Mithun 1992), and Ngandi (Australia, Heath 1978). Such languages used to be referred to in the generative literature as 'pro-drop' languages. This is a poor choice of term, since it implies that these languages had a subject pronoun at some synchronic or diachronic stage but that this pronoun has disappeared as a result of some historical or synchronic process.

Whatever the metaphor 'pro-drop' stands for now, its use results from a lack of understanding of the functions of various coding means available in languages. Meillet (1937) states explicitly that a clause with an independent subject pronoun in Latin has a different meaning from a similar clause without the pronoun. Similarly, the independent pronoun in Polish is the marker of switch reference and contrast. In the following example, the first-person singular pronoun *ja* is in contrast with *Pan* 'polite form of address, masculine':

(6) Dla Pana może nie mieć znaczenia. ale **ja** jestem człowiekiem
for Sir perhaps NEG have significance:GEN but 1SG be:1SG man:INSTR
poważnym.
serious:INSTR
'For you it may be without significance, but I am a serious man.'
(Sources)

Thus, subject coding on the verb in Polish is an independent coding means that is not triggered by any element in the clause and that interacts with other coding means in the same domain.

We must now address more explicitly why we do not consider cases in which coding on the verb and a potential trigger are both present in the clause to be agreement in the traditional sense. We do not consider these to be cases of triggered agreement because the coding on the verb must be present regardless of whether the potential trigger or controller is present or not. Moreover, with the same controller, viz. with the first- and second-person singular pronouns *ja* and *ty*, the verb may code masculine or feminine gender. These are features not present in the pronouns, so they cannot be triggered by the pronouns. It remains to be shown why, if the controller is present in the clause, the verb codes the same person and number features coded by the controller. The answer depends crucially on the forms of the verb in Polish. Every finite verbal form must include information about the gender, person, and number of the subject. Consequently, if there is an overt subject in the clause, whether nominal or pronominal, the verbal form must code the same features that this subject codes for person and number and, for the third person, gender. If this were not the case the clause would be inherently contradictory, the overt subject coding one value and the verb coding another value belonging to the same domain. Such a clause would be uninterpretable. Thus, although agreement does not exist, disagreement is disallowed, and the fact that two constituents code the same value within the same domain is not evidence for a cause-and-effect relationship.

Where markers of agreement occur is not really important. In Hausa (West Chadic), unlike in Polish, subject pronouns are not phonologically fused with the verb. However, they must be present whether or not there is a nominal subject in the clause:

(7) a. Taa je kasuwa.
3F:PRF go market
'She went to the market.'

b. *Binta je kasuwa.
Binta go market

c. Binta taa je kasuwa
Binta 3F:PRF go market
'Binta went to the market.' (Schwartz 1989: 57)

d. Sarki ya tashi.
chief 3M rise
'Chief he rose.' (Kraft 1963: 165) 'The chief rose.')

Hausa also has a class of independent pronouns, different from subject pronouns, which behave syntactically like free nouns. A clause with an independent pronoun also must have a subject pronoun:

(8) a. **Ni** bà-**n** yàrda ba.
1SG NEG-1SG agree NEG
'As for me, I don't agree.' (Kraft 1963: 165)

b. **Shi** zâ-**i** zama jàgàba.
3M FUT-3M become leader
'He will be the leader.' (Kraft 1963: 165)

Schwartz (1989: 57) argues that the 'subject pronominal features in INFL [coding on the verb, in the present framework] are dependent arguments when an independent subject NP is absent but agreement features when independent subject is present.' In contrast, within the present framework, subject pronouns always represent independent coding of the argument, regardless of what other elements appear in the clause. The illusion of agreement results from the fact that once a specific value in a given domain is coded on one element of a clause, no other value from the same domain may be coded within the same clause; i.e., disagreement is disallowed.

As further evidence for agreement as an independent coding means, consider object coding on the verb in Gidar (Central Chadic). In this language, the verb codes the information status of the object, with the known object being a marked category. The third-person masculine known object is marked on the verb either by *nə* or by high tone on the epenthetic schwa, depending on the phonological structure of the verb. An unknown object is not coded on the verb and the epenthetic schwa, if any, has low tone.

Known object:

(9) a. Tə̀-nzád-ə́-k ɗə̂fá.
3F-cure-3M-PRF man
'She cured the man.' (the man is known)

Unknown object:

(9) b. Tə̀-nzád-ə̀k ɗə̂fá.
3F-cure-PRF man
'She cured somebody.'

Since the presence of the object in (9b) does not trigger coding on the verb, the agreement coding in (9a) must be an independent coding means.

Superficially, English could be considered to provide a counterargument to the hypothesis that agreement is an independent coding means. In the present tense, the verb with the suffix *-s* cannot occur unless the clause has a third-person singular subject, whether nominal or pronominal. This may follow from the general principle that a clause in non-imperative mood has to have a subject. In English, unlike Polish, the verb cannot occur without an overt subject, whether nominal or pronominal. Compare the following Polish example with its English translation:

(10) Jeśli leży, to czego szukacie w tej zmarzniętej
if lie:3SG:PRES DEM what:GEN search:2PL in DEM:F:GEN frozen:F:GEN
ziemi. Niech spoczywa w Panu.
soil:GEN let rest:3SG:PRES in Lord.
'If he lies [here], what are you looking for in this frozen soil? Let him rest in Lord.' (Sources)

Since the suffix *-s* in English does not in itself code the subject but must be accompanied by an overt subject noun or pronoun, we must ask why the suffix *-s* is necessary. The answer lies in the explanation we have provided in Chapter 3. The marker *-s* on the verb codes the distinction between nouns and verbs because there are no other systemic markers that distinguish between the two categories. This distinction is necessary for the proper interpretation of the utterance. The marker *-s* on the verb thus codes a different domain from that coded on the noun, and the co-occurrence of the third-person singular subject noun/pronoun and the suffix *-s* on the verb provides only the illusion of agreement.

4. Which lexical categories can code agreement?

The type of agreement illustrated above, that of coding the subject on the verb, is the most familiar type. The coding of agreement elements on adjectives, numerals, and demonstratives is well known from Indo-European languages and represents another common agreement phenomenon. These types of agreement are also widespread in Bantu languages and in conservative dialects of Fula (West Atlantic, Niger-Congo). Many languages also exhibit coding of objects and adjuncts on the verb. One such system is described later in this section.

Less familiar is the coding of noun phrase features on the preposition. In Gidar, the associative preposition *də̀* codes the gender and number of the noun phrase that follows it. The masculine singular is unmarked, but the feminine and the plural (which is common to both genders) are marked by suffixes to the preposition. In phrase-internal position the vowel of the suffix is deleted and the associative preposition inherits the high tone of the suffix:

Masculine singular:

(11) a. Á jàaɓé ná-n **də̀** zə̀l wá.
PREP Djabe COP-1SG ASSC husband 1SG
'I live in Djabe with my husband' lit. 'I have a husband in Djabe.'

Feminine singular:

(11) b. Á jàaɓé ná-n **də́-t** glúk ná wà.
PREP Djabe COP-1SG ASSC-3F wife GEN 1SG
'I live in Djabe with my wife.'

c. Kàrmbáxà mə́zə̀líŋ **də́-t** gùlkú áw-sə̀ná-n bà.
turtle male ASSC-F female 3M:FREQ-know-3M NEG
'One cannot distinguish between the male and the female turtle.'

In the plural, which is coded by the suffix *ti*, the schwa of the associative is fronted before the suffix of the third-person plural agreement is reduced:

(11) d. Á jàaɓé ná-n **dí-t** gíl ná-wà.
PREP Djabe COP-1SG ASSC-3PL wife.PL GEN-1SG
'I live in Djabe with my wives.' (Frajzyngier (in press))

It would appear on the face of it that agreement on the associative preposition is triggered by the gender and number of the following noun, but this conclusion is not correct. In fact, gender and number marking on the associative preposition is an independent coding means. Evidence that the gender and number marker is not triggered by the presence of another argument in the clause is provided by clauses in which the associative preposition is not followed by a noun, as in questions about the associative argument. The existence of agreement markers enables the speaker to express his/her presuppositions regarding the potential gender and number of the questioned participants:

(12) a. **Dә́-t** náwá kә̀-l á wrá dì.
ASSC-3F who 2SG-go PREP field QS
'With whom (F) did you go to the field?'
b. **Dí-t** náwá kә̀-l á wrá dì.
ASSC-3PL who 2SG-go PREP field QS
'With whom (PL) did you go to the field?'

Two other prepositions in Gidar also code the gender and number of participants: The dative/benefactive preposition *sә́* and the causative preposition *gә̀*. Like the associative preposition, these prepositions can code gender and number without the potential trigger being present in the clause. This is the case in specific interrogative clauses. In the following examples, both prepositions and verbs code the gender and number of the dative argument:

(13) a. **Sә́-n** náwá kә̀-psә́-**n** bárdàwván dì.
DAT-3M who 2SG-give-3M hoe DEF QS
'To whom did you give the hoe?'
b. **Sә́-t** náwá kә̀-psә́-**t** bárdàw ván dì.
DAT-3F who 2SG-give-3F hoe DEF QS
'To whom (F) did you give the hoe?'
c. **Sí-t** mày náwá kә̀-psí-**t** bárdàw ván dì.
DAT-3PL ASSC.PL who 2SG-give-3PL hoe DEF QS
'To whom (PL) did you give the hoe?'

There are languages that have agreement markers on complementizers, e.g. East Dangla (Shay 1999), Lele (Frajzyngier 2001), and Nigerian Arabic (Owens 1993) as described in Chapter 8.

5. Functions of agreement

5.1. The issues to be discussed

Since agreement is an independent coding means rather than an automatically controlled consequence of the presence of some other constituent(s) in the utterance, it is necessary to explain functions of agreement. This question is especially important for a language like English, in which agreement appears to be an obligatory consequence of other characteristics of the clause. To accept the theory that agreement is an automatically controlled phenomenon in English or any other language would be to accept that there are structural elements in the language that do not have a function. Although this conclusion is theoretically possible, one should not reach it without thoroughly researching the potential functions of the structural elements in question.

Like any other independent coding means, agreement may have different functions in different languages, depending on what functional domains the language codes and what other coding means are available for these functional domains. Examining the functions of agreement helps to explain why some languages have agreement and other languages do not. In the present chapter we concentrate on the type of agreement that involves the coding of noun phrases on the verb. This includes subject coding, object coding, the coding of semantic (rather than grammatical) functions and the coding of adjuncts.

In the following sections we discuss why some languages, such as Romance, Slavic, Semitic, and some Chadic languages require coding of an argument on the verb even if that argument is also represented by a separate noun in the clause. In those languages, features coded on the verb and features represented by the noun may not have contradictory values. In other words, although agreement on nouns, verbs, and adjectives is an independent coding means, disagreement is not allowed.

Some of the functional domains coded by agreement on the verb include, but are not limited to: (1) information status of the participants (topic, focus and potentially other pragmatic categories); (2) grammatical roles of participants, such as subject or object; (3) semantic roles of participants, and (4) referentiality of participants. Agreement coding on other categories, such as adjectives, numerals, prepositions, and complementizers, enables those categories to function as heads of various phrases, as explained later in the present chapter.

5.2. Interaction between agreement and word order: coding the grammatical relations of the participants

In a right-branching language in which the arguments following the verb are not marked by case inflection or adpositions, agreement is one means of coding the roles of these arguments. Consider Krongo, a Kordofanian language in which the verb occurs in clause-initial position. Neither the nominal subject nor the nominal object is marked by inflectional markers (case). All remaining arguments are marked by case. The subject is coded on the verb through a system of prefixes. In the third person there is a distinction between masculine (unmarked); feminine, marked by the prefix *m*-; and plural, marked by the prefix *k*-. This coding of subject features on the verb allows the nominal subject to be distinguished from the object as long as the two arguments differ in gender and/or number:

(14) a. **Àssàlà** káaw àttúmántàará.
M:PRF:spot person hyena
'The man saw a hyena' (Reh 1985:267) (because 'hyena' is feminine, the reading 'a hyena saw the man' is ruled out)

b. **K**-állà kátù mòlòotò.
PL-IMPF:carry people belt(s)
'People carrry belts.' (Reh 1985:267; mòlòotò is not marked for number)

If a transitive verb occurs with only one argument and this argument is the subject, its role is indicated by the presence of subject coding on the verb. If the sole argument in the clause is the object and the object has same gender, person and number as the subject, the role of the object is computed from the presence of what Reh calls a transitizing suffix on the verb:

(15) Àpá-ŋ bílyáatà.
M:PRF:hit-TR child
'He hit a child.' (Reh 1986:211)

5.3. Encoding the semantic role of the argument

In this section we describe several cases in which coding on the verb encodes the semantic or pragmatic role of the argument. The goal of this section is to show that if the role of the argument is coded on the verb it is not coded on the noun by any other means such as linear order, adpositions, or case marking. We begin by discussing a language that codes semantic and pragmatic roles on the verb and showing that these roles are not marked on the arguments through other coding means. We then show that another, superficially quite similar, language does not code arguments' roles on the verb because these roles are coded by other means.

Tagalog is a verb-initial language. Every noun phrase is marked by a preposition indicating the pragmatic or semantic role of the following noun. In a clause containing a single argument, this argument is marked by the preposition *ang*. This preposition has a pragmatic function whose exact nature is still somewhat controversial but which may be conceived of as topic or perhaps clausal focus (cf. also Gil 1999). Somewhat arbitrarily, we shall gloss the marker *ang* as TOP for topic, with the understanding that this may not reflect its actual pragmatic function. Its actual pragmatic function is immaterial for the proposed hypothesis about coding on the verb (all data from Schachter and Otanes 1972, glosses ours):

(16) Biyudo ang maestro.
widower TOP teacher
'The teacher is a widower.'
Biyuda ang maestra.
widow TOP teacher
'The teacher is a widow.'

(17) Kinain ang pagkain.
eat TOP food
'The food was eaten'
Sumusulat ang istudyante.
write TOP student
'The student is writing.' (Schachter and Otanes 1972: 73)

In a clause containing more than one argument, all arguments not marked by *ang* are marked by prepositions. The preposition *ni*, for example, marks a human agent (AG):

(18) Kinain ni Juan ang pagkain.
eat AG Juan TOP food
'Juan ate the food.'

When the preposition *ang* precedes an argument, the preposition that would encode the semantic role of that argument is omitted and the semantic role of the argument is indicated by one of a number of affixes to the verb. Schachter and Otanes 1972 label this coding on the verb as the coding of focus, distinguishing among Agentive Focus (AF), Object Focus (OF), and Directional Focus (DF). The fact that it is the verbal unit that encodes the semantic role of the topicalized participant marked by *ang* is evident from correlations between changes in the form of the verbal piece and changes in the meaning of the sentences below (examples from Schachter and Otanes 1972:78–9):

(19) a. Naghugas ng pinggan ang bata.
wash plate TOP child
'The child washed the plate.' AF
b. Hinugasan ng bata ang pinggan.
'The child washed the plate.' OF

(20) a. Maglalakip ng kuwalta sa sulat ang istudyante.
will enclose money letter TOP student
'The student will enclose some money in the letter.' AF
b. Ilalakip ng istudyante sa sulat ang kuwalta.
'The student will enclose the money in the letter.' OF
c. Lalakipan ng istudyante ng kuwalta ang sulat.
'The student will enclose some money in the letter.' DF

(21) a. Nagmamahal sa dalaga ang binata.
love LOC young woman TOP young man
'The young man loves the young woman.' AF
b. Minamahal ng binata ang dalaga.
'The young man loves the young woman.' DF

While the Tagalog verb encodes a large number of semantic roles, the verb in Lango (Western Nilotic, Nilo-Saharan) encodes only two relationships: subject and benefactive. The subject, whether nominal or pronominal, precedes the verb and also is marked by a verbal prefix. The object is marked by the position following the verb. The benefactive argument also follows the verb but is marked by an affix added to the verb. Thus, the role of the argument following the verb is computed from marking on the verb (all examples and glosses from Noonan 1992:119ff):

(22) a. Án àdɔk.
1SG 1SG-go+back-PRF
'I went back.'

b. Án àdɔkkì dákô.
1SG 1SG-go+back-BEN-PRF woman
'I went back for the sake of the woman.'

c. Gwôk òtɔɔ.
dog 3SG-die-PRF
'The dog died.'

d. Gwôk òtɔɔyì lócə̀.
dog 3SG-die-BEN-PRF man
'The dog died on the man.'

e. Dákò òtèdò rìŋó.
woman 3SG-cook-PRF meat
'The woman cooked the meat.'

f. Dákò òtèddì lócə̀ rìŋó.
woman 3SG-cook-BEN-PRF man meat
'The woman cooked the meat for the man.'

In Turkana (Eastern Nilotic), a verb-initial language, the subject is marked by the nominative case marker but the other arguments are unmarked. The presence of a dative/benefactive argument in the clause is coded by means of an affix to the verb. If there is both a dative/benefactive (indirect object) and a direct object in the clause, the former precedes the latter. The order of arguments thus serves as the coding means enabling the proper assignment of semantic functions (only the dative example is illustrated; glosses as per source):

(23) E-ìn-a-kin-ì ŋesì i-tuanì lò a-k-ìmuj.
3-give-e-DAT-A she (N) person this food
'She will give this person some food.' (Dimmendaal 1983: 62)

The 'applicative' markers found in Bantu languages perform a similar function. In Kiyaka, the applicative form is in complementary distribution with the preposition marking the recipient. If the recipient is old information, it is marked on the verb by the applicative form and is not marked by a preposition (glosses as per source):

(24) Tu-ku-tum-**in**-íní yaándi mwaaná (ngé).
we-you-send-APPL-RP 1-him 1child you
'We sent you the child.' (Kidima 1987: 184) (RP = recent past)

(25) Taatá u-ba-thúm-**ín**-íní-kwa ku zaandú baaná (mené).
father he2-me-send-APPL-RP-17 17to market 2child 1me
'Father sent the children to the market for me.'

A recipient that is in focus also is coded on the verb and cannot be marked by preposition:

(26) Ngéyé tu-tum-**in**-íní mwaaná.
you we-send-APPL-RP 1child
'We sent a child to you.' (Kidima 1987: 184; the preposition *kwa* before ngéyé would make the sentence ungrammatical.)

A recipient that is neither old information nor in focus is marked by the preposition *kwa* 'to'. The applicative form may not be used when the recipient is marked by preposition:

(27) Tu-tum-*in-íní mwaaná **kwa** ngéyé.
we-send-APPL-RP 1child to you
'we sent a child to you' (Kidima 1987: 184)

Coding on the verb may even occur in verb-final languages, although such cases are not frequent (cf. Nichols 1986). In Choctaw, a verb-final language, all nouns in a clause are marked either by a nominative suffix *(a)t* or *sh* or by an oblique suffix *(a)n* (Davies 1986: 7). This inflectional system does not allow for much differentiation in the role of arguments, since several nouns in the clause may have oblique case. Affixes on the verb code the semantic roles of arguments, thus supplementing inflectional coding means:

(28) Hattak-at alla-ya towa-ya **i**-pila-tok.
man-NOM child-OBL ball-OBL 3DAT-throw-PAST
'The man threw the ball to the child.' (Davies 1986: 7)

6. Conclusions

In the languages we have examined, agreement is an independent coding means in the sense that it is not triggered by any other element present in the utterance. Even in instances where agreement appears to be automatic, e.g. third-person singular coding on the present-tense verb in English, the trigger and the product of agreement represent different functional domains. In this instance, the noun or pronoun represents the domain of reference while the verbal suffix *-s* represents the domain of coding categoriality. One cannot talk here about the trigger and the product of agreement. Cases in which both agreement and the potential trigger are present in the utterance are not instances of agreement but rather represent the coding of two (or more) different functions. Such examples illustrate the principle of language structure that disagreement is disallowed.

Inflection on the verb can code a number of functions, including grammatical relations, semantic roles of arguments, information status of arguments, and referentiality of arguments.

CHAPTER 7

Interaction of nominal classification with other coding means

1. Introduction

The purpose of the present chapter is twofold: (1) to describe the interaction between systems of nominal classification (including gender systems) and other coding means in a language; and (2) to argue against the widely held belief that the function of nominal classification is to fulfill some inherent human need to categorize the world.

We propose that nominal classification is a coding means whose overall function is to enable the operation of other coding means. We demonstrate that systems of nominal classification enable the existence of at least two coding means, viz. agreement systems as described in Chapter 6, and systems of deictic and anaphoric reference. Agreement systems may also participate in the coding of reference. In languages in which noun class is overtly marked on the noun, nominal classification may also have the derivational function of allowing the formation of new nouns having semantic characteristics similar to those of other nouns in the same class.

In what follows, we first discuss the prevalent approach to nominal classification and present our arguments against this approach. We then discuss the interaction of nominal classification with other coding means.

A system of nominal classification is a system whereby nouns in a language are divided into two or more classes and where each class has a corresponding element in the reference system and/or in the agreement system (cf. also Corbett 1991:4–5). Members of a class may be overtly marked by phonological means, as in Polish, or by morphological means, as in German (see below), Fula and most Bantu languages, or they may be phonologically and morphologically unmarked, as in English. In some languages the system of class distinctions varies from the singular to the plural. This is the case in many Bantu and Kwa languages as well as in Polish, German and English. Nominal classification systems frequently have corresponding elements in an agreement system; however, the language may evolve in such a way that the system of agreement disappears while the overt coding of nominal classes on the noun remains, as is the case in some dialects of Fula. In such a language the functions of the agreement system are taken over by some other coding means.

We exclude from our study systems of numeral classifiers like those found in some Southeast Asian languages (cf. Downing 1996).

2. Previous approaches to nominal classification

A systematic and thorough discussion of the many past and contemporary approaches to nominal classification is outside the scope of the present book. We concentrate on a single fundamental issue, that of the motivation for nominal classification. In the wealth of recent publications on nominal classification the reader may find typologies of classifier systems (Aikhenvald 2000) and discussions of a number of issues not addressed in the present chapter (Corbett 1991; Aikhenvald 2000; Senft 2000).

It has been claimed that one of the chief functions for nominal classification is a fundamental human need to organize and categorize reality: 'The classification of nouns can be thought of as a semantic (and grammatical) necessity, just as verbs must semantically (and grammatically) be classified with respect to tense/aspect' (Demuth 2000: 289). Talmy (1992: 131), as quoted in Senft (2000: 13), states that languages 'generally subcategorize nouns grammatically along certain semantic parameters, principally proper/common, count/mass, unitary/collective, and relative/absolute'. Senft (2000: 27) concludes his listing of various functions of classifiers with the following: 'However, besides all these functions the basic function of classifiers is to classify, and the choice of the objects to be classified is between the extralinguistic referents or the intralinguistic category 'noun' (Senft 2000: 27). Aikhenvald takes a similar approach: 'Almost all languages have some grammatical means for the linguistic characterization of nouns and nominals' (Aikhenvald 2000: 1). Nominal classification systems also have been identified as the expression of cognitively salient semantic categories in Denny (1986), Craig (1986), and Lakoff (1987).

All of the above approaches take nominal classification to be the product of a human need to categorize the world. The argumentation for these approaches usually consists of affirmative evidence, namely the presentation of nominal classes representing groups of objects with similar semantic characteristics. However, the mere presence of such classes in a language is not proof that the nominal classification system stems from some biological or cognitive factors, as implied by Senft. To show that the presence of a language phenomenon is the result of cognitive necessity, as claimed in the views presented above, it must be shown that: (a) all languages have such a system; and (b) all such systems are based on cognitive categories, i.e. categories having to do with the perceived characteristics of objects in the surrounding world. To demonstrate that the hypothesis about the cognitive motivation for nominal classification is not true, however, it is enough to show that: (a) there are languages without nominal classification systems; and (b) some systems of nominal classification are not based on the perception and analysis of the surrounding world or on human attitudes towards objects in the surrounding world. We demonstrate point (a), i.e. the existence of a language without nominal classification, on Mina, a Central Chadic language. We demonstrate point (b) through an examination of the gender system of Polish singular nouns.

Having shown that the emergence of nominal classification is not motivated by a need to categorize the surrounding world, we argue that the motivation for nominal classification is language-internal. A system of nominal classification, which may include a system of gender distinctions, is one strategy for solving the problem of anaphoric and deictic reference, or reference tracking. We thus make explicit the nature of the interaction between nominal classification, reference and agreement that has been indicated in Givón (1976), Frajzyngier (1985b, 1997), and Corbett (1991).

Although nominal classification is one of the strategies that languages have grammaticalized for the purpose of reference tracking across discourse, it is by no means a prerequisite for reference tracking. Languages can and do use other strategies, one of which is described in Chapter 11. Further, the domain of reference may have different subdomains in different languages and languages may have different means of coding these various subdomains. In sections below we illustrate the interaction between nominal classification and other coding means in systems of reference.

Finally, we provide an explanation for why nominal classes are often, but not always, organized in ways that suggest the existence of cognitive bases for nominal classification.

3. A language without nominal classification

Mina (Central Chadic), like many other Chadic languages, lacks a gender or noun class system. The language distinguishes among first-, second- and third-person pronouns. There is no formal distinction between human and non-human or animate and inanimate nouns. There are no nominal classes based on any other cognitively based criteria, nor are there any classes based on formal criteria. The language codes the distinction between singular and plural, with plural being the marked category. There is no agreement system in the sense that the presence of a noun in the clause requires the presence of certain markers on verbs, modifiers, quantifiers, or determiners. The language has only three productive derivational morphemes, but their presence on a noun has no morphological effects on any other coding means in the language.

The fact that a language has no system of nominal classification does not imply that all nouns in that language have the same syntactic properties. In fact, many languages have subclasses of nouns whose inherent properties pertain to their functions in specific domains. In Mina the relevant domain is that of locative predication. In locative constructions, nouns that are inherently locative have a different coding system from nouns that are not inherently locative. Nouns that are inherently animate and inherently human have yet another system of coding in locative predication, as described in Chapter 10. The existence of subclasses of nouns and verbs in the domain of locative predication is not a result of speakers' categorization of the world but rather of the grammaticalization of various functional domains and the means of coding them.

4. A language with nominal classes not based on cognitive criteria

In this section we consider the case of a language with noun classes as commonly understood, i.e. classes that are reflected in the agreement system and in other means of coding reference, but whose noun classes are based on formal rather than cognitive categories. Corbett (1991) describes several systems, including French, in which nominal classification is based on phonological features rather than on cognitive criteria. In this section we discuss in detail another such language, Polish.

All Polish singular nouns belong to one of three classes commonly referred to as masculine, feminine, and neuter. The basis of class membership is phonological: Nouns ending in a non-palatal consonant belong to the masculine class; nouns ending in a palatal consonant or in the vowel *a* belong to the feminine class; and nouns ending in the vowel *o* belong to the neuter class. In addition, there exists a class of masculine animate nouns that behaves differently from the class of masculine inanimate nouns with respect to the system of case marking. The nominal classification system in the plural is entirely different, being semantically based: All human masculine nouns belong to one class and all remaining nouns belong to another class.

Apart from the last phoneme of the word, there is no unifying characteristic among the nouns belonging to the same gender class. Here is a small sample of body-part terms, which are divided among the three classes according to solely phonological characterics, along with a few inanimate nouns. Among the feminine nouns are *ręka* 'arm', *dłoń* 'hand', *skroń* 'temple', *łapa* 'paw', *noga* 'leg' and *podłoga* 'floor', *małpa* 'monkey', *ściana* 'wall', *połapa* 'ceiling', and *stodoła* 'barn'. Among masculine nouns are *nos* 'nose', *palec* 'finger', *paznokieć* 'finger nail', *łokieć* 'elbow', *brzuch* 'belly', *ząb* 'tooth', *znój* 'fatigue induced by work and heat', *buk* 'beech tree', *dąb* 'oak', and *pomidor* 'tomato'. Among neuter nouns are *płuco* 'lung', *kolano* 'knee', *oko* 'eye', *ucho* 'ear' and *okno* 'window'.

Since the surrounding-world referents of these nouns cannot have any phonological characteristics, it is obvious that these characteristics have been assigned by the language. Why would a language assign such characteristics? To say that this assignment satisfies a human need to categorize would be circular, since these nouns did not have any common characteristics until the nouns were assigned final vowels or consonants.

Since gender assignment in Polish singular nouns is based on formal properties, it is clear that this assignment is not a product of the categorization of the world or of the imposition of cognitive categories on objects in the world. Instead, it is a means of organizing and coding nouns so that their formal characteristics can be used for other purposes or functions. One of these functions is to enable the operation of a system of reference. Another is to enable the operation of system of agreement, which in turn codes functions in various domains (cf. Chapter 6). A third function, which actually may develop after the emergence of the formal system of coding, is the derivational function of allowing for the formation of new lexical items having certain semantic characteristics. Since derivational morphology may be the source of a system of nominal classification (cf. Corbett 1991), derivational morphology may exist at the very beginning of the grammaticalization of nominal classes as well as at the end of the grammaticalization chain, when the formal characteristics of that morphology acquire semantic functions.

Not all nominal classification systems have all three functions. There are languages that have overtly marked nominal classes but lack agreement. English nominal derivational morphology is one such example. Different derivational suffixes such as *-ette*, *-ment*, *-tion*, *-ship*, *-er*, *-hood*, etc., mark nouns as belonging to different semantic classes, but these classes do not behave differently from other English nouns with respect to the agreement system and anaphors.

It is also possible to have a language in which nominal classes are not formally marked on the noun but are reflected in the agreement system. In such a language the system of nominal classification cannot have a derivational function, since noun class is not formally coded.

Languages that have nominal classification but no agreement system and whose systems of reference do not reflect nominal classes are products of an evolutionary process whereby the distinctions coded by agreement and by class-sensitive anaphors and deictic markers have been replaced by other coding means. This is the case in some dialects of Fula, where nouns have retained the formal characteristics of nominal classes but the system of agreement has disappeared, as has the system of reference based on nominal classes. Seen from an historical perspective, a language like English, with its rich system of derivational morphology, could be considered to have nominal classes even though these classes are not reflected either in the agreement system or in the reference system.

To support our hypotheses, we first demonstrate the use of a nominal classification system in the coding of reference. We then examine the discourse consequences of having nominal classes by contrasting a language that has nominal classes with a language that does not.

5. Nominal classification and anaphoric reference

Martinet (1967) explains that the gender system in French allows reference to two noun phrases by means of a system of pronouns coding gender distinction. Efficiency of reference is indeed the main outcome of the presence of nominal classes, regardless of the historical origin of these classes. How these classes are determined is certainly an interesting issue (cf. Aikhenvald 2000), but with respect to the synchronic functions of such systems it is a secondary issue. What is important is that there are several classes established in the language and that there are deictic and anaphoric elements that refer to those classes. When it comes to coding reference, even a system of two classes of nouns is more efficient than a system with no noun classes. This efficiency lies in the possibility of referring to a participant by means of an anaphor instead of a full noun or a noun modified by one or more determiners. Nominal classification thus enables both deictic and anaphoric reference.

In Polish, the existence of three genders makes it possible to refer to non-human, non-animate nouns through anaphors only, provided that no noun of the same number and gender occurs between the antecedent and the anaphor:

(1) Muszę wygrać tę bitwę, albo przynajmniej
must:1SG:PRES win DEM:F:ACC battle:F:ACC or at least
przegrać **ją** z jak najmniejszymi stratami.
lose ANAPH:F:ACC ASSC how smallest:PL losses
'I must win this battle, or lose it with the smallest possible losses.'

(2) Najpierw Pan wynalazł **to** wszystko swoim
first 2POL discover 3N all:N 3REFL:POSS:M:INSTR
naukowym umysłem.
scientific:M:INSTR mind:INSTR
'You have first discovered all of this with your scientific mind.'

(3) **To** nie był krzyk.
3N NEG be:PAST scream
'That was not a scream.' (Sources)

The existence of the three-class system allows the use of anaphors alone even if there are many nouns between the antecedent and its subsequent mention, provided that none of these is a potential antecedent of the same gender or number. In the following example *szubienica* 'gallows', a feminine noun in Polish, is mentioned in the first clause. It is referred to by the feminine anaphor *ją* six clauses later:

(4) Ktoś musiał wznieść tę szubienicę.
somebody must:PAST:3M erect DEM:F gallows:ACC
'Somebody must have erected those gallows.'

Ktoś zacięty i uparty, bo to nie była
somebody zealous CONJ obstinate because DEM:N NEG be:PAST:SG:F
łatwa robota.
easy:F:SG job
'Somebody zealous and obstinate. It was not an easy job.'

Stulpa już się nie wyliże z zapalenia płuc, a Subik
Stulpa already REFL NEG lick out:FUT from inflamation lungs CONJ Subik
z tego przeklętego strachu.
from DEM:M cursed fear
'Stulpa will never recover from his pneumonia and Subik from that cursed fear.'

Ktoś musiał ją zbudować.
somebody must:3M 3F:ACC erect:INF
'Somebody must have built those gallows.' (Sources)

The use of the demonstrative 'it' in the English translation of the last clause would not be felicitous, since it could have as its antecedent any of the singular nouns 'fear', 'work', 'pneumonia', but not the plural noun 'gallows'. The plural demonstrative 'them' could have as its antecedent two or more of the aforementioned antecedents; therefore, the English translation uses the full noun.

In the next example, use of the neuter demonstrative *to* rules out reference to any of the three nouns mentioned in previous discourse, since none of these nouns is neuter:

(5) Kiedy grasz na swoim saksofonie, jesteś dużo fajniejszy.
when play:PRES:2SG on POSS:REFL sax be:2SG more pleasant:M
'When you play on your saxophone you are much more pleasant.'

Chcesz, żebym zagrał?
want:2SG COMP-HYP-1SG play
'Do you want me to play?'

Chciałabym **to** zobaczyć.
want:PAST:HYP:1SG:F DEM:N see
'I would like to see that (i.e., your playing).' (Sources)

The existence of nominal classes thus allows for a system of anaphoric reference that includes as many anaphors as there are nominal classes.

6. Discourse consequences of nominal classification

The presence or absence of a system of nominal classification in a language has implications for its forms of discourse. In the domain of reference, a language without a system of nominal classification will use nouns more often than a language with a rich system of nominal classification. Consider two Chadic languages, Mina and Gidar, both belonging to the same branch of the Chadic family and both spoken in the same area of Northern Cameroon. Some Mina settlements are no further than 15 kilometers from the next Gidar settlement. The grammatical differences between these languages, unlike their similarities, thus cannot be attributed to common retention or to areal influences. We have shown above that Mina lacks a system of nominal classification. Gidar, on the other hand, distinguishes between masculine and feminine gender in third-person singular pronouns. The presence or absence of gender coding has predictable consequences for both languages. In Mina texts involving masculine and feminine protagonists, a full noun must be used each time there is a change of protagonist. In Gidar, a pronoun is used in the same discourse conditions. Following is a brief analysis of two short texts, each containing masculine and feminine protagonists, in the two languages.

In Mina, after the introduction of a full noun, its subsequent mention as a subject involves a third-person pronoun or no pronoun at all, depending on the aspect of the clause. However, the pronominal or zero-marked subject may be used only if no other potential subjects of the same number have been introduced. A new subject must be introduced by a full noun:

(6) Hìdí wàcíŋ íbə wàl ngən.
man DEM CONJ wife 3SG
'This man with his wife'

(7) Mbù mbù í mbù wəží gwáɗ.
give birth 3PL give birth children many
'had many children.'

(8) **Wàl** ngən à ndí ndə kə ɗá tìpíɗ.
wife 3SG 3SG HAB go INF fetch termites
'His wife had the habit of going to fetch termites.'

(9) Kə́ ndə zə́ fù ndə dzáŋ zàvàŋ-yíì í màr rà.
INF go AUX all go find guinea fowl-PL 3PL graze D.HAB
'Each time she went she found guinea fowl grazing'

(10) Zàvàŋ-yíì zá fəɗ-á ná tàlán kə́ gí.
guinea fowl-PL COMP shave-OBJ 1PL head AFF please
'The guinea fowl told [the woman] to shave their heads.' (Frajzyngier et al. MS)

If there is a change of subject and the new subject differs in number from the preceding subject, the new subject may be coded by a pronoun because pronouns code the distinction between singular and plural:

(11) Séy à ndí fəɗ-á-ŋ tə̀ tàlán fəɗ fəɗ fəɗ.
so(Hausa) 3SG HAB shave-OBJ-3SG 3PL head shave shave shave
'So, she would shave their heads. Shave, shave, shave.'

Later in the same narrative, the only participants are the husband and the wife. Here, a language with gender-marking in the pronouns would refer to the participants by means of third-person masculine and feminine pronouns. Mina, however, must use full nouns:

(12) Bə̀k bə̀k á bə̀k-á-ŋ ɓə̀ wìrnjík kə́ nə̀ mə̀ŋ.
fill fill 3SG fill-OBJ-3SG ASSC ash AFF PREP inside
'He filled them with ash.'

(13) Séy **wàl** ngə̀n táŋ á nd-rə̀ wàcín syì wìrnjík ɗíyà bə̀ká-há cìɗéʼ
so wife 3SG DEM 3SG go-D.HAB DEM COM ash start pour-GO pile
cìɗéʼ cìɗéʼ cìɗéʼ à kə̀tə̀f.
pile pile pile PREP road
'As his wife went along, ashes kept pouring out in little piles along the road.'

(14) Séy mə̀ **ngùl ngùl** tì á tìy-ù wàl tsú zə́ dàmú.
so REL husband husband see 3SG see-3SG wife went be bush
'So the husband saw that the wife went to the bush.'

In a similar situation in the Gidar texts, pronouns may be used because third-person pronouns code gender. In the following fragment there are two protagonists, a son and his mother. After the protagonists have been introduced they are subsequently referred to by pronouns, despite changes of subject:

(15) Də̀rbágà-nì wíin sə́-t də̀və́-t má-n à-tə́nə̀-k ə̀pél
after-3M boy PREP:3F inside-3F mother-3M 3M-start-PRF INF-talk
sə̀-tá.
DAT-3F
'During his absence, a boy started to talk to his mother from inside her.'

(16) **À**-ná sə̀-**tə́**-k ná ə̀mmá ní-gíl də̀ ngáa dì.
3M-say PREP-3F-PRF COMP mother 1SG-leave ASSC where Q
'He said to her, "Mother, by what exit do I leave?"'

(17) **Tə̀**-ná sə̀-**nə́**-k ná é-gìl klà krìí-wà.
3F-say PREP-3M-PRF COMP IMPER-leave by vagina-1SG
'She told him, "Leave by my vagina."'

Several sentences later, after yet another change of subject, the new subject is again coded by a pronoun:

(18) Tə̀-ná sə̀-**nə́**-k ə́mpá ná é-gìl klà má-wà.
3F-say PREP-3M-PRF again COMP IMPER-leave by mouth-1SG
'She told him again, "Leave by my mouth."'

English also codes gender in the pronoun system, distinguishing among masculine human, feminine human, and neuter pronouns:[6]

1_3_0 <1052 A> I [th] I ^felt **it** would be !c\ourteous#
1_3_0 <1053 A> to ^pop in and !t\/ell **him** a_bout it#

1_3_0 <288 c> – – – [h] ^hope **she**'d F/\ound _something#
1_3_0 <289 A> ^well !I would have th\ought#
1_3_0 <290 A> ^after seven y=ears#
1_3_0 <291 A> ^they ought to ^ch\/uck **her** _out in the _world#

In English one must use a full noun with a determiner if more than one inanimate antecedent has been mentioned in discourse. We see, therefore, the interaction between the presence or absence of a nominal classification system and the forms of discourse. If a language does not have nominal classes, it must use full nouns whenever there is a change of subject or object in discourse. If a language has nominal classes, it uses pronouns whenever there is a change of subject and the subject has been previously mentioned in discourse.

7. Why the illusion of cognitive function?

Given that the motivation for nominal classification is language-internal, one may ask why nouns belonging to the same class often code referents with similar characteristics. There are a number of possible explanations, as nominal classes in languages may emerge from a number of sources (cf. Corbett 1991). Perhaps the simplest is that noun classes may reflect old derivational morphemes that once coded semantic characteristics and that are no longer transparent. Alternatively, noun classes may be based on old demonstratives that came to be fused with the lexical items they marked, as suggested by Kuryłowicz (1964) (later elaborated on and incorporated into a grammaticalization sequence by Greenberg 1978). The proposal that noun classes originate from derivational morphemes provides a functional explanation for the presence of common semantic characteristics among nouns of the same class, but it fails to explain why the semantic properties once assigned by these morphemes have been lost while their phonological properties remain to play an important role in the language.

However, there is independent evidence that nouns may be classified by phonological criteria. In Polish, for example, the borrowed word *kometa* 'comet' was masculine until the 18th century; over time, however, its phonological characteristic of having the final vowel *a* won out, and the noun is feminine in contemporary Polish. There also is evidence that a child acquiring language is guided by phonological rather than semantic properties. The Polish word *tata* 'dad' is masculine despite the fact that it ends in the vowel *-a*, which elsewhere marks a noun as feminine. Polish-speaking children in the U.S. have been overheard saying:

(19) a moja tata
CONJ my:F dad
'and my (feminine) dad'

Cf. standard Polish:

a mój tata
CONJ my:M dad
'and my (masculine) dad'.

8. Functions of articles in French and German

Within French and German linguistics there is a long tradition of attempting to discover the basis for the assignment of masculine or feminine (or neuter, in German) gender. Such studies have revealed that the system of assignment is not completely arbitrary and that each gender class in both languages contains rather large blocks of nouns having common semantic or phonological characteristics (Corbett 1991). At the same time, in both languages nouns that have common semantic and phonological characteristics can belong to different genders.

We propose a drastically different approach to the problem of gender assignment in French and German. The function common to definite and indefinite articles in French and German is that of overtly coding the gender of a noun. The reason that gender is assigned to a noun is to enable anaphoric reference to that noun in discourse and deictic reference to that noun in the environment of speech.

Our argumentation is as follows. In French discourse, anaphoric reference to a noun may consist simply of a demonstrative coding gender, namely *le* (masculine) or *la* (feminine). The same demonstrative occurs with the noun as a definite article. Such reference is useful, of course, only if the gender of the noun being referred to is known. In other words, the gender of the noun must be marked in some way, especially if that noun does not belong to a block of nouns of the same gender and having common semantic characteristics. The function of the articles *le* and *la*, then, is to overtly code the gender of the accompanying noun, thereby making possible the subsequent use of the anaphoric demonstratives *le* and *la*.

The function of articles in German is quite similar. While there exist groups of nouns that share gender and that also share phonological and/or semantic characteristics, there are many nouns whose gender class cannot be deduced from characteristics of the noun itself. The presence of one of the articles *der* (masculine), *die* (feminine) or *das* (neuter) codes the gender of the noun and allows the noun to be referred to in subsequent discourse by pronouns or demonstratives that also code gender.

There is also an historical argument for the proposed function of articles. Latin did not have articles; however, the gender of every noun was marked by means of case/number/gender endings. When the language lost these markers as a result of phonological reduction, the coding of gender was taken over by articles, which did not become established in French until the 11th century (Jensen 1990). Finally, if nouns are not overtly marked for gender by articles, phonological characteristics or other means, their gender classification may disappear over time, as has occurred in English.

9. Conclusions

We have demonstrated that the primary function of nominal classification is to enable the operation of two formal systems of coding, agreement and systems of reference. The two systems obey the principle of functional transparency. Nominal classes, if overtly marked on the noun, also may have a derivational function. The illusion that nominal classification is motivated by some supposed cognitive need to categorize the world may be explained by the fact that synchronic nominal classes represent categorizations based on derivational morphemes that once coded semantic characteristics but that are no longer transparent.

CHAPTER 8

Matrix clause coding

1. Introduction

The purpose of this chapter is to describe the interaction of matrix clause coding ('subject-to-object raising') with other coding means. Since Rosenbaum (1967), many theoretical studies have been devoted to structures, collectively known as 'raising' constructions, in which the subject of the embedded clause appears as the object of the matrix clause. Theoretical interest in this issue is justified by the fact that such phenomena have been observed in languages as disparate as Romance (Bolkestein 1976a,b, 1977; Legendre 1986), Slavic (Nichols and Schallert 1983; Boniewicz 1982) and Indo-European in general (Holland 1982), Korean (Kim 1994), Japanese (Sells 1990), Semitic (the present work), and Nilo-Saharan (Jake 1979). Our analysis reveals that: (1) the same syntactic construction, namely raising, may code different functional domains across languages; and (2) the functional domains coded by raising in some languages may be coded by different means in other languages. Our analysis also illustrates how coding systems interact across clausal boundaries.

2. Previous approaches to coding in the matrix clause

Complex sentences in which the subject of the embedded clause is coded as an object of the matrix clause have been divided, in both traditional and contemporary theory, into several types: subject-to-object raising (SOR), EQUI constructions, and constructions involving 'small clauses'. The following sentences are examples of such constructions in English:

(1) I saw him run/running (EQUI)
(2) I heard him play a fiddle (EQUI)
(3) I want him to run (SOR)
(4) I believe her to be a good doctor (SOR)
(5) I consider the taxi driver entirely innocent ('small clause', Haegeman 1994: 172)

We use the term 'matrix clause coding' to refer to any construction in which the subject of the embedded clause is coded in the matrix clause. The term implies no assumptions about the functions or derivational histories of the various types of constructions. As we demonstrate, the raised argument may be coded as a free lexical item or as a pronoun affixed to the matrix verb. The verb of the embedded clause may be finite or nonfinite, depending on the language and the construction.

Some languages exhibit types of matrix clause coding that are beyond the scope of the present chapter, e.g., coding of the embedded clause subject as subject of the matrix clause; coding of the embedded clause object as object of the matrix clause; or coding of the embedded clause object as subject of the matrix clause. In other words, languages have exploited all of the logical possibilities for coding embedded clause arguments in the matrix clause. A preliminary examination reveals that each of these possibilities is an independent coding means having a semantic or a pragmatic function. These functions, as well as the possibility of coding matrix clause arguments in the embedded clause, are topics for further study.

2.1. Explanations of the form

Many attempts to explain matrix clause coding focus on the formal properties of the construction. These explanations can be divided into two types: Those that postulate that the matrix clause object is reanalyzed as the subject of the embedded clause and those that postulate that the embedded clause subject is 'raised' to become the object of the matrix clause (a summary of hypotheses about raising can be found in Holland 1982). The first view is represented by Ernout and Thomas (1972: 320), who state that the accusativus-cum-infinitivo (a.c.i.) construction in Latin had its origin in the conflation of two clauses.[7] The following sentence was said to have had its origin in the clauses *sentio eum* 'je l'aperçois' and *sentio uenire* 'j'aperçois venir':

(6) Sentio eum uenire.
feel:PRES:SG 3M:ACC come:INF
'I hear him come.' (Ernout and Thomas 1972: 320)

According to Ernout and Thomas, the object of the matrix clause was reanalyzed as the subject of the embedded clause as speakers of Latin forgot the origin of the accusative (for an insightful critique of this analysis, cf. Bolkestein (1979, 1976). Bolkestein (1977) proposes that the a.c.i. construction in Latin is a single unit that serves as a complement of the verb. While this analysis has some merit for Latin, it cannot be extended to other languages, especially those in which the verb of the embedded clause is not infinitive.

The view that the matrix clause object originated as the subject of the embedded clause and was 'raised' to the matrix clause is represented by early transformational theory, beginning with Rosenbaum (1967). An ample argumentation is provided in Postal (1974). According to GB theory, raising is motivated by the interaction of several properties: the Case filter requirement that all overt NPs be assigned abstract Case; the fact that the nonfinite form of the verb does not assign Case; and the Case-assigning property of the matrix clause verb. In this view, since the verb of the embedded clause is nonfinite, it cannot assign Case. Because the NP subject of the embedded clause must have Case assigned to it, it is 'raised' to the matrix clause where it is assigned Case by the matrix verb.

While older GB analyses explicitly state that SOR is a result of the need to satisfy Case assignment, more recent analyses merely imply this. In the Principles and Parameters approach, the raising portion of the explanation has been replaced by the notion of Exceptional Case Marking (cf. van Riemsdijk and Williams 1986: 31). In the sentence 'John believes Bill to be sick', it is said that "" Bill" is not an argument of "believes" even though "believes" gives "Bill" its case' (van Riemsdijk and Williams 1986: 242). This type of Case assignment is considered exceptional because Case is assigned across a barrier (for a discussion of the problems involved, cf. Haegeman 1994: 169–71 and Haegeman 1991, Chapters 3 and 10). While the Principles and Parameters approach may account for the assignment of Case, where 'Case' is an artifact of a theory rather than a coding means, it does not explain why the embedded verb occurs in the infinitive in the English SOR construction.

Horn (1985) also invokes the historical process of reanalysis, in this case from subject of the embedded clause to object of the matrix clause. Horn proposes that this type of reanalysis, hence the SOR phenomenon, is possible only in languages in which the appropriate syntactic conditions are present: namely, in which the subject of the embedded clause occupies the same position in the string that would be occupied by the object of the matrix clause. This claim is demonstrably untrue, as matrix-coding phenomena occur in a number of languages in which the subject of the embedded clause does not occupy the position of the object of the matrix clause. In Hdi (Central Chadic), for example, the subject pronoun *yù* of the embedded clause follows the verb of the embedded clause. Nevertheless, this argument may be coded as the object of the matrix clause by the first-person object pronoun *íxà*:

(7) Sn-**íxà**-snà tà dzàá-**yù**.
hear-1SG-hear IMPF go-1SG
'He heard me go.' (Frajzyngier with Shay 2002: 504)

The phenomena of EQUI deletion and 'small clauses' have received less attention in the literature than SOR. One posited distinction between SOR and EQUI deletion is that in the latter the object of the matrix clause is 'not raised to this position but is an original direct object of the verb; it is modified by a complement clause whose (understood, deleted) subject is coreferential to the direct object' (Nichols and Schallert 1983: 224). Since some analyses of SOR also posit the 'raised' argument as an original direct object of the verb, the distinction has little explanatory value. The term 'small clause' is invoked in contemporary GB theory to explain the structure of sentences like (5). Small clauses are 'projections of a functional head AGR... the AGR head of a small clause fails to assign case... the verb "consider" case marks the subject of the small clause' (Haegeman 1994: 172). This explanation is entirely motivated by theory-internal assumptions concerning the status of AGR as a head and the Case filter requirement that every argument be assigned Case. It fails to explain why some matrix verbs take small clause complements while others do not.

2.2. Explanations of the functions

Very little work has been devoted to the function(s) of matrix clause coding. It has often been assumed that matrix clause coding is motivated by the lexical verb of the matrix clause. From the study of Latin through early transformational grammar, verbs have been divided into the categories 'raising' and 'non-raising'. More recently, the raising verbs have been termed Exceptional Case Marking verbs (cf. Baker 1988: 180). Why some verbs cause raising while others do not has never been explained.

The GB theory that Case assignment requirements motivate raising is a kind of functional explanation, if one accepts the notion of abstract Case assignment. Unfortunately for this explanation, matrix clause coding also occurs in languages in which the verb of the embedded clause is finite and can therefore assign Case to its subject. This is illustrated in example 7 and in the following construction, also from Hdi, in which matrix clause coding occurs and the verb of the embedded clause has its own subject and its own aspect marker:

(8) Sná-n-sná t-íí tà dzàá-yù.
hear-3SG-hear OBJ-1SG IMPF go-1SG
'He heard me go.' (Hdi, Frajzyngier with Shay 2002: 504)

Case assignment requirements also fail to explain why the same embedded clause proposition may occur with or without raising. Examples 7 and 8 contrast with 9, in which the two clauses are separated by the deontic complementizer *káɮái* and the embedded clause subject is not coded in the matrix clause:

(9) Sná-ghá-sná káɮái tà dzàá-íyù káá.
hear-DIST-hear COMP IMPF go-1SG COMP
'He heard that I should go.' (Hdi, Frajzyngier with Shay 2002)

A few other functional explanations have been proposed, none of which is either fully explanatory or accounts for formal variations in matrix clause coding across languages. In her exhaustive studies of complementation, for example, Bolkestein (1976a) postulates that the a.c.i. construction in Latin is a subordinating means with no other semantic or pragmatic function, but this account clearly fails to explain the functions of similar constructions in other languages.

Nichols and Schallert (1983) raised, but were unable in the end to answer, the question whether the main function of raising in Common Slavic or Indo-European languages is to make 'embedded clauses accessible for pragmatic parameters'. Nevertheless, they did isolate certain pragmatic functions associated with raising, namely focus in Finnish and the more specific 'focus of counterfactual implicature' in Old Russian.

Givón (1990) offers a putatively functional explanation for raising, defining it as 'a process of analogical extension, where the verb-sense that takes a propositional object adjusts its structure to resemble the structure of the verb-sense that takes a nominal object' (Givón 1990: 777). This explanation, which has as its motivating locus the vague notion of 'verb-sense', does not explain the function of raising at the sentence level, at the clause level or at the level of pragmatics. It seems that the functional motivation for raising remains to be discovered.[8]

3. The forms and functions of matrix clause coding

This chapter explains both the forms and the functions of matrix clause coding. The fundamental element of the explanation is that matrix clause coding of the subject of the embedded proposition is an independent grammatical means. It is not an automatically controlled result of some formal requirement, as suggested in GB theory, or a process triggered by some property of the matrix verb. It is not the result of reanalysis, as postulated by Horn (1985), or of any kind of structural adjustments to the verb, as postulated by Givón (1990). Before we begin to discuss what raising is, we may deal briefly with the question of whether matrix clause coding in one language is formally the same as matrix clause coding in another. This question was raised by Sells (1990) in his analysis of SOR in Japanese. Here is the solution: If different coding means, such as linear order, case marking, and adpositions, carry the same functions across languages, then it is legitimate and appropriate to compare those means. That is, if different means are used to code an argument of the embedded clause as object of the matrix clause, then these means have the same function. Viewing all types of matrix clause coding as instantiations of the same formal coding means allows us to compare constructions that have often been considered unrelated, both within and across languages.

In a given language, matrix clause coding interacts with and is complementary to other lexical, syntactic and morphological means available for the coding of a given functional domain. Matrix clause coding is, therefore, an independent coding means in exactly the same sense in which case marking, linear order, verbal inflection and adpositions are independent coding means. Like other coding means, matrix clause coding may have functions ranging from the syntactic, such as the coding of a dependent clause after a verb of saying in Latin, to the semantic, such as the coding of epistemic modality, to the pragmatic, such as coding focus and topicalization. The functional domain and functional range of matrix clause coding in a given language can be understood only by studying the interaction of matrix clause coding with other coding means and with the inherent properties of the matrix verbs with which matrix clause coding occurs.

The hypothesis that matrix clause coding is an independent coding means allows us to address the following questions, which prove troublesome for traditional and contemporary analyses of raising phenomena: Why do some verbs in some languages require matrix clause coding? Why is matrix clause coding apparently optional with some verbs in some languages? Why do some languages have matrix clause coding while others do not? There can be no exhaustive answer to the last question, since our current knowledge of the evolution of grammatical systems does not allow us to explain why a certain construction did or did not grammaticalize in a certain language, nor does it allow us to predict which grammatical constructions will or will not emerge in a language.

4. Matrix clause coding as an independent grammatical means

This section has three aims: to argue against Exceptional Case Marking by showing that matrix clause coding is not motivated by the absence of a Case assigner in the embedded clause; to show that the embedded clause subject is not 'raised' to the main clause; and to counter Horn's (1985) claim that raising occurs only in languages displaying certain syntactic conditions. There are two main arguments against Exceptional Case Marking. The first is based on the fact that some languages have 'double coding'; i.e., they overtly code the same argument as object in the matrix clause and subject in the embedded clause. This demonstrates that matrix clause coding is not motivated by Case assignment requirements, since any argument that appears overtly in the embedded clause would already be assigned Case by the embedded clause verb. In some languages, the argument of the embedded clause may even be coded in three places: in the matrix clause, in the embedded clause and in the complementizer. The second argument is that, in many languages, matrix clause coding is optional; therefore, it cannot be the automatically controlled result of the presence or absence of any other element in the sentence.

4.1. Double coding of arguments

Languages that allow double coding of the subject of the embedded clause cannot be said to involve 'raising' of any kind, since the subject is still present in the embedded clause. Such languages fully justify the neutral term 'matrix clause coding', since the relevant parameter has to do with whether or not the subject of the embedded clause also appears in the matrix clause. In this section, we use data from a number of languages that allow double coding to argue against hypotheses that invoke Exceptional Case Marking, raising, and appropriate syntactic conditions as the motivation for matrix clause coding.

In Nigerian Arabic, the subject of the embedded clause may be coded only once, in the embedded clause (as in (10)), or it may be coded twice (as in (11)), as the object of the matrix clause and the subject of the embedded clause (data and analyses from Owens (1993: 160–1); glosses slightly modified):

(10) Ána 'aaríf **t**-íji.
I know 3F-come
'I know that she is coming.'

(11) Ána 'aaríf-**ha** **t**-íji.
I know-3F 3F-come
'I know that she is coming.'

The embedded clause subject may also be coded on the complementizer by means of a suffix:[9]

(12) Ána 'aaríf bee-**ha** **t**-íji.
I know that-3F 3F-come
'I know that she is coming.'

In one dialect of Nigerian Arabic, the subject of the embedded clause may be encoded in all three places in the same sentence:

(13) Ána 'áarfa-**ak** bée-**b** **íntá** baxíit.
I know-2 M.SG-COMP-2M.SG 2M.SG rich
'I know that you are rich.' (Owens 1993: 161)

These constructions cannot be explained in terms of Exceptional Case Marking, since Exceptional Case Marking is motivated by the presence of a nonfinite verb in the embedded clause and the verbs in these examples are finite. They cannot be explained in terms of raising, since the subject remains in the embedded clause. For the same reason, it can hardly be said that the subject is originally an argument of the matrix clause. Traditional syntactic analyses thus fail to account for the phenomenon.

Hdi (Central Chadic) allows double coding of arguments in independent clauses in the perfective aspect. In such clauses, a pronominal object may be marked either by a verbal affix or by the preposition *tá*, depending on the pragmatic status of the object. When the subject of the embedded clause is coded as the object of the matrix clause, this subject may be marked either by the preposition *tá* or by affixation to the verb (all data from Frajzyngier with Shay 2002):

Coding by preposition:

(14) Nghá-n-nghà **tá** **íí** tà dzàá.
see-3-see OBJ 1SG IMPF go
'He saw me go.'

Coding by affixation:

(15) Ngh-**íxà**-nghà tà dzàá.
see-1SG-see IMPF go
'He saw me go.'

The subject of the embedded clause may be coded in both the matrix and the embedded clause, where it appears as a suffix to the embedded clause verb (examples (7) and (8), repeated here for convenience):

(16) Sn-**íxà**-sná tà dzàá-**yù**.
hear-1SG-hear IMPF go-1SG
'He heard me go.'

(17) Sná-n-sná t-**íí** tà dzàá-**yù**.
hear-ANAPH-hear OBJ-1SG IMPF go-1SG
'He heard me go.' (Frajzyngier with Shay 2002: 504)

In East Dangla (East Chadic), the subject of the embedded clause is coded as the object of the matrix clause and also as the subject of the embedded clause (data and analysis from Shay 1999):

(18) a. No dòr-**ga** ák-**dyi**.
1SG hear.PRF-3M come.IMPF-3M
'I heard him come.'
b. No tal-**tya** kát-**tí**.
1SG see.PRF-3F leave.IMPF-3F
'I saw her go.'
c. No dòr-**ga** dàbsay-gì-**dyi** bèrka.
1SG hear.PRF-3M slaughter.IMPF-IMPF-3SG cow
'I heard him slaughter a cow.'

In Pero (West Chadic), the pronominal subject of the embedded clause may be coded twice, once as an object pronoun suffixed to the matrix verb and once as a subject pronoun preceding the embedded clause verb (all examples from Frajzyngier 1989a):

(19) a. Ka-a-men-ji-**mu** **minu**-n-cu dugun-i-m-a.
2M-NEG-want-HAB-1PL 1PL-SEQ-eat fig-DEF-NEG-Q
'Don't you want us to eat the figs?' (Frajzyngier 1989a: 258)
b. Nì-mén-jì-**cí** **cì**-n-púnd-ínà à-té-m.
1SG-want-HAB-2F 2F-SEQ-cook-VENT NEG-3F-NEG
'I want you to cook, not her.' (Frajzyngier 1989a: 258)

The behavior of third-person pronominal subjects in Pero provides additional evidence against the existence of a raising rule. The third-person singular pronominal subject of the matrix or independent clause is unmarked, unless the subject is in contrastive focus. But when a third-person singular pronoun is the subject of an embedded clause, it is coded as an object in the matrix clause. There is no subject pronoun preceding the verb of the embedded clause:

(20) Nì-mén-jì-ée-**nì** mù-n-cù.
1SG-want-HAB-OBJ-3M.OBJ COMP-SEQ-eat
'I want him to eat.' (Frajzyngier 1989a: 257; OBJ refers to the vowel marker -ée preceding some object pronouns)

The presence of the object suffix cannot result from raising, since there is no overt argument in the embedded clause to be raised. It cannot result from the syntactic position of the embedded subject, as suggested by Horn (1985), for the same reason.

Gidar (Central Chadic) also allows double coding of the embedded clause subject. Moreover, Gidar allows matrix clause coding even when the embedded clause has its own tense/aspect coding, which are considered within the Principles and Parameters approach to be Case assigning categories. Therefore, matrix clause coding in Gidar cannot be motivated by the need to assign Case to the embedded clause subject. In the following sentences, the subject of the embedded clause is marked by the suffix *tà* and by the coreferential object suffix *tə* in the matrix clause. In the first example, the embedded clause verb has the habitual aspect marker *dà*. In the second, the embedded clause has the present tense marker *tà*: (all data from Frajzyngier in press):

(21) Nə̀ wùlə́-**tə̀**-k dà-ddá-**tà**.
1SG see-3F-PRF D.HAB-go-3F
'I saw her going.'

(22) Nə̀ pə́rm-**tə́**-k tà-**tə̀** zá-t.
1SG hear-3F-PRF PRES-3F come-3F
'I heard her coming.'

Matrix clause coding occurs in Gidar even if there is a complementizer between the matrix and the embedded clause:

(23) À-wlú-**wə̀**-k ná **nə̀**-dé-kè.
3M-see-1SG-PRF COMP 1SG-come-PRF
'He saw me come.'

The preceding example provides evidence against Exceptional Case Marking, since the Principles and Parameters approach considers the presence of a complementizer to be a barrier to raising.

In Mina (Central Chadic), the auxiliary *za* follows the verb and the direct object, if any (all data from Frajzyngier, Johnston with Edwards, MS):

(24) Ká-mə̀sár hlí zà.
PRF-fry meat AUX
'He/she fried the meat.'

In a complex sentence, the subject of the embedded clause may be coded as a direct object in the matrix clause. This object occurs before, rather than after, the auxiliary of the matrix clause, making the subject of the embedded clause clearly an element of the matrix clause. This coding cannot be motivated by Exceptional Case Marking, since the embedded clause verb is marked for aspect and the subject of the embedded clause also occurs as a prefix to the verb of the embedded clause. Nor can it be motivated by appropriate syntactic conditions (cf. Horn 1985), since the auxiliary *za* should serve as a barrier to these conditions:

(25) Ká-lìm-á-**k** zà sə̀-ndə́ rà.
PRF-see-OBJ-1SG AUX 1SG-go-1SG PROG
'He saw me going.'

4.2. Optional matrix clause coding

With some verbs in some languages, matrix clause coding is optional. Since matrix clause coding may or may not occur with exactly the same matrix verb and exactly the same arguments in exactly the same linear order, it cannot be argued that matrix clause coding is triggered by Case marking requirements, appropriate syntactic conditions or any other structural factor. In such cases, matrix clause coding also cannot be motivated by the lexical nature of the matrix verb. The following examples are from Pero (example 20 is repeated here for convenience). In the first, the matrix verb is 'want' and the embedded clause subject appears as an object suffix to the matrix clause verb. In the second, all verbs and arguments are the same, but the embedded clause subject does not occur either in the matrix clause or in the embedded clause. The information that the subject of the embedded clause is third person is computed from the fact that the clause has deontic complementizer *mù* (example 26 repeated from 20):

(26) Nì-mén-jì-ée-**nì** **mù**-n-cù.
1SG-want-HAB-OBJ-3M.OBJ COMP-SEQ-eat
'I want him to eat.'

(27) Nì-mén-jì **mù**-n-cù cíinà dákàm mù-n-gbúdì.
1SG-want-HAB COMP-SEQ-eat food much COMP-SEQ-grow
'I wish he would eat more, so he would grow.'

In Mina, the embedded clause subject may or may not be coded within the matrix clause. In the following sentence, the embedded clause subject *Zroumba* is part of the matrix clause verb phrase and is also coded by a pronoun in the embedded clause. The auxiliary *zà* (with vowel reduction) marks the end of the matrix clause verb phrase:

(28) Sà-ká-hlìm **zrə́mbà** zà **á**-nd-á rà.
1SG-PRF-hear Zroumba AUX 3SG-go-GO PROG
'I heard Zroumba coming.'

In exactly the same syntactic conditions, with exactly the same lexical items, matrix clause coding may not occur. In the following example, *Zroumba* appears only in the embedded clause. (In Mina, a clause with a nominal subject also must have a pronominal subject, here represented by *á*):

(29) Sà-ká-hlìm zà **zrə́mbə́** **á**-nd-á rà.
1SG-PRF-hear AUX Zroumba 3SG-go-GO PROG
'I heard Zroumba coming' or 'I heard that Zroumba is coming.'

Since matrix clause coding is optional in Pero, Mina and some other languages, matrix clause coding is not an automatically controlled result of any condition or set of conditions but rather an independent grammatical means. The functions of that means are the subject of the next section.

5. Functions of matrix clause coding

We have said that matrix clause coding is not triggered by the presence of a certain verb in the matrix clause, since in some languages the same matrix verb may occur with or without matrix clause coding. However, it is true that in some languages matrix clause coding is confined to certain classes of matrix clause verbs. For example, the a.c.i. construction in Latin occurs mainly with verbs of saying, volitional verbs, and verbs of perception (Gildersleeve and Lodge 1971: 335; Ernout and Thomas 1972: 320ff; Bolkestein 1976a, 1977). While matrix clause coding with verbs of saying is infrequent across languages, matrix clause coding with verbs of perception and volitional verbs occurs in many unrelated languages. In a few languages, it occurs with verbs outside these classes.

We show in this section that matrix clause coding may have different functions in different languages. Moreover, matrix clause coding in the same language may have different functions with different verbs, though these functions have common characteristics. The discussion of the functions of matrix clause coding demonstrates the application of the principle of functional transparency in the following way. Matrix clause coding indicates the modality of the embedded clause within the functional domains coded in the individual language. These domains are to certain degree constrained by matrix clause predicates such as verbs of perception, verbs of saying, volitional verbs and cognitive verbs. With predicates of this type, the hearer expects a certain range of subdomains to be indicated in the clause. These domains and subdomains are described in the following sections.

5.1. The coding of epistemic functions

With verbs of perception and volitional verbs, matrix clause coding often codes epistemic modality. Since the types of epistemic modality coded differ from one class of verb to the other, we discuss each class separately, beginning with verbs of perception. Epistemic modality is not the only function performed by matrix clause coding with verbs of perception. When epistemic modality is coded by other means, matrix clause coding may have a pragmatic function (cf. Section 7). In this section, we describe only its epistemic functions.

5.1.1. Epistemic coding with verbs of perception

Matrix clause coding with verbs of perception has the modal function of coding direct, as opposed to indirect, perception. When this is the case, matrix clause coding may contrast with the absence of matrix clause coding or with the presence of some other coding means, such as a *de dicto* complementizer. Our evidence comes both from languages that have matrix clause coding and from those that do not.

In English, matrix clause coding with verbs of perception codes direct perception or the *de re* status of a proposition (Frajzyngier 1991; Frajzyngier and Jasperson 1991). Evidence for this is that matrix clause coding cannot be modified by a clause indicating inference, word of mouth or indirect evidence:

(30) 1_6_0 <1021 B> and ^I've !heard him — 'talking in the re!f\/ectory#

*but I don't recall who told me so

(31) 2_13_0 <947 (A> it was the ^casual ‘way that [@m] I :overheard ‘Ella ‘telling !J\oan#

*but I don’t recall who told me so

(32) 2_7_0 <1297 b> [m] . I [ha] overheard a man in Barkers today .asking for a wok — and . I apparently was the only other person there who knew what a wok *was — (laughs)*

*but I don’t recall who told me I overheard it

(33) 1_8_0 <341 A> I ^thought I :saw you :d\/o something ‘with *them#*/

*because they had been disturbed

Indirect perception is coded in English by the absence of matrix clause coding and the presence of the complementizer ‘that’:

(34) 2_9_0 <1132 B> +”^signs+ are the :only _things you can obs\erve#
2_9_0 <1133 B> ^like !if you ‘took an /X-ray#
2_9_0 <1134 B> and ^saw **that** ‘things were :blocked !\up or *something#*

(35) 2_10_0 <588 B> ((we‘ve)) ^heard **that** :Front P\age#
2_10_0 <589 B> was ^frightfully F\unny#
2_10_0 <590 c> yes
2_10_0 <591 B> but we‘ve “^m\issed it#
2_10_0 <592 B> we ^can‘t ‘find !where it‘s \on ‘now#

(36) 6_6_0 <602 a> we were ^\ordered to ‘go#
6_6_0 <603 a> “^h\ad to o_bey _orders#
6_6_0 <604 a> but ^when they :saw **that** ‘they were :g\/oing# -
6_6_0 <605 a> **that** ^we were l\eaving them# — -
6_6_0 <606 a> a ^dreadful _thing !h\appened#

Even if the complementizer is omitted, the absence of matrix clause coding codes only indirect perception:

(37) 2_14_0 <922 A> ^having ‘heard **her ‘super’visor was c/oming#**
2_14_0 <923 A> and so there was ^no s\uper’vision to ‘do#

(38) 6_5_0 <260 w> ^but I'm ^quite c\/ertain#
6_5_0 <261 w> that ^when you'd 'heard **he'd :d\/ied#**
6_5_0 <262 w> there ^must have 'been a :b\/it of you#
6_5_0 <263 w> that have ^s/aid# -
6_5_0 <264 w> ^I k\illed him# – – –

In Gidar, matrix clause coding also implies direct perception:

(39) Nə pə́rm-**tə̀**-k də̀ ə́tàw wùlá wàhlìyà.
1SG hear-3F-PRF ASSC cut neck cow
'I heard her slaughter a cow.'

(40) À pə́rm-**wə̀**-k də̀ tàw wùlá wàhlìyà.
3SG hear-1SG-PRF ASSC cut neck cow
'he heard me slaughter a cow.'

Matrix clause coding implies direct perception even if the matrix clause is separated from the embedded clause by a complementizer. Thus, the presence of the complementizer with matrix clause coding in Gidar has no effect on the coding of the nature of perception:

(41) N-úlə̀-**tə́**-k **ná** tə̀-dè-kè.
1SG-see-3F-PRF COMP 3F-come:VENT-PRF
'I saw her come.'

The absence of matrix clause coding in Gidar indicates indirect perception, regardless of whether the complementizer *ná* is used.
Indirect perception without the complementizer:

(42) Nə̀ pə́rmə̀-k **à** tàw wùlá wàhlìyà.
1SG hear-PRF 3M cut neck cow
'I heard that he slaughtered a cow.'

(43) À pə́rmə̀-k **nə̀** tàw wùlá wàhlìyà.
3SG hear-PRF 1SG cut neck cow
'He heard that I slaughtered a cow.'

Indirect perception with the complementizer:

(44) N-úlə̀-á-k **ná** tə̀ dè-kè.
1SG-see-PRF COMP 3F come:VENT-PRF
'I saw that she came.'

(45) À-wl-á-k **ná** **kírtì-n** dә-ɓà-n gèsín.
3M-see-PRF COMP children-3M 3M-burn-PL truly
'He saw that in fact it was his children that burned.'

In Mandara (Central Chadic), matrix clause coding of the subject of the embedded clause indicates direct perception. The embedded clause subject appears as an object infix in the reduplicated matrix verb but is absent from the embedded clause (all Mandara data from Frajzyngier's fieldnotes):

(46) Yà cìná-**n**-cínà kɓ-vá ùzá-rà.
1SG hear-3SG-PRF break-SEP hoe-3SG
'I heard him break his hoe.' (SEP-separative extension)

The absence of matrix clause coding indicates indirect evidence. In the following example, the subject of the embedded clause is marked by the third-person subject pronoun *á* and the matrix verb does not have the object marker *n*:

(47) Yà cìná **á** kɓ-vá ùzá-rà.
1SG hear 3SG break-SEP hoe-3SG
'I heard that he broke his hoe.' (Frajzyngier, fieldnotes)

5.1.2. Matrix clause coding and different types of complementizers

Additional evidence for the epistemic function of matrix clause coding is provided by data from languages that have a distinction between two complementizers, one coding direct perception and the other indirect perception (cf. Frajzyngier 1995b). If a language having two such complementizers also has matrix clause coding, it occurs with the complementizer that codes direct perception but not with the complementizer that codes indirect perception.

In Lele (East Chadic), the direct perception complementizer is *gō* and the indirect perception complementizer is *nā*. When the complementizer *gō* is used, the matrix clause verb must have an object pronoun suffix that is coreferential with the subject of the embedded clause:

(48) Ŋ̄-gòl-í gō jè wàl-**dí** kúlbà.
1SG-see-3M COMP IMPRF slaughter-3M cow
'I saw him slaughtering a cow'

(49) Ŋ̄-gòl-**dù** gō jè wàl-**dú** kúlbà.
1SG-see-3M COMP IMPRF slaughter-3M cow
'I saw her slaughtering a cow.' (Frajzyngier fieldnotes)

Matrix clause coding is not allowed with the indirect perception complementizer *nā*:

(50) Cànìgé ɗēŋlí **nā** gírbí-dú jè kòjò kò-rò.
Canige hear COMP forget-3F PRF hoe POSS-3F
'Canige heard that she forgot her hoe.' (Frajzyngier fieldnotes)

If the embedded clause is equational, no complementizer is used and the subject of the embedded clause is not coded on the verb of the matrix clause. Instead, the whole embedded clause is a complement of the matrix verb:

(51) È-gé dà túgú kóŋ nī àlá kùrmbàlò gòl kāmdā-ì sùbù né
go-3PL LOC village certain LOC then chief see wives-3M three COP
gō láy wà tú.
REL beautiful PL all (French)
'When they arrived at a certain village, the chief saw that the three wives of the man were all beautiful.'

5.1.3. *Epistemic coding with volitional verbs*

When matrix clause coding occurs with a volitional verb in the matrix clause, the modality of the embedded clause is *realis*, i.e., the speaker considers the event to be possible or real. When matrix clause coding is optional, the absence of matrix clause coding indicates the *irrealis* or hypothetical mood. We provide evidence from a number of languages.

In Pero, volitional sentences having matrix clause coding of the embedded subject have *realis* mood; i.e., the speaker can expect the event to occur and/or has control over the event (examples 19 and 20 are repeated here for convenience):

(52) Ka-a-men-ji-**mu** **minu**-n-cu dugun-i-m-a.
2M-NEG-want-HAB-1PL 1PL-SEQ-eat fig-DEF-NEG-Q
'Don't you want us to eat the figs?'

(53) Nì-mén-jì-**cí** **cì**-n-púnd-ínà à-té-m.
1SG-want-HAB-2F 2F-SEQ-cook-VENT NEG-3F-NEG
'I want you to cook, not her.'

The absence of matrix clause coding indicates the hypothetical mood. The following sentence is hypothetical because the speaker has no control over the event, especially over its outcome. Note also that subject is not overtly marked in the embedded clause because the third-person subject is not overtly marked in pragmatically neutral clauses in Pero (repeated from 27):

(54) Nì-mén-jì **mù**-n-cù cíinà dákàm mù-n-gbúdì.
1SG-want-HAB COMP-SEQ-eat food much COMP-SEQ-grow
'I wish he would eat more, so he would grow.'

In Hdi, when the subject of the embedded clause is coded as a direct object of the volitional matrix clause, the embedded complement is in the *realis* mood; i.e., the speaker believes his wish may come true (all Hdi data from Frajzyngier with Shay 2002):

(55) Tà kúmà-í **tá** **kághá** ngá dzá'á dà vàghù mù
IMPF like-1SG OBJ 2SG PREP go PREP-to spend the day PREP-at
vwàx-á-ɗà.
field-GEN-1SG
'I want you to go and work in the field of my in-laws.' (Frajzyngier with Shay 2002: 520)

When the embedded subject is not coded in the matrix clause, the embedded clause is in the hypothetical mood. Most elicited sentences containing volitional matrix verbs are coded in this way, since the elicited complement is not a genuine wish of the speaker's:

(56) Tà kúmà-yù tá vàghá-tà-**ghá** mà màrwá.
IMPF like-1SG OBJ spend the day-REF-2SG PREP-at Maroua
'I would like you to spend a day in Maroua.' (Frajzyngier with Shay 2002: 480)

5.2. Obligatory matrix clause coding with volitional verbs: Why 'want' in English requires matrix clause coding

The most compelling argument in favor of the epistemic function of matrix clause coding with volitional verbs is that it allows us to explain why the verb 'want' in English requires matrix clause coding while semantically similar verbs in other languages not only do not require matrix clause coding but often do not allow it. Our hypothesis is as follows: The verb 'want' in English is inherently *realis*. Since matrix clause coding implies *realis* modality and the absence of matrix clause coding implies *irrealis*, matrix clause coding is the only possible choice with the verb 'want':

(57) 1_2_1 <828 B> he ^wanted **me** to be in a good !m\ood for th/at# *.*/
1_2_2 <1053 A> ^well I'd I ^wanted **you** to [@] you ^kn/ow#

1_2_2 <1054 A> *. ((to)) "^kn\ow#*
1_3_0 <648 A> ^where do you want **me** to s\it# *-*

1_1_0 <351 B> ^if they :wanted **a :man** to do :medieval !l/iterature# — - -

(58) and the ^others 'said they 'wanted :**me** to !t\alk a'bout it#

1_7_0 <273 A> I ^mean you 'want **the !g\irls** to 'drink it# .

Similarly, in written texts (all data from Brown 1_A.Txt):

(59) but that the board would cooperate so far as possible to get the children to where the parents wanted **them** to go.

(60) Ol' Case wanted No. 7 to be not only the best homerun hitter,
Because neither of them really wanted **their marriage** to break up

Evidence that 'want' is inherently *realis* is provided by the fact that the complement of 'want' cannot be unattainable:

(61) *I want to be Julius Caesar [not in the context of a theatrical play].
*I want Julius Caesar to visit my class.
*I want to have eight lifetimes.

The verb 'wish', on the other hand, is inherently *irrealis* and is thus incompatible, except in very marked discourse contexts, with matrix clause coding. The complement of 'wish' may be fantastic, unattainable or merely out of the speaker's control:

(62) Wish **I** was 40, and a top-grade big leaguer.

1_10_0 <1187 A> I ^wish I had !eight l\/ifetimes#

1_8_0 <267 A> I* ^wish I :d\/id# .

1_8_0 <1021 (A> ((I ^think)) she said 'something a'bout [i ? a:] she ^wished that :everybody would 'take . [@:] the'thing":s\/eriously#

1_10_0 <980 A> I ^wish I'd kn\/own I'd be 'coming 'here this 'week#

1_10_0 <245 A> +I ^wish you'd 'asked me what+ :escort . :would have !b\ /een#

2_10_0 <1013 B> +((yes)) ^actually I !!wish+ ^I !!wish ((you were a/ h\ elp)) 'actually /Arthur#

The verb 'like', coupled with the auxiliary 'would', is also inherently *irrealis* and incompatible with matrix clause coding. It is most felicitous with complements that are attainable but out of the speaker's control:

(63) a. I would like her to be here.
?I would like her to have three hands.
b. Ideally, the President would like the French to agree on a 'status quo ante'. (Brown Corpus)
c. however the President, who would like to woo the former Chinese province away from both Peking and Moscow. (Brown Corpus)

Matrix clause coding thus performs the same function in English and in Chadic languages, that of coding *realis* modality. However, while English has the inherently *realis* verb 'want' and the inherently *irrealis* 'wish' and 'would like', volitional verbs in Chadic languages are neither inherently *realis* nor *irrealis*. In Chadic languages, therefore, it is matrix clause coding alone that codes the *realis* mood, while the absence of matrix clause coding indicates the *irrealis* mood.

One could argue that the fact that matrix clause coding in Chadic languages, Nigerian Arabic and in Polish (as shown in the following sections) is not triggered by formal requirements of case assignment and does not involve movement out of the embedded clause does not mean that exceptional case assignment or movement out of the embedded clause must be ruled out in English. However, given that we are dealing with the same formal phenomenon, an explanation that accounts for all instantiations of this phenomenon in different languages is preferable to one that differs from one language to the next. The most compelling evidence that matrix clause coding is not a result of formal requirements, as postulated in previous theories, is provided by constraints on the occurrence of matrix clause coding. These constraints, and similar effects of matrix clause coding on semantic interpretations, indicate that matrix clause coding in English is a coding means with a specific function, just as it is in Polish, Nigerian Arabic and Chadic languages.

5.2.1. *Other 'raising verbs' in English*

A number of other verbs in English allow matrix clause coding. The distribution of such verbs in the London–Lund corpus supports our hypothesis that matrix clause coding is an independent grammatical means. The functional distinctions coded by the presence or absence of matrix clause coding vary with the semantics of the matrix clause verb; however, the examples we have found show that these distinctions correspond broadly with the *realis/irrealis* and *de re/de dicto* distinctions illustrated above. We provide here a few examples of such distinctions.

One verb that allows matrix clause coding is 'consider'. The presence of matrix clause coding with this verb appears to code the *de re* domain. When 'consider' is not accompanied by matrix clause coding, the meaning of the construction is 'to think over', 'to ponder' (the first line of the following example contains two intransitive clauses with the first-person subject):

11_3_1 <50 a> and I ^**considered** I ^l\ay 'back#
11_3_1 <51 a> and ^s\ipped my c/ocoa#
11_3_1 <52 a> and **con^sidered** the :pets I could :h\ave

However, when the complement of 'consider' is coded in the matrix clause, the construction describes an option or conclusion in the *de re* domain:

5_4_0 <204 II> (in view of the demand for stringent economy by the/ Government does the panel **consider** the time opportune for the expenditure of time and money in putting Stonehenge upright)

6_7_0 <730 a> now these were two men you greatly liked obviously Brockhouse and Orton but can't you bring yourself to **consider** the possibility that Brockhouse in his old age in a sense denied Orton the full prospect of being Chief Officer that by . clinging on and *making ((the))* point

A similar situation obtains with the English verb 'expect'. When the complement is not coded in the matrix clause, this verb has the meaning 'to think it likely (that)', 'to entertain the thought (that)', especially in some dialects of English; it does not refer to an awaited *realis* event:

2_7_0 <813 b> oh I **expect** he got a penny or two for it

The verb 'expect' with matrix clause coding indicates an anticipated outcome or event in the *realis* domain:

1_9_0 <123 A> one ^always **exp/ects** them#
1_9_0 <124 A> *to ^come to one*

2_5_1 <254 a> you mean you **expect** [@] . Marines to go everywhere at a trot .

1_9_0 <126 (a> and **expects** — to be visited
1_9_0 <128 A> *of ^c/\ourse#

1_10_0 <1086 b> you mustn‘t **expect** to be entertained you just go in/and out and do your thing .

The construction with the English verb ‘believe’ has similar constraints. With non-raised subjects the verb *believe* indicates belief in a statement, the domain de dicto. With raised object the belief is held with respect to some reality rather than with respect to a statement:

2_1_3 <1465 B> there‘s ^no reason ((to **believe**)) he‘s a !c\ommunist _mind#

1_7_0 <332 a> . . . cos I **believe** you can get it on the National Health can‘t you**

2_3_0 <82 B> *I ^**believe** it‘s a :bit of [@m@] . an a:m\algam#
2_3_0 <83 B> ((^this m/ap#))*

11_4_0 <348 a3> it has al^ready ‘been !m\/ade ‘clear#
11_4_0 <349 a3> that Her ^Majesty‘s ‘government are op!posed to .:and de!pl\ /ore#
11_4_0 <350 a3> the ^Arab b\oycott# .
11_4_0 <351 a3> ^I **believe** that !more is to be ‘gained in this :m\/atter#
11_4_0 <352 a3> by sup^porting !policies and ‘actions :aimed at[dhi:] . ‘reso!l\ ution of the ‘Arab-’Israel c/onflict# .

7_1_3 <866 A> hel^l\o ((‘Jane))# .
7_1_3 <867 b> [@:m] I **believe** you rang me up
7_1_3 <868 A> ^y\es#

Some verbs of cognition may not only allow but require matrix clause coding. Possible examples are the verbs ‘hold’ (in the cognitive sense) and ‘deem’. The latter appears in the London–Lund corpus only with matrix clause coding:

12_7_0 <838 a> and their ^represen’tation in p\/ublic#
12_7_0 <839 a> [?]are ^**deemed** to be !both im’moral“!![?]\/and of’fensive#

Further study of the coding of complements of cognitive verbs across languages may reveal and refine the types of distinctions coded by the presence or absence of matrix clause coding. Verbs that are used to code dubitative mood, such as ‘think’ do not allow matrix coding in English, Polish, and other Western Indo-European languages.

5.2.2. *Deontic function with volitional verbs*

Matrix clause coding with volitional verbs sometimes codes deontic rather than epistemic modality. In English, the verb 'want' is very often inherently deontic. In some dialects, however, it appears to have lost its deontic function. In this case, the deontic function is assumed by some other marker, such as a deontic auxiliary in the embedded clause:

(64) Do you want I should go with you? (some American dialects)

In some languages, volitional verbs are not inherently deontic and the mood of the embedded clause is coded by some other means, which may include matrix clause coding. In Mupun (West Chadic), deontic complements of volitional verbs are coded by a complementizer consisting of the sequence *kə n* followed by the pronominal or nominal subject of the embedded clause and sometimes by the complementizer *ɗi*. The structure of the whole sentence is S V (x) *kə n*-N_1 (N_1) V (*ɗi*) (y), where the first N_1 represents the matrix clause coding of the subject of the embedded clause and the second N_1 represents the coding of the same argument in the embedded clause. The variables *x* and *y* represent any other sentence elements:

(65) An mbə ɗem **kə** **n-ha** **a** ji (**ɗi**) n-jiŋ.
1SG FUT want COMP PREP-2M 2M come COMP PREP-Jing
'I want you to come to Jing.'

(66) An mbə ɗem **kə** **n-yi** **yi** cet mbise **ɗi** n-an.
1SG FUT want COMP PREP-2F 2F cook food COMP PREP-1SG
'I want you to cook for me.'

In 67, the subject of the embedded clause is coded only once, after the complementizer *kə*:

(67) N-ɗem **kə** **n-war** cet mbise **ɗi** n-darap.
1SG-want COMP PREP-3F cook food COMP PREP-Darap
'I want her to cook for Darap.' (Frajzyngier 1993: 444)

If the deontic complementizer *kə* is replaced by the *de dicto* complementizer *nə*, the embedded clause has indicative mood and the verb *ɗem* is not construed as volitional:

(68) N-ɗem **nə** wa cet mbise n-Darap.
1SG-want COMP 3F cook food PREP-Darap
'I agree that she cooks for Darap.' (Frajzyngier 1993: 444)

6. Systems interaction in the coding of *realis* modality

In this section we describe how one language uses means other than matrix clause coding to code the epistemic or deontic modality of certain complements. We then demonstrate how this allows matrix clause coding to be used for pragmatic functions.

Polish does not have matrix clause coding after volitional verbs. It is theoretically possible that Polish does not code the distinction between *realis* and *irrealis* wishes. It is also possible that the language codes this distinction but uses different means, and in fact this is the case. The verb *chcieć* 'want' may be used for both *realis* and hypothetical wishes. In either case, if the subject of the matrix clause is identical with the subject of the embedded clause, the embedded clause has an infinitive verb:

(69) Kochany Karol-ek sam tam chciał **wejść.**
dear Charles-DIMIN INTENS there want:PAST:3M enter:INF
'Dear Charlie himself wanted to enter there.' (Sources)

The hypothetical mood is coded by the past tense form of the matrix clause verb and the hypothetical marker *by*:

(70) Pan **chciał-by** tu zaprowadzić nowe porządki, a to
Sir want:PAST:3M-HYP here introduce:INF new order:PL CONJ DEM
się nie da.
REFL NEG give
'You would like to introduce new rules here, but that will not work.' (Sources)

Wishes with respect to persons other than the subject of the matrix clause must have the marker *by* following the *de dicto* complementizer *że*. The role of *by* is to code the deontic modality. The distinction between *realis* and *irrealis* wishes is coded by the tense of the matrix clause verb: The present tense codes a *realis* wish while the past tense form codes a hypothetical wish.

Realis wishes:

(71) Ja **chcę,** że-by oni wiedzieli, że-by nie
1SG want:1SG:PRES COMP-HYP 3PL know:3PL:PAST COMP:SUBJ NEG
przestawali podejrzewać.
cease:PAST:3PL suspect:INF
'I want them to know, I want them to keep suspecting.' (Sources)

(72) Ale **chcę**, że-by miała jakiś swój kąt,
but want:1SG:PRES COMP-HYP have:PAST:3F some POSS:REF:M angle
kiedy wróci.
when return:FUT:3SG
'But I want her to have her own place when she returns.' (Sources)

Hypothetical wishes:

(73) Chcesz, że-by-m zagrał?
want:2SG:PRES COMP-HYP-1SG play:PAST:M
'Do you want me to play?'

Chciała-by-m to zobaczyć.
want:PAST:F-HYP-1SG DEM see:INF
'I wish I could see that.' (Sources)

(74) A ja by-m coś chiała.
CONJ 1SG HYP-1SG something want:PAST:3F
'I would still want something.'

Co?
'What?'

Żeby jeszcze raz **było** jak w niebie.
COMP:SUBJ yet once be:PAST:N as in heaven
'For it to be once again as it was in heaven.' (Sources)

With verbs of perception, direct perception is coded in both literary and non-literary varieties of Polish by the preposition/subordinator *jak*, glossed 'how':

(75) Słyszałam **jak** mu radziłaś.
hear:PAST:F:1SG how 3M:DAT advise:PAST:F:2SG
'I heard you advise him.' (Sources)

(76) Nie usłyszałem, **jak** wszedłeś.
NEG hear:PAST:M:1SG how come in:PAST:M:2SG
'I didn't hear you come in.' (Sources)

(77) Nie wiem, czy widział, **jak** się śmiałem.
NEG know:1SG:PRES whether see:3M how REFL laugh:1SG:PAST
'I do not know whether he saw me laughing.' (Sources)

(78) I ujrzał **jak** jakiś nieznajomy mężczyzna
CONJ see:3SGM:PAST:PRF how some unknown:SGM man
obcina ogon jego koniowi.
cut off:PRES tail his horse:DAT
'And he noticed an unknown man cutting off his horse's tail.' (Sources)

Indirect perception is marked by the complementizer *że*:

(79) Zauważył, **że** Pan Romański lubi tak samo
notice:PAST:PRF:3M COMP Mr. Romanski like:PRES:3SG so also
zapatrzyć się pod wirującą karuzelą jak on.
stare:INF REFL under spin:GER:F merry-go-around like 3M.SG
'He noticed that Mr. Romanski also liked to stare under the spinning merry-go-round.' (Sources)

(80) Widzimy więc wyraźnie, **że** telewizja w Ameryce nie jest
see-PRES:1PL therefore clearly COMP television in America NEG be
bynajmniej dobrodziejstwem świadczonym społecznie na wielką
at all benefit provide:PAST:PASS:M socially on grand
skalę.
scale
'We see, therefore, quite clearly, that TV in America is not a benefit provided on a socially grand scale.' (Sources)

Thus, the semantic functions performed in English and Chadic languages by matrix clause coding are performed in Polish by the presence or absence of morphemes from other classes.

7. Pragmatic functions of matrix clause coding

Boniewicz (1982) claims that matrix clause coding in Polish occurs only with the verbs *wydawać się*, *zdawać się* 'seem' and *uważać za* 'consider (to be)'. In the 130,000-word corpus of sources to the frequentative dictionary of Polish, we have found only the verb *uważać za* 'consider to be' with a construction resembling subject raising:

(81) Dlaczego Pani nie wystarczy, że on nie
why Madam:DAT NEG suffice:FUT:3SG COMP 3M NEG
uważa Pani za chorą?
consider:PRES:3SG Madam as sick:INSTR:F
'Why is it not enough for you that he does not consider you ill?' (Sources)

There is a fundamental question, however, whether this construction truly represents matrix clause coding rather than modification of the object.

Contrary to Boniewicz (1982), many verbs in non-literary Polish, including verbs of perception, allow matrix clause coding of an argument of embedded clause. This coding, however, has pragmatic rather than modal functions. For example, a focused embedded clause subject is coded as an object of the matrix clause (transcription simplified for typographical reasons; j = palatal glide, c = voiceless affricate, dz = voiced alveolar affricate):

(82) Cy-ś ty, xłopce, vidźał **kogo** budovać stavańec proci
Q-2SG 2SG boy:VOC see:PAST:M anybody:ACC build:INF prop against
xalnemu v́atru?
halny wind
'Did you, my lad, ever see anybody build a prop against the mountain wind?' (Nitsch 1960: 81. We take *stavańec*, a noun not listed in dictionaries, to mean a standing protection against something.)

Another function of matrix clause coding is to topicalize the embedded subject in order to make it available as a topic in subsequent discourse. With verbs of perception, matrix clause coding may be accompanied by the subordinator *jak* 'how' to code direct perception:

(83) Że tam som jacysik cygani f kośćele, że **ig** vidźał
COMP there are some Gypsies in church COMP 3PL see:PAST:3SG
oknem **jako** se **woṕekajo** spyrke.
window:INSTR COMP REFL:POSS bake:PRES:3PL salted pork
'That there are some Gypsies in the church, that he saw them through the window baking salted pork.' (Nitsch 1960: 79)

(84) Coź-va vidz'eli **tyx** **dvux, jak** śe
when-1DU see:3PL DEM:PL:ACC two COMP REFL
provadźyli woba pijane s karcmy.
accompany:PAST:3PL:M both drunk:PL from tavern:LOC
'When we (dual) saw those two, drunk, accompanying each other on the way from the tavern.' (Nitsch 1960: 159)

Matrix clause coding also may be accompanied by the complementizer *że* (*ize*, in the following dialectal example), coding indirect perception:

(85) Jag won **ḿe** uisdrzi, **ize** **jow** ta zebrza, to won ḿe
when 3M 1SG see:PRF COMP 1SG here beg then 3M 1SG:ACC
fsadzi do xarestu.
put in:FUT:3SG to detention
'If he sees me begging here, he will arrest me.' (Nitsch 1960: 66)

Matrix clause coding may even involve the object of the embedded clause. Here again, the function of matrix clause coding is topicalization:

(86) A **bajek** to co dzień **inksom** v'edział pedźeć.
CONJ tale:PL:GEN COM QUANT day another know:PAST:3SG say:PAST:3SG
'And folktales, he was capable of telling a different one every day.' (Nitsch 1960: 83)

8. Conclusions

We have shown that matrix clause coding, or coding the subject of the embedded clause as the object of the matrix clause, does not involve raising, movement out of the embedded clause or Exceptional Case Marking, but instead is an independent coding means. We have shown that the functions of this means may differ from language to language and within individual languages. Matrix clause coding may have different functions with volitional verbs, verbs of saying, and verbs of perception. In some languages matrix clause coding codes epistemic and deontic modalities. In other languages matrix clause coding has pragmatic functions, as when it makes an argument of the embedded clause available for various pragmatic operations (cf. Nichols and Schallert 1983).

In some languages matrix clause coding with verbs of perception indicates direct perception. For volitional verbs that are inherently [+deontic], matrix clause coding indicates the speaker's belief that the wish will be realized or has the potential of being realized. For the same verbs, the absence of matrix clause coding indicates the *irrealis* modality. For volitional verbs that are not inherently [+deontic], matrix clause coding indicates the deontic modality of the complement while the absence of matrix clause coding indicates indicative modality.

CHAPTER 9

Determining the function of a linguistic form: the indirectly affected argument and the external possessor

1. Introduction

1.1. Theoretical issues with respect to meaning

Many contemporary discussions of semantics are characterized by an *a priori* approach wherein the meaning of a linguistic form is based on inferences about some non-linguistic reality to which it is tacitly assumed the form refers. When the meaning of a form in a foreign language is described, this description is based on the translation of the form into one of the familiar languages of scientific discourse. The language of symbolic logic was developed as a means of avoiding the pitfalls inherent in this methodology. However, the language of symbolic logic is ultimately based on the functional domains of westerm Indo-European languages. A description of a linguistic form in the language of symbolic logic is nothing more than a translation of that form into one more language.

Approaches based on *a priori* assumptions about meaning create the impression that the linguist already knows the meaning and function of a linguistic form, and that all that remains to be done is to represent the meaning within some linguistic theory. This approach can be found across a wide spectrum of linguistic theories, e.g. Jackendoff (2001); Wierzbicka (1992); Van Valin and LaPolla (1997). In the present work we propose a method for discovering the language-specific meaning of a linguistic form and a method for providing proof of the meaning of a linguistic form.

The foundation of the proposed approach is that meaning does not exist outside of the linguistic forms that code it. The meaning of each linguistic form must be formulated as a hypothesis for which evidence must be provided. In other words, a statement about the meaning of a linguistic form in a given language should be an empirical statement, the evidence and counterevidence for which should be sought in the same language.

In this chapter we illustrate the proposed methodology for determining the function of a linguistic form. For this illustration we have selected the category coded by the dative case in a language with rich inflectional coding on nouns. We have chosen to examine this particular category for two reasons: First, our study contributes to the development of a systematic picture of the functions of inflectional case marking; and second, our study addresses a hypothesis concerning the dative case that has recently received much attention in the literature, a hypothesis based on identifying the meaning of the linguistic form in terms of inferences about non-linguistic reality.

1.2. External possessor hypothesis

König and Haspelmath (1998) propose that various European languages have a construction whose formal properties include the presence of two noun phrases, one marked by the dative case and the other by some other case (nominative, accusative, etc.), and whose semantic function is to code possession. König and Haspelmath (1998) propose that such constructions in these languages code 'external possessor' or 'external possession':

(1) Die Mutter wäscht dem Kind die Haare.
ART:NOM mother wash.3SG ART:DAT child ART:ACC hair
'The mother washes the hair of her child.' (König and Haspelmath 1998:526)

In this view, the external possessive construction is understood as a means of coding possession that is supplemental to 'internal possessive constructions' like those coded by the genitive case:

(2) die Haare des Kindes
ART:NOM hair ART:GEN child:GEN
'the child's hair'

Similar claims have been made by other scholars for a variety of Indo-European languages.

1.3. Our hypothesis and the types of argumentation

We propose that in a language that has a system of cases that includes the accusative, the dative, and the genitive case, the semantic relationships coded by the dative case include the indirect affectedness of an argument. In such a system, the accusative case codes direct affectedness.[10] We also show that, contrary to recent claims in the literature, the coding of possession is not one of the functions of the dative case in such a system. Any possessive interpretation of the dative case is a product of an analysis of the situation described by the construction rather than of the function of the construction within the grammatical system of the language.

The present chapter examines the claim that the construction with one argument marked by the dative case and another marked by the accusative or some other case codes possession. In showing that the construction codes indirect affectedness, we demonstrate why the coding of possession is not a function of the construction. We also show why the situation described by the construction may lend itself to a possessive interpretation. Argumentation for our hypothesis that the dative case codes indirect affectedness of the object is drawn from an analysis of the relevant facts in Polish, one of the languages said to have external possessor constructions (cf. König and Haspelmath 1998). To illustrate the coding of indirect affectedness through marking on the verb we have selected Hdi, a Central Chadic language. To illustrate the coding of indirect affectedness through prepositions we have selected Hausa, a West Chadic language, and Gidar, a Central Chadic language. The proposed analysis not only accounts for the functions of the indirect object category in many languages but also allow us to explain why English does not have the grammatical category of indirect affectedness.

2. Theoretical underpinnings and methodology

There are two fundamental elements in the description of a linguistic construction: its form and its function. With respect to form, the crucial questions concern those elements of the form that are distinguishing, hence obligatory, in a given construction. Although König and Haspelmath (1998) are not very explicit about the formal properties involved, all of their examples of external possession constructions involve one argument marked by the dative case, coding the possessor, and another argument marked by either the nominative or the accusative case, coding the possessum. No other formal characteristics of the external possession construction are given or are apparent from the data included in König and Haspelmath (1998).

With respect to function, the most important question is to what functional domain, as defined in Chapter 1, a given construction belongs. Since the common constituent in all constructions claimed to code external possession is an argument marked for the dative case, the fundamental questions to be addressed in this chapter concern the functions of the dative case.

König and Haspelmath (1998) define the notion of external possession only by analogy with 'internal possession'. In the present chapter, the working definition for the functional domain of possession is as follows: The coding of a relationship between two nouns such that one noun is interpreted as the possessor or owner of the other noun or as the whole entity in a part-whole relationship with the other noun. The broad outlines of this definition are widely accepted in linguistic literature and practice (Marouzeau 1951) and appear to be the basis for König and Haspelmath's selection of examples. Possessive constructions in some languages may be divided into several subcategories, such as alienable and inalienable, but this is not an issue in the present chapter.

Examples 1 and 2, and others cited as examples of 'external possession', give rise to the following questions:

- Does the construction really code possession?
- If the construction does not code possession, what does it code?
- If the construction does not code possession, what makes the possessive interpretation of the relationship between two arguments possible?
- How does one go about determining the function of a given construction?

A construction *C* that codes a function *F* should not occur when function *F* is not possible. Thus, a construction that codes possession should not be used when no possessive relationship is possible, e.g. with an intransitive verb and no potential possessum:

(3) a. *John's went
 b. *Jana idzie
 John:GEN go:PRES:3SG (Polish)

If a construction codes possession, it should not be used when a potential possessum is present but the possessive interpretation is ruled out. A potential possessor is not marked genitive when the other noun(s) in the clause are not potential possessums:

(4) *Something amuses John's.

A potential possessor should not be marked for possession if another possessor is present in the clause, since the presence of different possessors with the same possessum would be contradictory:

(5) *I saw John's my wife.

However, if a construction *C* belongs to a functional domain or subdomain other than that of possession, it is free to occur with possessive constructions (or with any other constructions outside its domain or subdomain), provided there is no functional tautology or contradiction. If *C* belongs to the subdomain of coding the indirect affectedness of an argument, it may co-occur with possessive constructions and will be in complementary distribution with other means of coding semantic relationships between the verb and its arguments. Specifically, it will be in contrast with means of coding the affectedness of arguments.

In what follows we apply this methodology to dative case marking in Polish. Dative case marking is in complementary distribution with accusative case marking in several types of constructions. The accusative case in Polish marks direct affectedness with verbs that allow such an interpretation. We show that the dative case marks indirect affectedness of an argument. The existence of this semantic relationship is established through an empirical examination of the semantic functions actually coded in Polish.

The fundamental difference between the proposed approach to semantic relations and that which is offered by some contemporary theories is that the former is grounded in the coding means available in specific languages. Consequently, it does not assume the existence of semantic categories obtained through the analysis of other languages or the existence of *a priori* theoretical categories such as 'Agent', 'Theme', 'Patient', 'Actor', 'Undergoer', etc. In what follows, we show that the semantic roles of directly and indirectly affected argument are coded in Polish by case marking. We also show that the 'external possessor' interpretation for clauses containing arguments marked dative is an artifact of analyzing the situation described by the construction rather than analyzing the linguistic construction itself.

3. The notion of indirect affectedness

A construction that codes 'indirect affectedness' represents an event as indirectly affecting, either positively or negatively, a person or other animate being. This effect may be physical, mental or emotional. The coding of indirect affectedness is possible even if the person so affected is not a participant in the event or is not present at the place or time of the event. This semantic relationship, called 'ethic dative' (*dativus ethicus*) in traditional grammars, is most easily illustrated using intransitive verbs. Here, the indirectly affected argument does not have to be present at the scene of the event:

(6) Uciekł mi tramwaj.
run away:PAST:3M 1SG:DAT streetcar:NOM
'I missed the street car.' (Polish; lit. 'The street car ran away on me.')

(7) Dobrze jej życzę, ale uważam, że trzeba
well 3F:DAT wish:PRES:1SG but consider:PRES:1SG COMP need
tamto powiedzieć.
DEM:REM say
'I wish her well, but I think that that thing needs to be said.' (Sources)

Other arguments in the clause may or may not be affected by the event. The distinction between direct and indirect affectedness is illustrated by the following examples from Polish.

Direct affectedness, coded by accusative case:

(8) a. A jak **mnie** rozpoznałaś, powiedz dziecinko.
CONJ how 1SG:ACC recognize:PAST:2F tell:IMPER child:DIMIN:VOC
'And how did you recognize me, my child?'

Indirect affectedness, coded by dative case:

b. Ja **mu** nie rozpoznałem symptomów.
1SG 3SG:M:DAT NEG recognize:PAST:1SG symptom:PL:ACC
'I did not recognize the symptoms for him.' (the dative argument could be either the patient himself or another examiner seeking confirmation of a diagnosis)

The function of indirect affectedness subsumes the benefactive function, traditionally considered to be the fundamental function of the dative case:

(9) Ja **mu** oddam te kluczyki,
1SG 3SG:M:DAT give back:FUT:1SG DEM:PL:ACC key:DIMIN:PL:ACC
Pani pozwoli.
Madam allow:FUT:3SG
'Madam, allow me to return those keys to him.'

The notion of indirect affectedness is value-neutral; it does not imply whether the effect on the argument is beneficial, detrimental, or otherwise. This is illustrated by the following examples:

Neutral:

(10) a. Czy-ś **jej** nie wyczytał wczoraj z gwiazd.
Q-2SG 3F:DAT NEG read:PAST:M yesterday from star:PL
'Haven't you read for her [the destiny] from the stars?'

b. Nie dorównam **jej** w polu.
NEG equal:FUT:1SG 3F:DAT in field
'I will not match her [strength] in the field.'

Detrimental:

(11) a. Mam nadzieję, że nie zrobi **jej** jakiejś krzywdy.
have:1SG hope COMP NEG make:FUT:3SG 3F:DAT some harm
'I hope he will not harm her.' (Sources)

b. Zanadto dokucza **jej** reumatyzm.
too much bother:PRES:3SG 3F:DAT rheumatism
'Rheumatism bothers her too much.' (Sources)

Beneficial:

(12) Panna Janeczka miała wtedy trzy latka, kaszki **jej**
Miss Jeannie have:PAST:3F then three year:PL porridge 3F:DAT
warzyli.
cook:3PL
'Miss Jeannie was three years old at that time. They cooked porridge for her…' (Sources)

Evidence that indirect affectedness is indeed the function coded by the dative case is provided by the fact that an argument marked by the dative case in an active clause cannot function as the subject of the corresponding passive clause.

Dative argument, active clause:

(13) a. Niech jej wódz nie wierzy.
let 3F:DAT chief NEG believe
'The chief should not believe her.' (Sources)

Cf. the ungrammaticality of the corresponding passive clause:

(13) b. *__Ona__ nie powinna być wierzona.
3F:NOM NEG should:3F be believe:PASS
for 'She should not be believed.'

Dative argument, active clause:

(14) Taka chytrość, że się **człowiekowi** w głowie nie mieści.
such cunning COMP REFL man:DAT in head NEG fit
'such cunning you couldn't imagine' (Sources)

There is no possible corresponding passive sentence with *człowiek* 'man:NOM' as subject.

In contrast, an argument marked by the accusative case in the active clause, i.e., a directly affected argument, can serve as the subject of the corresponding passive clause:

Accusative argument, active clause:

(15) Jahu uduchowił **człowieka** i wygnał
Jahu provide soul:PAST:3M man:ACC CONJ chase away:PAST:3M
go z raju.
3M:ACC from paradise
'Jahu gave man a soul and chased him away from paradise.' (Sources)

Cf. the corresponding passive:

(16) **Człowiek** został uduchowiony przez Jahu i
man:NOM become:PAST:3M provide soul:PAST:PASS:3M by Jahu CONJ
wygnany z raju.
chase:PAST:PASS:3M from paradise
'Man had a soul put into him by Jahu and was chased from paradise.'

Further evidence for the function of indirect affectedness is that the subject of an intransitive clause coding the point of view of the subject must be marked dative. The point of view of the subject is coded by the reflexive form:

(17) Zostawcie **sobie** narazie mój długopis.
leave:PL:IMPER REFL:DAT for the time my pen:ACC
'For the time being you can keep my pen.' (Sources)

(18) Może gdzieś człowiek dalej zajechać niż na cmentarz.
can:PRES:3SG somewhere person further go:INF than PREP cemetery
'Can a person go any further than to a cemetery?'

Jak dobrze **mu** się jedzie to może.
if well 3SG:DAT REFL travel:3SG:PRES DEM can:3SG:PRES
'If the going is good, he can.' (Sources)

The second line of the above example describes the event from the point of view of an indirectly affected argument rather than a controlling subject. If the dative and reflexive markers were omitted, the clause would code a controlling subject:

(19) Jak dobrze jedzie to może.
if well travel:3SG:PRES DEM can:3SG:PRES
'if he is going well, he can.'

Here are other examples of intransitive predicates with indirectly affected arguments marked by the dative case:

(20) a. Niech się **im** w życiu darzy.
let REFL 3PL:DAT in life:LOC succeed:PRES:3SG
'May they prosper in life.' (Sources)
b. **Komu** tu dobrze.
who:DAT here well
'But who is well around here?' (Sources)
c. **Młodemu** to wszystko służy.
young:M:DAT DEM everything:NOM serve:PRES:3SG
'Everything works to the advantage of a young man.' (Sources)

4. Against the possessive function of the dative case

We have argued above that the function of dative marking in Polish is to code the indirect affectedness of the argument. In this section, we show that 'external possession' is not a possible function of the dative case.

4.1. The dative argument is not necessarily a possessor

In a Polish clause containing an argument marked dative and another argument marked accusative, the accusative argument is not necessarily the possessum of the dative argument. The importance of this fact is that the structural characteristics of such clauses, namely the dative coding of one argument and the accusative coding of another, are identical with those of so-called external possessor constructions. In (21), the accusative argument is not necessarily the possessum of the dative argument:

(21) a. Ważne jest to, **co** Ty **mi** odpowiesz.
important be:3SG DEM what:ACC 2SG:NOM 1SG:DAT reply:2SG:FUT
'What is important is what you will reply to me.' (Sources)

b. Jeśli moja córka życzy **sobie** **ciastko**.
if my daughter wish:PRES:3SG REFL:DAT pastry:ACC
'If my daughter desires a pastry…' (Sources)

c. Pani **mi** tylko wyrzuci **kabelek** przez okno.
madame 1SG:DAT only throw:FUT:3SG cable:DIMIN:ACC through window
'You, Madam, should only throw me the cable through the window.' (Sources)

Example (22) contains an argument marked by the dative and an adjunct marked by the instrumental, where no possessive relationship obtains between the dative and instrumental noun phrase:

(22) A nie zawsze **wdzięcznością** za to **mu** płacą.
CONJ NEG always gratitude:INSTR for DEM:ACC 3M:DAT pay:PRES:3PL
'And it is not always with gratitude that they reward him.' (Sources)

For some clauses containing both a dative and an accusative argument, no possessive interpretation is possible at all:

(23) O Boże, jak **mi** **ich** żal.
oh God:VOC how 1SG:DAT 3PL:ACC pity:NOM
'Oh God, how I pity them.' (Sources)

4.2. The dative argument can occur with a possessive construction

An important argument against the possessive function of the dative argument is that such an argument can occur with a possessive construction. If the dative argument were the possessor, the presence of another possessor in the clause would be contradictory. This is the case when two possessive markers occur in a clause with a single possessum:

(24) a. *mój jego rower
my his bike
(no interpretation possible)

b. *samochód policjanta studenta
car policeman:GEN student:GEN
(no interpretation possible)

However, an argument marked by the dative case can occur with either a coreferential possessor or a different possessor. These constructions are neither tautological nor contradictory because the dative case does not code possession. Here are examples of dative arguments occurring with possessive constructions in which the possessor is coreferential with the dative argument:

(25) Chcemy **Ci** tylko przypomnieć **twoje najlepsze lata**.
want:1PL:PRES 2SG:DAT only remind:INF your best years:ACC
'We just want to recall for you your best years.' (Sources)

(26) To ja myślałam, że wyskoczyłaś przez okno,
DEM 1SG think:1SG:F:PAST COMP jump:2SG:F:PAST through window
bo zbrzydło **Ci** już to **Twoje życie**.
because grow ugly:3SG:N 2:DAT already DEM your life:ACC
'I thought that you jumped through the window because you were sick of that life of yours.' (Sources)

If the possessive pronoun *twoje* 'yours' were omitted, the word *życie* 'life' would still be interpreted as belonging to the addressee, i.e. the argument marked by the dative case. This interpretation is possible, even obligatory, not because of the presence of a dative argument but because the noun *życie* 'life', when not within a possessive construction, is interpreted as belonging to a previously mentioned animate noun. Replacing the word *życie* 'life' in the above example with another noun that is not inherently linked with an animate noun does not allow for a possessive interpretation:

(27) bo zbrzydła Ci już
because grow ugly:PAST:3F 2:DAT already
pogoda/muzyka/lingwistyka/moja koszula.
weather/music/linguistics/my shirt:ACC
'because you were sick of the weather/music/linguistics/my shirt'

An argument marked by the nominative or accusative case may have its own overtly coded possessor that is different from the argument marked by the dative case. If the dative case in fact coded possession, such sentences would be ungrammatical.

Dative and nominative case:

(28) Nic **mi** te **twoje** **proszki** nie pomagają.
nothing 1SG:DAT DEM:PL 2SG:POSS potions:NOM NEG help:3PL
'Your potions do nothing for me.'

(29) Potrzebna **mi** jest **twoja** **pomoc**.
need:3F 1SG:DAT is your:NOM help:NOM
'I need your help.' (Sources)

Dative and accusative case:

(30) **Komu** mogłabyś powierzyć **swoją** **tajemnicę**.
who:DAT can:PAST:F:HYP:2SG confide:INF F:REFL:ACC secret:ACC
'In whom could you confide your secret?' (Sources)

(31) Ale co, mam **ludziom** **moje zasługi** w oczy rzucać.
but what have:PRES:1SG people:DAT my merits:ACC in eyes throw:INF
'What, shall I throw my merits in people's faces (i.e., shall I toot my own horn)?'

(32) Dlaczego pozwoliłaś **mi** poczuć **Twoją** **bliskość**.
why allow:2SG:F:PAST 1SG:DAT feel:INF:PRF your:ACC closeness:ACC
'Why did you allow me to experience your closeness?' (Sources)

In French as in Polish, a noun marked for the dative case can occur with a possessive construction whose possessor is different from the noun marked by the dative. The dative case again codes indirect affectedness:

(33) Et je tremblais pour la France, car je crains
CONJ 1SG tremble:IMPF for DEF France because 1SG fear:PRES
qu'elle ne **me** dévalue encore **son franc**.
COMP:3F:SG NEG 1SG:DAT devalue again her franc
'And I trembled for France, for I feared that she would again devalue her franc on me.' (Cohen 1965:34)

A similar function of the dative case is to be found in German, as illustrated by many examples in Smith (1987). Here, the dative case is a means of coding the semantic relationship between the verb and an argument and is not a means of coding possession. The evidence that the dative case belongs to the domain of the relationships between the verb and its arguments is that it is in contrast with other means of coding this relationship rather than with other means of coding possession. In German, the dative case is used when the subject is affected, e.g. when the subject is in direct physical contact with the object:

(34) a. Der Mantel ist **mir** zu gross.
DEF coat be 1SG:DAT too large
'The coat is too big for me.' (said by a customer while wearing the coat)

The benefactive preposition, in contrast, does not code affectedness of the argument:

b. Der Mantel ist **für mich** zu gross.
DEF coat be for 1SG:ACC too large
'The coat is too big for me.' (said by a customer before trying the coat on; examples, translations, and interpretations from Smith 1987:409)

In Polish, the dative case is used when the event is represented from the point of view of the subject (as coded by the reflexive form) but it is another argument, marked by the dative case, that is affected:

c. Pomóż włożyć kapotę, bo **mi** się rękawy
help:IMP put:INF coat:ACC because 1SG:DAT REFL sleeve:PL:NOM
pomyliły.
mix:PAST:3PL
'Help me put on the coat, because the sleeves got all mixed up on me.' (Sources)

In Polish, French and German, a clause containing a noun phrase marked by the dative case and a noun phrase marked by the accusative or instrumental case neither codes nor implies a possessive relationship between the two noun phrases. The function of dative case marking in such a clause is not to code possession but to code the indirect affectedness of the dative argument.

5. Why is the possessive interpretation possible?

In this section, we show how a study of clauses containing body-part or kinship terms, as well as the inherent meanings of some verbs, imply possession and how they may have given rise to the 'external possessor' interpretation.

If a language codes the indirect affectedness of an argument through inflectional means, this coding must be used if the speaker intends to indicate that an argument is indirectly affected. In a clause containing a noun referring to a body part, the body as a whole is usually affected and so is marked dative:

(35) I ci wszyscy, **którym** wierciłeś dziurki
and DEM:PL all REL:PL:DAT drill:PAST:2SG hole:DIMIN:PL
w karkach.
in neck:PL:LOC
'And all those for whom you had drilled little holes in their necks.' (Sources)

(36) Widział-em, jak **mu** oczy zachodził-y bielm-em.
see:PAST-1SG how 3SG:M:DAT eyes fill:PAST-3PL cataract-INST
'I saw [his] eyes filling with cataracts.' (Sources)

(37) Dusza **mi** się z czułości do Pana kraje.
soul 1SG:DAT REFL from tenderness:GEN to you:POL:LOC cut:PRES:3SG
'My soul aches with tenderness for you.' (Sources)

(38) Ja **mu** gębę zamknę.
1SG 3M:DAT mouth:ACC shut:1SG:FUT
'I will shut his mouth.' (Sources)

The possessive interpretation of such clauses does not result from the presence of the dative case but rather from the use of a body-part term as an argument. Evidence for this hypothesis is that a clause containing a nominative argument and a body-part term marked accusative also is interpreted as coding possession. This is because body-part terms entail the existence of a possessor, the organism to which the body part belongs:

(39) Ojciec myje głowę.
father:NOM wash:PRES:3SG head:ACC
'Father washes his head.' (Karolak 1984: 108)

Like the use of a body-part term, the use of a kinship term usually forces a possessive interpretation with some available argument, regardless of how that argument is marked. This is because kinship terms entail the existence of other kin:[2]

(40) Matka czesze córkę.
mother:NOM comb:PRES:3SG daughter:ACC
'The mother combs her daughter's hair.' (Karolak 1984: 108)

(41) Nie zapominaj, że jesteś świętokradcą i mordercą
NEG forget:2SG COMP be:2SG sacrilegious person CONJ murderer
własnego syna.
own son:ACC
'Do not forget that you are guilty of sacrilege and that you are the murderer of your own son.'

Even in a clause containing both a dative argument and a body part marked accusative, there is not necessarily a possessive relationship between the dative and the accusative arguments. In the following example, the accusative-marked noun *ręka* 'hand' does not belong to the dative-marked argument *mu* 'to him' but rather to the nominative-marked subject. Thus, the assignment of possessum to possessor is not a function of the dative case:

(42) Koło niego siedziała taka czarna, no, taka dziewczyna i
next 3M:LOC sit:PAST:3F such:F black:F well such:F girl:NOM CONJ
trzymała **mu** **rękę** przez szyję.
hold:PAST:3F 3M:DAT hand:ACC through neck:ACC
'Next to him was sitting a brunette, well, a girl, and she was holding her hand on his neck.' (Sources)

In short, the presence in a clause of a noun referring to a body part simply implies some possessor. The fact that the possessor is sometimes marked by the dative case reflects the fact that the possessor of a body part is usually indirectly affected in any event involving a body part:

(43) A tamtego roku Irka mu łopatą do **głowy** rozum
and DEM:REM year:GEN Irka 3M:DAT shovel:INSTR into head wisdom
kładła.
put:PAST:3F
'And last year Irka was shoveling wisdom into his head.' (Sources)

Another factor that may have led to the 'external possession' interpretation is that some verbs inherently imply at least temporary possession. The Polish verb *wyrwać* 'pull out (forcibly)' obligatorily affects the argument from which something is pulled out. This is especially true when the object pulled out happens to be a body part:

(44) Co diabeł chciał babie łeb urwać.
what devil want:PAST:3SG:M woman:DAT head:ACC pull out:INF
'How the devil wanted to pull out the woman's head.' (Nitsch 1960: 155; transcription simplified)

6. Coding direct affectedness with body parts

When the possessor of a body part is directly rather than indirectly affected, the possessor is marked accusative and the body part involved is part of a locative complement coded by preposition:

(45) Gdyby oni wiedzieli, kopali-by mnie w brzuch.
COND:HYP 3PL know:3PL kick:3PL:IMPF-HYP 1SG:ACC PREP belly:ACC
'Had they known [that], they would have been kicking me in the belly.' (Sources)

The relationship between the object of the preposition and the argument marked by the accusative case is interpreted as one of possession for the simple reason that the accusative case codes the argument as affected. Since body parts do not occur in isolation but call for a possessor, the argument marked accusative is interpreted as the possessor. The role of the prepositional phrase is to specify where the argument is affected.[12]

(46) Jak postrzał, który kiedyś musiałeś dostać,
like bullet-wound REL:M:SG:ACC once must:2SG:M:PAST get:INF
w brzuch, w usta, w oczy.
in belly:ACC in mouth:ACC in eyes:ACC
'Like a bullet wound that you must once have once suffered in the belly, in the mouth, in the eyes.' (Sources)

The possessive interpretation of 46 does not result from the presence of a nominative argument and a prepositional phrase but follows from the nature of the lexical items in the prepositional phrases. If the body-part noun is replaced by another noun, the possessive interpretation is not possible:

(47) Jak postrzał, który kiedyś musiałeś dostać w lesie.
like bullet-wound REL:M:SG:ACC once must:2SG:PAST get:INF in forest
'Like a bullet wound that you must once have received in the forest.'

In English, which has not been claimed to have an external possessor construction and which has not grammaticalized the function of indirect affectedness (see below), similar clauses involving body-part terms and a human direct object also demand a possessive interpretation:

(48) They poked him in the eyes.
They hit him on the nose.
They slapped him in the face. (Elicited)

The direct object in these sentences is construed as affected not only because it is marked as object but because of the semantic nature of the verb and the arguments involved.

7. Indirect affectedness through other means

In Hausa, a West Chadic language, an indirect object noun is coded by the preposition *wà* and an indirect object pronoun by the prefix *má*. The function of this coding is to code the indirect affectedness of an argument. The possessive interpretation is available only if the object is a body part (all examples and translations from Newman 1982: 59, glosses ours). The indirect object may be affected beneficially or adversely:

(49) Sun yi **mu-sù** dariya.
3PL:PRF make DAT-3PL laughter
'They laughed at them.'

(50) Kàaka taa macèe **ma-nà**.
grandma 3F:PRF die DAT-1PL
'Grandma died on us.'

(51) Zaa-tà kaawoo **ma-kà** ruwaa.
FUT-3F carry:VENT DAT-2M water
'She will bring you water.'

In some cases a possessive interpretation is possible:

(52) Sun gyaràa **wà** **Muusaa** mootàa.
3PL:PRF repair DAT Muusa car
'They repaired the car for Musa.' or 'They repaired Musa's car.'

Gidar (Central Chadic) has also grammaticalized the function of indirect affectedness. Gidar is a SVO language with no inflectional marking of case. A pronominal argument that is indirectly affected is marked by the preposition *sə̀*, whose vowel can undergo rounding or fronting and tonal changes. The indirect object phrase is formally part of the verbal complex, as evidenced by the fact that the perfective marker *kà* occurs after the indirect object. Evidence that the construction is not possessive is that it co-occurs with the inalienable possessive construction:

(53) a. Nə̀-plá-n sù-kú-k wàhlí ná-wà.
1SG-leave-3M PREP-2SG-PRF cow GEN-1SG
'I left you my cow.'

b. Wá-n plá-t krə́-k ná-w sú-kó.
FUT-1SG leave-3F dog-F GEN-1SG DAT-2SG
'I will leave you my puppy.'

The preposition *sə̀* can be used with the indirectly affected argument of both benefactive and adversative events:

Benefactive:

(54) Mà-m tə̀-mbát-ə̀k á gàgám ə́kày sə́-m ə̀zə̀m.
mother-1PL 3F-go-PRF PREP Gagam search DAT-1PL eat
'Our mother went to Gagam to look for something for us to eat'

Adversative:

(55) À-dí sə̀-nə̀-k óffò sə́-n bíinà.
3M-put DAT-3M-PRF fire DAT-3M roof
'He set fire to the inside of the roof'

Evidence that the preposition *sə́* does not code possession is that it does not occur in a clause containing a body-part noun belonging to the subject:

(56) Tə̀-tìlìk-í-k ɮə̀má-tà.
3F-pierce-3M-PRF ear-3F
'She$_i$ pierced her$_i$ ears.'

Further evidence that the dative preposition codes indirect affectedness rather than possession is that it can co-occur with a possessive construction in which the possessor is different from the subject:

(57) Tə̀-tìlik-í-k śə́-tə̀-k ɮə̀má-tà.
3F-pierce DAT-3F-PRF ear-3F
'She$_i$ pierced her$_j$ ears.'

In Hdi, Central Chadic, indirect affectedness is coded through tonal changes on the verb and tonal changes on object pronouns. High tone on the morpheme preceding the object pronoun codes indirect affectedness of an argument (all examples from Frajzyngier with Shay 2002). An intransitive verb may have an indirect object added to the verb complex:

(58) Dz-ù-gù-dú-ɗú-s-dzá kághá ná xgà-n-tì-í tá rvér wà
go-SO-INN-ALL-1SG-INV-go 2SG DEM call-3-REF-1SG OBJ lion NEG
káʼ-á.
COMP-3SG
'"If you come there for me, I will not invite Lion," he said.' (Frajzyngier with Shay 2002: 206)

The direct object is not necessarily the possessum of the indirectly affected argument:

(59) Ndá sná-ká rí sárák, hləv-í-ɗí-p-hləvá tá índà m̀ndú-xà.
STAT know-2SG Q club hit.PL-AWAY-1SG-OUT-hit.PL OBJ all man-PL
'Do you understand, Stick? Hit everybody for me!' (Frajzyngier with Shay 2002: 206)

If the clause contains an object, an analysis of the situation described may cause the object to be interpreted as belonging to the indirectly affected argument, as in the following example:

(60) ɓl-í-ɗí-ɓlá tá pìtsákw.
break-AWAY-1SG-break OBJ hoe
'He broke my hoe.' (Frajzyngier with Shay 2002: 201)

The possessive interpretation does not result from the presence of an indirect object but from the supposition that the speaker would not be affected by the breaking of the hoe if it were not his/her hoe. The evidence that the construction does not code possession is provided by the fact that it can occur with an argument marked by a possessive pronoun:

(61) Kl-í-g-í-ɗá-ghà wá kɗix-á-ɗá, ká-ʼá kà wàxú.
take-EP-INN-AWAY-1SG-D.PVG NEG donkey-GEN-1SG COMP-3SG like cry
'"Bring me back my donkey," he said, crying.' (Frajzyngier with Shay 2002: 195)

8. Languages without the category of indirect affectedness

English does not have a grammatical means of coding the indirect affectedness of an argument. Instead, it has one means to code the beneficiary of an event and another, much less productive, means to code an argument adversely affected by the event. Since the notion of beneficiary in English is not widely accepted, the following discussion explains the notion and provides evidence for its existence. The beneficiary is coded by the position directly after the verb when there is another noun following it, i.e. in the construction V NP NP. This construction indicates that the event has a positive (or at least non-negative) effect on the object following it. The same function may be coded by the preposition 'for' (original data from London–Lund corpus; contrasting examples built upon the original data):

1_8_0 <358 A> are you ^going to 'leave **him** a m/essage#

Cf. *Are you going to hang him a message?

1_5_0 <632 B> ^well — ^he 'ought to 'make **him'self** a !t\ime'table#

Cf. *He ought to destroy/burn/tear himself a timetable

1_10_0 <998 b> well if you can really very handsomely lend **me** your/- car on Wednesday…

Cf. *well if you can really very handsomely ruin me your/ — car on Wednesday

1_12_0 <271 B> ^no they !just used to _pass **me** !n\otes

Cf. *no they !just used to ruin/tear/burn me !n\otes

In contrast, an adversely affected argument may be coded by the preposition 'on' followed by the affected argument.

3_3_0 <155 A> from ^four or :five or :six 'books 'simul:t\aneously# .
3_3_0 <156 A> ^spread 'round a !t\able **'on you#** .

1_14_2 <981 A> where ^all the /aerodromes 'were and \everything# -/
1_14_2 <982 b> *good God*
1_14_2 <983 A> *^and the* !Irish '[gav] ^somebody spl\it **on him#** ./
1_14_2 <984 A> and the ^Irish 'government :kept it to them'selves and 'didn't 'tell the Br/itish# .

^following which !she walked :\/out **on him#**

9. Conclusions

In this chapter we have applied the proposed methodology for establishing the functional domain of a construction by examining the construction that has been analyzed elsewhere as coding 'external possession'. We have shown that this construction, which contains an argument marked for the dative case and (usually) some other argument, in fact codes the relationship of indirect affectedness between the verb and the dative argument. It has been shown that the function of external possession does not exist in Polish, a language for which this construction has been claimed, and that Polish and other languages have grammaticalized the function of indirect affectedness. The explanation provided for Polish accounts also for the alleged external possessive constructions in German, Czech, and Spanish in the Indo-European family and for all examined languages in the Chadic family of Afroasiatic.

We have shown that the dative argument in such a construction may be interpreted as the possessor of a potential possessum provided that (a) the potential possessum is a body-part or kinship term, and (b) the possessum does not have another possessor in the clause. The 'external possessor' interpretation for clauses involving dative arguments in Western Indo-European languages is an artifact of an analysis that fails to examine the data in terms of the interaction of the construction in question with other constructions in the same grammatical system.

Our analysis of the dative case marker as coding indirect affectedness enables us to explain why English does not have constructions similar to those found in Polish, German, Czech, Spanish, Gidar, Hausa and many other languages: English has not grammaticalized the category dative as encoding indirect affectedness.

CHAPTER 10

Systems interaction in the coding of locative predication

1. Introduction

The purpose of this chapter is to demonstrate the interaction between the inherent lexical properties of nouns and verbs and the functions and properties of various grammatical markers, including prepositions. This interaction will be demonstrated within the domain of locative predication, which involves propositions describing the location of an object, the location of an event, or movement to or from a location. The domain of locative predication in a given language is determined by the existence of specific formal means that distinguish it from other types of predication. The form of the locative predication is subject to the principle of functional transparency in that the locative function of the predicate and the locative function of the complement must be transparent to the hearer. This transparency is achieved through a number of means, some lexical and others grammatical. Thus, a complement may be considered to be locative only if it is coded by means different from those used to code other types of complements. It will be shown that the study of locative predication allows us to distinguish between direct object complements and locative complements even when the latter are not marked by locative prepositions.

The chapter focuses on locative predication in Mina (Central Chadic, spoken in the Far North Province of Cameroon). In this language, grammatical relations are coded by the word order Subject–Verb–Object. Various modalities are coded through tonal changes on the verb, auxiliaries (which may occur before the verb, after the verb or after the direct object), and clause-final modal particles. Coding means within the domain of locative predication in Mina include inherently locative lexical items that function as predicates and complements, several prepositions, and one auxiliary verb. The properties of these coding means have interesting implications for the syntax of the language and for grammatical categories in general.

2. Locative features in the lexicon and grammar

2.1. Problem 1: Inherent locatives, prepositions and predicators

The system of coding locative predication includes linear order, the particles *á* and *kə́*, the preposition *n* and the auxiliary *za*. A locative predication may be coded by linear order alone:

(1) Ábə̀ nd-á ngə̀n wùtá.
ASSC go-GO 3SG village
'Then she returned to her village'

Some locative predications are marked by the preposition *n*, which is followed by a schwa in predictable phonological environments:

(2) Tsáy mə̀ tí tì nd-á nástə́ **nə̀** yə̀m.
then REL look look go-GO enter (Fula) PREP water
'Then the one who was good at looking entered into water.'

Other locative predications contain the particle *á*, glossed PRED (predicator) for reasons explained below:

(3) I ŋ kə ndəv-a **a** kayak.
3PL PREP INF fall-GO PRED earth
'They will fall down on the ground.' (Edwards's notebooks)[13]

Finally, some locative predications contain both the particle *á* and the preposition *n*:

(4) Ván ʤə̀ rà mə̀ná **á** **nə̀** lùmò.
rain fall D.HAB like PRED PREP market
'It was raining from the direction of the market.' (D.HAB-dependent habitual)

These data present us with two sets of questions. The first has to do with the conditions under which the particle and/or the preposition are used, while the second has to do with the categoriality of the forms *á* and *n*.

2.2. Problem 2: Locative predication and possessive constructions

A problem that has received little attention in the literature has to do with the dependence of the internal structure of a constituent on the structure of some higher constituent. It is usually assumed that the form of a syntactic structure *A* is independent of the higher syntactic constituent *B*. For example, the structure of a noun phrase is assumed not to depend on the syntactic structure of which the noun phrase is a part. In Mina, however, the structure of a phrase coding the possessive function does depend on the higher constituent of which the phrase is a part. A possessive construction that functions as a subject or object argument must contain the marker *tə́*, glossed GEN 'genitive' for ease of reference:

(5) **Hìdə̀ tə kwáykwáy-yíì** wàcíŋ.
house GEN hyena-PL DEM
'house of those hyenas'

In some locative predications, however, a possessive construction functioning as a locative complement does not occur with the marker *tə́*:

(6) Hós á **ídə̀ kwáykwáy-yíì** wàcíŋ.
arrive PRED compound hyena-PL DEM
'She arrived at the compound of the hyenas.'

This alternation must be explained, since there is no theoretical reason why the internal structure of a construction should depend on the type of a higher construction in which it occurs. As will be shown, the solution to problem 1 allows us to postulate a hypothesis explaining problem 2.

3. Solution to problem 1

Recall that problem 1 concerns the conditions under which the locative predication includes the preposition *n*, the marker *a*, both of these markers, or neither of these markers. The solution to problem 1 lies in discovering the functions of the various coding means belonging to the domain of locative predication. These coding means include the lexical items occurring as predicates and complements; linear order; the prepositions, alone or in combination; and any combinations of these means. Lexical items involved in a locative predication may be inherently locative or not. Toponyms are inherently locative nouns, as is the word *dámù* 'bush'. Items like these are referred to as 'locative complements'. Inherently non-locative nouns include [+human] nouns and pronouns. Directional verbs of movement and stative locative verbs are inherently locative and are referred to as 'locative predicates'.

Following is a summary of the interactions among coding means in the domain of locative predication:

- Locative predicate and locative complement: Coding through linear order, specifically through juxtaposition (example 1, above);
- Locative predicate and non-locative complement: Predicate *n* Noun (example 2);
- Non-locative predicate and locative complement: Predicate *á* Noun (example 3);
- Non-locative predicate and non-locative complement: Predicate *á n* Noun (example 4).

3.1. Locative predicate and locative complement: Coding through linear order

When both the predicate and the complement are inherently locative, no locative prepositions are used. Instead, the properties of the lexical items involved ensure a locative predication interpretation:

(7) Í-bə̀ nd-á tə̀tə̀ bìn.
PL-ASSC go-GO 3PL.POSS room
'They went into the room'

(8) Ábə̀ nd-á ngə̀n wùtá.
ASSC go-GO 3SG village
'Then she returned to her village.'

The evidence that a locative argument after a verb is a complement rather than a direct object in Mina is provided by the behavior of the auxiliary *za* (phrase-internal forms *z*, *zə*), glossed as 'AUX' and coding the end-of-event. This marker occurs **before** a locative complement (9a,b) but **after** a direct object (10):

(9) a. Hídí kə́ ndə̀ **zə̀** **dámù** mə̀ pə́r kə́ bày í **n** kə̀
man INF go AUX bush REL first PREP chief 3PL PREP INF
ɗál-á-ŋ mà.
do-OBJ-3SG mouth
'If anybody goes to the field before the chief, they will cause him a lot of problems.'

b. Tséy hìdì wàcíŋ táŋ **z** **wútà** à ɓá **á** **n** médíg ngə̀ŋ
so man DEM return AUX house 3SG say PRED PREP neighbor 3SG
wàcíŋ ngámbù há kə̀ déɓ-é-ŋ dál nə̀ hìdə̀ wà dál
DEM friend 2SG INF bring-OBJ-3SG money PREP man DEM money

vànú.
how much
'When the man came back to the house, he said to his neighbor, "Friend, you brought money to this man. How much money?"'

Auxiliary marker after a direct object:

(10) Áá wàl nə̀ kə́ dzán-á **skə̀n pár** zə̀ bàdáp.
ah wife 1SG INF find-GO thing another AUX again
'Ah, my wife found another thing again.'

3.2. Locative predicate and non-locative argument: Predicate *à* Noun

When the predicate is locative but the complement is non-locative, the complement must be marked for its locative role. This is done by the preposition *n* (or its phonologically predictable variant *nə̀*), whose function is to mark a non-locative noun as a locative complement:

(11) Mìnjée mbə̀ mə̀ mármàr kə́ nàz-á kw-yíì zə́ **nə̀** láy.
now boy REL pasture INF abandon-GO goat-PL AUX PREP field
'Now the shepherd left the goats in the field.'

Evidence is that *láy* is inherently non-locative is that it may be used, without additional marking, as the subject or object of a clause:

(12) Taŋ a nda-ha nda tii a tii **lay** mi dish-yi tseey za.
go 3SG go-GO go see 3SG see field REL cultivate-STAT finish AUX
'She came to see that the field had been cultivated completely.' (Edwards's notebooks)

(13) Guzak naŋ kə vəl-a-k **lay** za.
uncle 1SG INF give-OBJ-1SG field AUX
'My uncle gave me a field.' (Edwards's notebooks)

Mina has a locative anaphor *mə̀ŋ* that is used to refer to inherently non-locative nouns. Unlike inherently locative anaphors, *mə̀ŋ* is treated as inherently non-locative, as evidenced by the fact that it requires the preposition *n*:

(14) Bə̀k bə̀k á bə̀k-á-ŋ ɓə̀ wìrnjík kə́ **nə̀** **mə̀ŋ**.
fill fill 3SG fill-OBJ-3SG ASSC ash AFF PREP ANAPH
'He filled them [the shoes] with ash.'

3.3. Non-locative predicate and locative complement: Predicate á *Noun*

A locative predication whose predicate is non-locative must be marked by the particle *á*, whose function is to indicate that an inherently non-locative predicate has a locative function. The particle *á* follows the direct object, if any. If the complement is inherently locative, it occurs without the preposition *n*. The verb *yà* 'call' is inherently non-locative, but in 15 the particle *á* signals that *yà* has a locative function:

(15) Nd-á yà ngùl ngə̀n **á** bìŋ.
go-GO call husband 3SG PRED room
'And [she] called her husband into the room.'

The verb *fàt* 'skin' also is inherently non-locative and so is marked by *á* when functioning as a locative predicate:

(16) Ǹkwə̀ tə́ ləvéŋ hì kə́ skə̀m-á zà hì fàt kà **á** káyàk.
goat GEN black 2PL INF buy-GO AUX 2PL skin AFF PRED earth
'A black goat, when you have bought it, you skin it on the ground.'

The verb *tíl* 'leave, move' also is inherently non-directional and non-locative and so must be marked by *á* if followed by a locative complement:

(17) Til ngən **a** wta.
leave 3SG PRED house
'He returned home.' (Edwards's notebooks)

Similarly, the verb *déɓ* 'carry':

(18) Bày ǹ kə́ɗə̀m ngə̀n ɓə̀t déɓ á déɓ ká **á** ìdá.
chief PREP calabash 3SG take carry 3SG carry AFF PRED home
'The chief$_i$ took his$_j$ calabash and carried it home.'

A non-directional verb, such as *yán* 'move house', must be followed by the particle *á*:

(19) Kwáykway-yíì wà zá ŋ´gə̀ há mbàl-ù há yàn á **kàcíŋ**.
hyena-PL DEM COMP if 2SG want-3SG 2SG move PRED here
'The hyenas told her, "If you want to, you can move in here."'

(20) Èe hìd-yíì wà í-bə̀ yáŋ tə̀tə̀ á **màcíŋ**.
eh, man-PL DEM 3PL-ASSC move 3PL:POSS PRED there
'Those people moved over there.'

The particle *á* is used after the verb *ɗáhá* 'exist' when this verb has a locative complement:

(21) Háɓ̰əm ɗáhá á bìŋ ngə̀n.
daughter exist PRED house 3SG
'There is a girl at her house.'

Although the particle *á* participates in locative predication, the scope of the particle is limited to the predicate rather than the whole proposition. It codes only the predicate, and not the complement, as locative. We term this particle a 'local predicator' because its scope is not the whole proposition but rather a fragment of the proposition.

If the clause has no predicate, the notion of locative predication is coded by the presence of the local predicator *á* and a locative complement. Thus, the local predicator *á* alone may function as a locative predicate:

(22) Kwáyàŋ zá ɓ̰í mə̀ mə̀ts-yíì bàytáŋ **á** dámù.
squirrel COMP meat REL die-STAT large PRED bush
'The squirrel said, "There is a lot of dead meat in the bush."'

(23) Séy mùà bàytáŋ **á** dámù zìbìr zìbìr.
so tamarind large PRED bush dark
'There is a large tamarind tree in the bush; it is dark.'

(24) Mìméŋ à zá àmmá bìɓ̰áv à mbál-á-kù nd-á ɓ̰í gwáɗ
leopard 3SG COMP truly God 3SG like-OBJ-1SG go-GO meat plenty
á bìŋ nàŋ.
PRED room 1SG
'The leopard said, "God truly loves me, as there is a lot of meat in my room."'

3.4. Non-locative predicate and non-locative complement: Predicate *á n* Noun

If neither the predicate nor the complement is inherently locative, the locative predication is marked by both the local predicator *á* and the preposition *n*:

(25) Séy tàkár tíl **á** **nə̀** yə̀m mə́l mə́l á mə́l-á dzə̀ɓə́ŋ.
so turtle leave PRED PREP water seize seize 3SG seize-GO five
'So, the turtle went in the water and caught five [fish].'

(26) Séy wàl wàcíŋ kúl skù à dál-áhà séy dáɓ íi dáɓ
so woman DEM able NEG 3SG make-GO so take 3PL take
á nə̀ lə̀ptál kə́ hùrgə̀ tán.
PRED PREP hospital INF cure 3SG
'This woman was not well, she was sick. So she was brought to a hospital for treatment.'

(27) Í n kə̀ zə́m ábə̀ bày mə̀tázàngár á nə̀ lày mə̀ ntá.
3PL PREP INF eat ASSC chief lizard PRED PREP place REL one
'They will eat with the lizard in the same place.'

(28) Hà táŋ tə́wə̀r á nə̀ fálà tə̀tàŋ.
2SG DEM suffer PRED PREP among 3PL
'As for you, you suffer [a lot] among them.'

The local predicator and the preposition also are used to code the addressee of the verb of saying, evidence that the verb of saying and its addressee are inherently non-locative:

(29) Hà ŋ kə́ lùw-á-ŋ žín á nə̀ ví.
2SG PREP INF say-OBJ-3SG then PRED PREP who
'Who are you going to tell it to?'

(30) À zá á nə̀ gímíɮíɗ áz tùmù médìgì ngáɮ ngáɮ í
3SG COMP PRED PREP monkey go 1DU neighbor pull pull 3PL
ngáɮ-á pám á mìdìgìɗ kwáyàŋ.
pull-GO until PRED court squirrel
'He said to the monkey, "Let's go, neighbor." They went to the squirrels' courtyard.'

To sum up the rules of forming locative predication in Mina: The fundamental criteria for forming the locative predication are the semantic class of the predicate and the semantic class of the noun serving as the locative complement. If the predicate is inherently locative, in the sense described earlier in this section, nothing else is required to code the locative nature of the predicate. If the predicate is not inherently locative, the predicator *a* must follow the predicate. If the noun that is to serve as a locative complement is inherently locative, nothing else is required to mark the noun as a locative complement. If the noun is not inherently locative, the preposition *n* must be used to mark it as a locative complement. The use of the preposition *n* and the locative predicator *a* in locative predications thus depends on the value of the feature [locative] in both the complement and the predicate.

3.5. Human and animate nouns as locative complements

A [+human] noun that is used as a locative complement is marked by one of several nouns derived from body-part terms. The body-part term may occur with or without the locative preposition *n*.The choice of body-part term depends on the type of movement or spatial configuration being described. The marker *mə̀* 'mouth' has been grammaticalized as 'on the edge of' or 'around':

(31) Yàɗírì ɓéɓé ɗáhá í ndì ɓə̀k **á** **nə̀** **mə̀** kúlmbón-yíì.
millet long time ago exist 3PL HAB plant PRED PREP mouth black ant-PL
'A long time ago, they used to plant millet around the black ants' nests.'

With the marker *kə̀bə̀m* 'face', the locative expression means 'in front of':

(32) Séy kə́ɗə̀m wá dà dà á d-á-ŋ wùdə ǹə́nà wà
so calabash DEM cook cook 3SG cook-OBJ-3SG food much DEM
mbá pè hlè hlè hlè hlè **á** **mə̀** **kə̀bə̀m** (n)gə̀n.
so much spread spread spread spread PRED mouth face 3SG
'So the calabash made a lot of food, spread in front of her.'

The concept 'above' is coded by the marker *táláŋ* 'head':

(33) ɗíy-á téwél ɗíy-á téwél ɗíy-á téwél **á** **táláŋ** ngə̀n.
put-GO twirl put-GO twirl put-GO twirl PRED head 3SG
'He twirled [the stick] above him.'

Movement towards a human goal is coded by *r(ə́)*, probably derived from *rá* 'hand':

(34) Ángə̀ há sə̀n bə́ts tə́ syì há ngàɓ-á-k **á** **rə́**
if 2SG know blow DEM COM 2SG accompany-OBJ-1SG PRED PREP
ngə̀n.
3SG
'If you know how to blow, you will accompany me to him.'

A [+human] noun whose function is that of attained goal is coded by the noun *kə́sə́m* 'body':

(35) Séy sə̀ n kə́ ngíž á káyàk séy ngíž ngíž ká á
so 1SG PREP INF urinate PRED earth so urinate urinate AFF PRED
káyàk **á** **kə́sə́m** **hìd-yíì** mə̀ nzə̀ tə́ kə̀ɗáŋ páy wàcíŋ.
earth PRED body man-PL REL sit GEN under tree DEM
'"I'm just going to urinate on the ground." So, he urinated on the ground, on the people who were sitting under the tree.'

To summarize: If the noun to be used as a locative complement is [+human], additional markers must be used to mark it as a locative complement. The means used depends on the spatial configuration of the event with respect to the locative complement.

4. Solution to problem 2: Prepositionless possessive constructions

It is generally assumed that the form of a syntactic structure *A* does not depend on the higher syntactic structure *B* of which *A* is a part. Genitive constructions in Mina contradict this assumption. Here, the same semantic relationship between two nouns is coded in two different ways, depending on the higher form in which this relationship is realized. If the possessive construction involving two nouns is an argument of a clause, the possessive relationship is coded by the preposition *tə́*:

(36) a. Dúwəŋ̀ **tə́** mədìngwərzé ábə məlá.
back GEN donkey ASSC wound
'The back of the donkey has a wound.'

b. Kə́ nzlà dúwəŋ **tə́** mədìngwərzé (zà).
INF cure back GEN donkey (AUX)
'He cured the back of the donkey.'

If the possessive construction is part of a locative phrase, however, the possessive relationship is coded by juxtaposition alone and the possessive particle is not allowed:

(37) a. Kə̀ dí dúwə̀n mədìngwərzé.
INF put back donkey
'He put it on the back of the donkey.'

b. Tíl zà á bìŋ kű́l-yíì.
leave AUX PRED room ancestral spirit-PL
'He went into the house of the kulis and ...'

The situation is further illustrated by contrasting natural discourse phrases containing a possessive phrase (38a, 39, 40a) with elicited sentences in which the same phrase is used as the subject or object of the clause (38b, 40b). The possessive relationship between nouns occurring within a locative phrase is coded by apposition. The same relationship in a noun phrase serving as an argument is coded by the marker *tə́*:

(38) a. Á **bìŋ** **wàl** náká wà.
PRED room wife REM DEM
'into room of that wife'

Cf.

(38) b. **Bìŋ** **tə́** **wàl** náká wà nék.
room GEN wife REM DEM good
'The room of that wife is good/nice.' (elicited)

(39) Á **wtə̀** **wàl** náká wàcíŋ.
PRED home woman DEM DEM
'into the home of that woman'

(40) a. Hós á **ídə̀** **kwáykwáy-yí** wàcíŋ.
arrive PRED compound hyena-PL DEM
'She has arrived at the compound of hyenas.'

Cf. the modifying construction as an argument of a clause:

(40) b. **Hìdə̀** **tə́** **kwáykwáy-yíì** wàcíŋ.
house GEN hyena-PL DEM
'house of those hyenas' (elicited)

An explanation for the intriguing behavior of the possessive construction lies in the inherent properties of locative predicates and the local predicator *á*. As shown in Section 2, *á* is a local predicator that is used in a locative clause whose predicate is not inherently locative.

An important component of the proposed solution to problem 2 is the hypothesis that the marker *tə́* also is a local predicator, but it is a modifying predicator. This predicator says 'this head noun has a property *X*', where the property *X* is coded by the modifier in the possessive construction. The marker *tə́* cannot follow the locative predicate in a locative construction because this would mark the same argument — the head noun of the construction — as part of two different predications: The locative predication, as marked by the presence of an inherently locative verb or the local predicator *á*, and the possessive predication, as marked by *tə́*. Thus, there appears to be a constraint that prevents the same noun from being a constituent of two different predications at the same time.

The evidence for the proposed hypothesis consists of several facts. First, in some contexts, the forms *á* and *tə́* are interchangeable, providing evidence that they have the same categorial function, that of predication:

(41) a. ɓ̰ə̀ tə́ ngìɗ **á** təkóŋ.
COW GEN DEM PRED GEN:1PL
'The cow over there is ours.'

b. ɓ̰ə̀ tə́ ngìɗ **tə́** təkóŋ.
COW GEN DEM GEN GEN:1PL
'The cow over there is ours.'

Second, the two forms cannot co-occur, providing evidence that they perform functions in the same domain:

c. *ɓ̰ə̀ tə́ ngìɗ á tə́ təkóŋ.
COW GEN DEM PRED GEN GEN:1PL
'The cow over there is ours.'

In a locative construction whose complement is not inherently locative, the complement is marked by the preposition *n* (cf. Sections 3.2, 3.4). This preposition may co-occur with the marker *tə́*. However, if the complement of the locative construction is inherently locative and therefore is not marked by the locative preposition *n*, the possessive marker is omitted in the locative predication. Both situations are illustrated in 54. In this example, the first modifying construction, *də́wə́ŋ kwàykwàyà* 'back of the hyena', has no possessive marker, while the second, *mə́ tə́ kwàykwàyà* 'mouth of the hyena', is marked by *tə́*. The local predicator *á* cannot co-occur with *tə́*, since the presence of *tə́* would mark the noun *də́wə́ŋ* as both part of the locative predication and head of the possessive construction. The verb of the second clause, 'put', is inherently locative and so has the same properties as the predicator *á*. But there is an important difference between the locative complements of the two predicators. The expression *də́wə́ŋ tə́ kwàykwàyà* 'back of the hyena' is inherently locative while the expression *mə́ tə́ kwàykwàyà* 'mouth of the hyena' is not. The evidence for the inherently locative nature of 'back of the hyena' is that *də́wə́ŋ tə́ kwàykwàyà* is not marked by the locative preposition *n*, while *mə́ tə́ kwàykwàyà* 'mouth of the hyena' must be preceded by the locative preposition *n* in a locative predication. Since the locative predicate *də́m* 'put' is separated from the possessive construction *mə́ tə́ kwàykwàyà* by the locative preposition *n*, the possessive head *mə́* cannot be construed as the argument of two different predications. For this reason, the marker *tə́* is not omitted, but marks *mə́* as head of a possessive predication:

(42) Séy ɓə̀t skə̀ŋ-yíi wàcíŋ dzáw dzáw cìké á **də́wə́ŋ kwàykwàyà** ɓə̀t
so take thing-PL DEM tie tie all PRED back hyena take

líjì dэ́m nə **mə́ tə́ kwàykwàyà.**
bit (Fula) put PREP mouth GEN hyena
'He took those things and attached them all to the back of the hyena. He took the bridle and put it in the hyena's mouth.'

The natural discourse data fully support the proposed explanation. Here are a few more examples of possessive constructions in which the complement is inherently locative, so there is no preposition *n* and the marker *tə́* is consequently omitted:

(43) Wàl wà kə dzáŋ rùkút tətə kə á **bìŋ ngùl** ngə̀n.
woman DEM INF close clothes 3PL AFF PRED room husband 3SG
'The woman$_i$ has locked their$_j$ clothes in the room of her$_i$ husband.'

(44) À zá á nə gímíɮíɗ áz tùmù médìgì ngáɮ ngáɮ í
3SG COMP PRED PREP monkey go 1DU neighbor pull pull 3PL
ngáɮ-á pám á **mìdìgìɗ kwáyàŋ.**
pull-GO until PRED court squirrel
'He said to the monkey, "Let's go, neighbor." They went to the squirrel's courtyard.'

A spatial specifier followed by a noun is an inherently locative construction. It is not marked by the preposition *n*, so the possessive marker is not used:

(45) Nd-á ɗéw ká á **bə̀r málùm** wàcìŋ.
go-GO sit AFF PRED side teacher DEM
'He came and sat down next to the teacher.'

A possessive phrase following the preposition *kə́* also does not contain the marker *tə́*. In (46)–(47), each possessive construction is part of a locative phrase marked by *kə́*, and the possessive relationship is coded by apposition alone. From this, it follows that the preposition *kə́* also is an inherent predicator:

(46) À zá wàcíŋ nék skù náz **kə́ dùwə́ŋ dà.**
3SG COMP DEM good NEG throw AFF behind house
'He said this isn't good. He threw it behind the house.'

(47) Gìmíɮíɗ kə́ts wàl ngə̀ŋ-yíì ábə̀ wə̀z-yíì táŋ nd-á cìké **kə́**
monkey gather wife 3SG-PL ASSC child-PL DEM go-GO all PREP
dùwə́ŋ də̀ kwáyàŋ.
behind compound squirrel
'The monkey gathered his wives and children. They all stayed behind the squirrel's house.'

5. Conclusions

The Systems Interaction method allows us to discover the semantic categories grammaticalized in the lexicon of the language and the functional domains encoded in its grammar. This study has focused on one functional domain, that of locative predication. The existence of this domain in Mina is evidenced by the interaction between three coding means, namely inherently locative lexical items, local predicator *á*, and locative prepositions. These means are in complementary distribution within the same domain, as follows: If both the predicate and the complement are inherently locative, locative predication is coded by linear order, wherein the locative predicate is followed by the locative complement. If the predicate is not inherently locative, the local predicator *á* must be used. If the complement is not inherently locative, the preposition *n* must be used before the locative complement. If neither predicate nor complement is inherently locative, the local predicator *á* and the preposition *n* both must be used. Specific spatial relations are coded by other prepositions, an auxiliary verb, and body-part nouns, a coding means unique to human and other animate nouns functioning as locative complements.

The Systems Interaction approach also allows us to establish that the particle *á* and the marker *tɔ́* are both local predicators, the first coding a locative function and the second coding a modifying function. It provides an explanation for the fact that the possessive phrase changes its form depending on the function it performs in a larger construction. The marker *tɔ́* may not be used when the possessive phrase is an immediate complement of a locative predication because this marker, like an inherently locative verb or the particle *á*, is a local predicator, and a noun that is an argument of one predicator cannot serve at the same time as an argument of another predicator.

The interaction of the various coding means in the coding of locative predication is driven by the principle of functional transparency, assuring that the role of every element remains transparent in the domain of locative predication.

CHAPTER 11

Systems interaction in the coding of reference

1. Introduction

The goal of the present chapter is to demonstrate that in order to understand the function of a given coding means in a language it is necessary to understand what place this means has within a given functional domain. This goal is achieved through a description of the interaction of various means in the coding of reference in a few selected languages, viz. English, Polish, Mupun, and Mina. The notion of reference as 'the relation between a part of an utterance and an individual or set of individuals it identifies' (Matthews 1997) is expanded in the present approach to include any and all means of identifying the individual or individuals represented in the given utterance. Not all of the means that are traditionally assumed to be markers of reference actually belong to the domain of reference. The form *this* in English, for example, may function in the domain of topicalization (cf. Givón and Wright 1987). For a cross-linguistic typology of the functions of demonstratives, cf. Diessel (1999).

The discussion of reference in contemporary syntactic theories is characterized by a piecemeal approach wherein a single coding means is discussed in isolation from other coding means or a single function is discussed in isolation from other functions. In Frajzyngier (1997b), however, it is shown that the functions, properties, and distribution of pronouns, anaphors, and agreement cannot be explained without taking into consideration other means that participate in the coding of reference.

Coding means in the domain of reference direct the hearer to identify the referent as belonging to some subdomain in the domain of reference. These subdomains include deixis; previous mention; 'known' referent (see below); the domains *de dicto* and *de re*; definiteness; 'deduced' referent (see below); and perhaps others. Each of these subdomains may have subdomains of its own. The subdomain of previous mention, for example, may contain the further subdomains of proximate and remote mention, while the subdomain of deixis may include the further subdomains of point of view and distance. Brief definitions of each subdomain of the domain of reference follow, with full descriptions to be provided later in the chapter. We stress that this listing is not exhaustive.

Deixis is the coding of a referent as present in the environment of speech. The specific properties of deictic systems, such as reference points (speaker, hearer, both or neither) and distances encoded, may differ significantly from language to language.

Previous mention is the domain in which a referent is coded as having been mentioned previously in the same or in another discourse. Some languages distinguish between proximate mention and remote mention (terms other linguists use for these phenomena may vary), and there may be additional distinctions between these two extremes.

Switch reference explicitly codes an element as referring not to the immediately preceding referent but to another, previously mentioned referent. Switch reference does not code the introduction of a new participant in discourse.

A '*known*' referent is a referent that the hearer is directed to treat as a known entity. The hearer may know the referent through his/her cognitive system, through previous mention, or even through deixis. In some cases, the hearer may not actually know the referent at all, but the coding of referent as known indicates that its identity is not subject to further inquiry.

The subdomains *de dicto* and *de re* divide the universe of reference into two types of entities: Those that have their existence only in the domain of speech, and by extension in the hypothetical domain, and those that have their existence in the domain of reality. These domains are discussed in Frajzyngier (1991, 1997b).

The subdomain '*deduced*' directs the hearer to deduce the identity of referent *A*, which may or may not have been mentioned in discourse, from the mention of an element *B*, which bears some relationship to *A*. This deduction may be based on preceding discourse or on general knowledge.

Coding for *definiteness* directs the hearer to identify the referent by any means available, without specifying where this identification is to be sought.

A speaker may use one or more coding means in the domain of reference to direct the hearer to identify a referent within one or more subdomains. These means include nouns; deictic markers; anaphors, in the wide, pre-GB sense of the word; agreement; linear order of elements in the utterance; case marking; and combinations of these means. There is no one-to-one correspondence between the coding means and specific functions. As in all other functional domains, one cannot predict what means are involved in the coding of reference in a given language, nor can one predict which subdomains are coded by a given means. The same means, e.g. pronouns or agreement, may code different subdomains from one language to another or may code opposite values within the same subdomain in different languages.

An approach that examines all of the means and functions involved in the domain of reference offers significant advantages over an approach that looks only at a given formal means or a given function within this domain. For example, we can explain why modifying constructions in some languages may contain both a definite article and a deictic while other languages prohibit this combination, an issue discussed by Haspelmath (1999). According to our analysis, a noun may be modified by more than one determiner provided each determiner codes a different functional domain. For example, if one determiner codes previous mention and another codes deixis, the two determiners may co-occur with a single noun. The same is true if the domains of previous mention and 'known' are coded by different determiners. The specific function of any determiner cannot be assumed from its translation but must be discovered through an analysis of the individual language.

In what follows we first provide evidence for the existence of the proposed subdomains in the domain of reference. We then describe how various means interact in the coding of these subdomains. If it can be shown that some formal means codes a given subdomain in the domain of reference and no other subdomain within that domain, this is taken as evidence for the existence of the first subdomain. We limit the discussion to a few languages which have relatively rich coding systems, for which we have abundant natural language data, and for which we have a global view of all of the means used in the coding of reference.

One of the fundamental questions with respect to the given means is to find out to what domain it belongs. It has been often assumed that demonstratives belong automatically to the domain of reference and that non-referential uses are somehow extensions of the referential uses (cf. Diessel 1999).

2. Deictic systems

Deictic systems identify a participant as present in the environment of speech. All references to the first and second person are deictic; however, not every instance of the first- or second-person plural pronoun (or singular/plural pronoun, in languages that do not distinguish number in the first and second person) has a deictic function.

In referring to the third-person singular and plural and in referring to locations, many languages use the same coding means for deictic and anaphoric referents. It is possible that such languages have no formal means to distinguish between these two domains. This would account for the practice in English, where the third-person [+human] pronouns 'he' and 'she' may refer to persons mentioned previously in discourse or to persons present in the environment of speech. In the following fragments, all uses of third-person pronouns that have been bolded are deictic:

(1) Paula: About…five miles, but I've been trying to run part of that
Michelle: Hmmm
Paula: …which doesn't come easy
Michelle: Wow, (whistle)
Sarah: You should do the Bolder Boulder [a race] with us next year. Mom and I are gonna walk it.
Mom: **She**'ll, **she**'ll leave us in dust unless we really start…

(2) Sarah: See, that's what I was saying.…that's what I was saying
Michelle: See, that's what I was saying. I'm was like he's gonna come get me.
Sarah: So **she** brings **her** cat down who has no front claws. That's not gonna do any good.
Sarah: We're gonna work on it' (conversation transcript provided courtesy of Barbara Fox)

In some languages third-person pronouns are anaphoric only. This is the case in Polish. Analysis of a 126,000-word corpus of literary Polish reveals not a single example of a third-person pronoun in a deictic function with the referent present in the conversation. There are, however, many examples in which the third-person pronoun is used in an anaphoric function:

(3) A cóż **ona** tam robi?
CONJ what 3F there do:3SG
'And what is she doing there?' (about a person mentioned in a previous sentence; Sources)

Similarly, Mupun (West Chadic) lacks independent third-person human deictic markers. The third-person deictic system is limited to non-human referents and locatives (all Mupun data come from Frajzyngier 1993):

	Non-human referent	Location
Proximate	ɗə́-sə̀	-sə̀ sə̀ sə̀
Remote	ɗə́-sə́	-sə́ pùen sə́

Here is the evidence for the deictic function of these markers.

(4) A kuɗaŋ sə mo pet ha a la mis ɓe se a
PREP before DEM 3PL call 2M COP child man CONS only (Hau.) 2M
cin mbi ɗə vəl **ɗə-sə** mo.
do thing REL two REL-DEM PL
'Before they call you a man you must do these two things: [a list follows].'

The next two examples illustrate the contrast between deictic and anaphoric locative reference in Mupun:

(5) Wu wa sə́.
3M come there (Deictic)
'He came from there.' (only deictic)

(6) Wu wa **ɗi.**
3M come there (Anaph)
'He came from there.' (only anaphoric)

3. Coding previous mention

Coding means in the domain of previous mention instruct the hearer to seek the referent for some noun or pronoun in the preceding, or even in some other, discourse. In many languages, coreference with the closest preceding referent of the same gender, number, person, and case requires the least morphological marking. Coreference appears to be the default situation in sequential constructions of the type S [SEQ] S, consisting of two clauses that may or may not be joined by a sequential marker.[14]

Within the subdomain of previous mention, some languages distinguish between proximate reference, in which a participant *x* is coded as having been mentioned relatively recently, and remote reference, in which the previous mention of *x* is considerably removed in discourse or may be found in another discourse entirely. The exact textual dimensions required for proximate and remote reference differ significantly among languages.

In what follows we first present evidence for the existence of previous mention as a distinct subdomain within the domain of reference and illustrate an instance of proximate vs. remote previous mention. We then examine the coding of coreference and switch reference within two syntactic situations: sequential clauses and complements of verbs of saying. With respect to the latter, we first show the coding of such reference through logophoric pronouns and then show how such reference may be coded in languages that do not have logophoric pronouns.

3.1. Evidence for the subdomain of previous mention

In this section we provide evidence from Mupun showing that previous mention exists as a subdomain distinct from other subdomains within the domain of reference.

Mupun has a marker *ń*, glossed as DEF in Frajzyngier (1993). In accordance with the new analysis we propose here, we gloss the marker as PM (previous mention). The first piece of evidence that the marker *ń* codes previous mention is provided by examples in which only the first mention of a noun in discourse lacks the marker. In the following sentence, the word *túl* 'house' occurs first without the previous mention marker and only later with the marker:

(7) Kat jep mis mo yo wet mo dəm n-**tul** siar fur
when young man PL go spend day 3PL go PREP-house friend 3PL
ɗan jirap mo n-**tul** **nə**.
and girls PL PREP-house PM
'If young men go to spend the day at their friends' house, and there are girls in the house.'

In the next example (part of which is repeated from 4), the first mention of the entity 'things' is marked by a deictic demonstrative, while subsequent mentions of this entity are marked by previous mention markers:

(8) A kuɗaŋ sə mo pet ha a la mis ɓe se a cin mbi
PREP before DEM 3PL call 2M COP child man CONS only 2M do thing
də vəl **ɗə-sə** mo.
REL two REL-DEM PL
'Before they call you a man you must do these two things:

də n-**sie** **nə** a naa nawar;
REL PREP-first PM 2M see smallidol
'First, you must see a small idol;

ɗə **vəl nə** a lap kum.
REL two PM 2M take ritual
'second, you must go through the ritual.'

Further evidence for the previous mention function of *ń* is that this marker cannot occur with participants of hypothetical events or events that have not yet happened:

(9) Kat tar fuan ***nə** ji ɓe mo ya cin siit.
when month rain PM come SEQ 3PL begin do work
'When the rainy season comes, they begin to work.'

Evidence that the marker *nə* codes previous mention as opposed to deixis is that *nə* can modify proper names and toponyms to indicate that these have been previously mentioned in discourse, regardless of whether the referent is present in the speech environment. In the following two examples, the previously mentioned place names 'Zaria' and 'Germany' are followed by the marker *nə*. The first mentions of these places in the discourse were not followed by this marker:

(10) N-dəm n-kes ɓe wa ba n-dəm ɗi n-**Zaria** **nə**.
1SG-go 1SG-finish SEQ return go 1SG-go there PREP-Zaria PM
'I went, finished [the school], and then returned to Zaria.'

(11) Yaksə mu dəm ɗi n-**Germany** **nə**.
then 1PL go there PREP-Germany PM
'Then we went to Germany.'

Following is the first reference to a toponym, which therefore lacks the previous mention marker:

(12) Manaja fun ɗə n-**pyanya** wa ji kaat an.
manager 1PL REL PREP-Panyan 3F come meet 1SG
'Our manager who was in Panyan came and met me.'

In the following examples, the previous mention marker follows proper names that have already been mentioned in discourse:

(13) Səm wur a **M.G. ń**.
name 3M COP M.G. PM
'His name is M.G.'

(14) Me reep mpuo wur kut ɗi-e ba da **namwes ń**-e.
some daughter another 3M COMP yet-Q NEG ? Namwes PM-Q
'Does he have another daughter apart from Namwes?'

Marking for previous mention does not necessarily mean that the marked element itself, i.e. the very same lexical item, has occurred in the discourse. Instead, previous mention marking instructs the hearer to look in the previous discourse for the referent for the marked lexical item. Thus, a previously unmentioned item that is associated with the referent may be marked for previous mention:

(14) Kaɗan me mat tok sik kə́ mo ɗaŋ me gwar lap ɓe
if QUANT woman greet CONJ 3PL then QUANT man answer CONS
yen nə tep.
medicine PM break
'If a woman greets them and one of the men answers, the medicine will break down.'

3.2. Proximate versus remote previous mention

In addition to coding unspecified previous mention, Mupun codes a distinction between proximate previous mention and remote previous mention. Proximate previous mention is coded by the deictic marker *ɗə́-sə̀* 'proximate' followed by the previous mention marker *nə*, while remote previous mention is coded by the remote deictic *ɗə́-sə́* followed by the previous mention marker *nə*. The following sentence has the proximate marker *ɗə́-sə̀* followed by the previous mention marker (reduplicated to code focus), indicating that the referent has its antecedent in the immediately preceding discourse:

(15) Kaɗ wur naa ngo ɗə ba wur ɓal kas ɓe wur dəm pe
when 3M see man REL NEG 3M strong NEG CONS 3M go place
mənə kə wur put ɗi.
ANAPH COMP 3M leave COMP
'When it [the leopard] sees a man who is not strong then it goes in that direction so that it can get out.'

(16) Amma kaɗan mo ɗaar ɓalɓal ɓe mo n-pus lusim **ɗəsə nə nə**.
but if 3PL stand firmly CONS 3PL FUT-shoot leopard DEM PM
'But if they stand firmly they will shoot this very leopard.'

In the next fragment, the proximate deictic followed by the previous mention marker refers to the activities just listed:

(17) A ɓuon **ɗəsə nə** a ɓuon ɗə mo cin mbi **ɗəsə** mo kes.
after DEM PM after REL 3PL do thing DEM PL finish
'After that, after they have done all those things ...'

Compare the following sentences. The first has the remote deictic marker followed by the previous mention marker, while the second, elicited, has only the deictic marker and so codes spatial deixis only:

(18) Wu ye nə a soot mo tue **ɗəsə nə** mo.
3M think COMP COP devil PL kill-PL DEM PM PL
'He thought that the devils killed the other ones.'

(19) Wu ye nə a soot mo tue **ɗəsə** mo.
3M think COMP COP devil PL kill-PL DEM PL
'He thought that the devils killed these ones.'

Polish codes the category of association with another situation known to the hearer, by means of a remote demonstrative composed of the locative remote marker *tam* followed by a deictic pronoun coding gender and person: *tamten* (3M) *tamta* (3F) and *tamci* (3PL). Evidence that this form codes neither deixis nor definiteness is provided by the fact that the form can be used with proper names even when the person referred to is present in the environment of speech. In the following example, the person named *Pionka* has been a topic of preceding discourse and is present in the speech environment:

(20) Ja to mam na myśli niech **tam-tyn Pionka** dołozy się.
1SG COM have:1SG on thought let there-DEM Pionka contribute REFL
'What I think is that Pionka should contribute.' (Nitsch 1960:226) (*tam-tyn* is a dialectal variant of *tamten)*

(21) Pan dyrektor Kukuła dostał nagrodę za **tamten** wynalazek
Mr. director Kukuła receive:PAST:3M prize for that invention for
dla hutnictwa.
foundry industry
'Director Kukuła received a prize for that invention for the foundry industry.' (The invention has not been mentioned in at least the preceding seven sentences, and probably has not been mentioned at all in the preceding discourse.) (Sources)

Evidence that the remote demonstrative codes the association with some situation or mention is provided by instances in which the remote demonstrative is used and the referent does not belong to the domain of knowledge common to the speaker and hearer. This situation is explicitly stated in the following example. The situation itself might have been mentioned in the preceding discourse:

(22) A **tamta** druga Zosia to dobra twoja przyjaciółka. Bo ja
and that other Zosia COM good 2SG:F friend:F because 1SG
jej chyba nie znam.
3F:GEN probably NEG know:1SG
'And that other Zosia, is she a good friend of yours? I don't think I know her.' (Sources)

We discuss the interaction of remote previous mention with other means of coding reference in the section devoted to the case study of Mina.

4. Coding switch reference

The coding of switch reference has the very specific function of switching reference from the closest potential referent to another referent previously mentioned in discourse. This definition explicitly does not include switching to a completely new referent, a function coded in many languages by the introduction of a new noun phrase.

Our study of the domain of switch reference reveals that a given formal means may have opposite functions in this domain in different languages. In what follows, we discuss two syntactic environments in which some languages code switch reference. The first environment is the sequential clause, i.e. a clause indicating a temporal sequence of events or a cause-effect relationship, with or without a conjunction. The second environment is the complement of a verb of saying.

4.1. Switch reference in sequential clauses

In sequential clauses having the structure S_1 [SEQ] S_1, the argument having the role of subject in S_1 is taken to have the same referent as the subject of S_1 unless explicitly marked otherwise; thus, coreference in the sequential clause is the default situation (cf. Comrie 1999). Evidence for this assertion is that the coding of subject coreference requires the least morphological marking. In the English conjoined clause, for example, the absence of overt coding of the subject codes coreference with the subject of the preceding clause:

2_11_1 <120 A> +well well ^Amy '[w@:]+ ^Amy 'kept sort of . :hugging her 'little white :sh\/awl 'round her#
2_11_1 <121 A> and **saying** I ^wish I hadn't 'knitted h\oles into 'this#

1_1_0 <50 B> ^you give* them the :l\ot {^you s=ee#}# *.*
1_1_0 <51 B> ^that's the **p/oint#**
1_1_0 <52 B> ((and)) ^**make** sure that there's :s\/omething#
1_1_0 <53 B> [@:] ^fairly :cl\osely rel/ated#

Switch reference in English sequential clauses is coded by the use of pronouns:

1_1_0 <81 A> ^now . !A he may not . send it . quite as soon as ./ :th/at#
1_1_0 <82 A> and ^=B#
1_1_0 <83 A> **it** ^may take a hell of a long time to !c\ome
1_1_0 <39 A> be^cause you see ((I)) — [@] ^some of our p\eople#
1_1_0 <40 A> (. clears throat) ((who)) are ^d\oing LEs# — -
1_1_0 <41 A> [@:m] ^have to consider which !{p\aper} . to "d\o# .
1_1_0 <42 A> and **I** ^wondered . whether . [dhi] . gra:phology

In Polish, subject coreference in the sequential clause is coded by agreement on the verb, an obligatory element in any Polish clause. This coding means is used even when another potential subject argument intervenes between the previous mention and the new mention, provided this argument has different features for gender, number, or person. This situation may be described as $x_a y$-$_b x_a$ where x and y are different nouns and 'a' and 'b' are different values for the features gender, number, and person:

(23) **Oszukał** mnie. Człowiek z epoki metali ciężkich
cheat:PAST:3MSG 1SG:ACC man from era metal:PL heavy:PL
oszukał mnie w dyskusji.
cheat:PAST:3MSG 1SG in discussion
'He cheated me. A man from the era of heavy metals cheated me in the discussion.

Sądziłem, że **jest** zwolennikiem inseminacji i rozsądku.
judge:1SG COMP be:3MSG proponent:INSTR insemination CONJ reason
Nie **był** taki.
NEG be:3M:SG such:M:SG
'I thought that he was a proponent of insemination and reason. He wasn't like that at all.'

(24) **Poszła** po dziecko do Teresy, **zrobi** zdjęcia
go:PRF:PAST:3F:SG PREP child to Teresa make:FUT:3SG pictures
a la minute i tu **przyniesie**.
minute and here bring:FUT:3SG
'She$_i$ went to Teresa to fetch her child. She$_i$ will make instant photo pictures and bring them here.' (Sources)

In Polish as in English, switch reference in the sequential clauses is coded by the use of pronouns or gender-coded deictic elements:

(25) **Anna** zadrżała z przerażenia, że lada chwila popłyną
Anna tremble:PAST:3F from fear COMP any moment pour:FUT
łzy, których pełno było w oczach przyjaciółki. lecz **ta**
tears REL:PL plenty be:N in eyes:LOC friend:F:GEN but DEM:F
opanowała się na siłę i zaczęła powoli mówić.
compose:3F:PAST REFL PREP force:ACC and start:F:PAST slowly talk
'Anna feared that at any moment tears that filled her friend's eyes would pour out. But she [the friend] had composed herself, and started to talk slowly.' (Sources)

(26) To bardzo podłe wino. Może i **oni** się napiją.
DEM very vile wine maybe CONJ 3PL REFL drink:FUT:3PL
'That is a very vile wine. Maybe they will drink some as well?'

(27) Pewnie nadciągnęło nasze wojsko, aby otworzyć drogę do
perhaps arrive:PAST our army in order to open road to
Warszawy. I **oni** polecieli z tym wojskiem.
Warsaw CONJ 3PL run:3PL:M with DEM army
'Perhaps our army has arrived in order to open the road to Warsaw. And they ran with the army.'

(28) Są przecież bezdzietne małżeństwa, dla których dziecko nie
exist:PL nevertheless childless marriages for REL:PL child NEG

jest konieczne. Bez potomstwa bywają szczęśliwe i kochają
be necessary without progeny be:FREQ:PL happy:PL CONJ love:PL
się, a **ja** nie mam co kochać.
REFL CONJ 1SG NEG have:1SG what love
'There exist, nevertheless, childless marriages, for which a child is not necessary. They are happy and loving. And I do not have anything to love.' (Sources)

(29) Krzesnomatka przysła do niego i muwi mu zebyś
godmother come:PAST:F to 3M CONJ say:3SG 3M COMP:SUBJ:2SG
sie nie godził na przysły rok a **on** muwił.
REFL NEG agree PREP coming year CONJ 3M say
'The godmother came to him and says, "Do not agree for the next year." And he says …' (Nitsch 1960: 114)

In both Polish and English sequential clauses, subject switch reference is coded by means of pronouns, and switch reference is more morphologically marked than subject coreference.

4.2. Coreference and switch reference with verbs of saying

Complements of verbs of saying provide an interesting challenge to the notion of the default situation. In many languages, the coding of coreference between the subject of the main clause and the subject of the embedded clause is the marked situation in that it requires additional coding means that are not used elsewhere in the language.

Some languages have special sets of pronouns referring to the arguments of the matrix verb of saying and sometimes, though less frequently, to verbs of thinking. Such pronouns have been observed in Adamawa languages (Hagège 1974), in Bantu (Hyman and Comrie 1981), in Kwa (Clements 1975), and in Chadic (Frajzyngier 1989c, 1993, 1997b). Hagège 1974 uses the term 'logophoric' for a pronoun whose antecedent is the subject of the verb of saying in the matrix clause. We extend the term to include pronouns whose referent is the addressee of the matrix clause. The term 'non-logophoric' thus refers to complement clause pronouns whose antecedent is outside matrix clause of saying (cf. Frajzyngier 1985c, 1993, 1997b).

The common characteristic of logophoric pronouns, i.e. pronouns coding coreference, is that they are formally different from their counterparts in the matrix clause. Thus, coreference is coded by the use of two different forms to refer to the same referent. Switch reference, on the other hand, is coded by the use of the same pronoun form used in the matrix clause; thus, the same pronoun form has different referents in the matrix and the embedded clause. We illustrate the phenomenon of logophoricity using data from Mupun, which has separate sets of logophors referring to the subject and addressee of the matrix clause (from Frajzyngier 1993).

Logophoric subject:

(30) **Wu/wa/mo** sat nə ta **ɗi/ɗe/ɗu** ɗee n-jos
he/she/they said that stop he/she/they stay PREP-Jos
'He$_1$/she$_1$/they$_1$ said that he$_1$/she$_1$/they$_1$ stopped over in Jos.'

Non-logophoric subject:

(31) **Wu/wa/mo** sat nə **wu/wa/mo** ta ɗee n-jos
he/she/they say COMP he/she/they stop stay PREP-Jos
'He$_1$/she$_1$/they$_1$ said that 'he$_2$/she$_2$/they$_2$ stopped over in Jos.'

Logophoric addressee:

(32) N-sat n-**wur** nə **gwar** ji.
1SG-say PREP-3SG COMP 3SG come
'I told him$_1$ that he$_1$ should come.'

Non-logophoric addressee:

(33) N-sat n-**wur** nə **wur** ji.
1SG-say PREP-3SG COMP 3SG come
'I told him$_1$ that he$_2$ should come.'

The matrix clause in the following example does not contain an addressee. However, the use of the logophoric pronoun *gwar* in the relative clause indicates that the referent is also the addressee of the matrix clause:

(34) An nə ko a iri ɗak ɗə **gwar** sin an ɓe an mbə cin nə.
1SG COMP any COP kind work REL 3SG give 1SG CONS 1SG FUT do it
'I said that any kind of work which he gives me, I will do it.'

Languages without logophoric pronouns have other means of coding coreference and switch reference in the complement clause. In English, coreference in the complement clause is coded by use of the same pronoun as that used in the matrix clause. This phenomenon is partly explained by the fact that the finite complement clause in English always requires overt coding of the subject, but the interesting fact remains that the coding of coreference in the embedded clause employs the same means as the coding of switch reference in the sequential clause:

4_1_0 <70 b> **she** ^said **she** didn't . 'think we were upst\airs# -

4_1_0 <332 b> but **she** ^said **she**'d 'got a Boots t\oken#
4_1_0 <333 b> and ^so **she**'d 'use !th\at# — - -

4_2_0 <49 a> **he** ^said that **he** :thought this :might be d\ifficult#

Switch reference between the subject of the matrix clause and the subject of the complement clause may be coded by a pronoun, provided the two referents differ in person, gender or number:

4_3_0 |<792 A> ^I said !what about gr\andad#
4_3_0 <793 A> ^**she** said well **!h\e** won't eat {^m\uch#}#

1_1_0 <454 B> ((and **he** said)) **I**'ve ^got some :h/ere# -

However, if the subject of the matrix and the embedded clause have the same features for person, gender, and number, switch reference is coded by the use of a full noun, even if that noun has been previously mentioned in discourse:

6_7_0 <678 a> remember **Brockhouse** had said that **Frank Jones** made a great mistake in not retiring from politics at the end of the First World War

If the noun is not a proper name, it must be coded by the definite marker 'the' or the deictic marker 'this':

1_1_0 <77 A> [@:] I ^did get **a !p\ostcard** fr/om him# — -
1_1_0 <78 A> ^saying that [@:m] **the !thing** is now :r/eady# .
1_1_0 <79 A> and that he will ^send it by the :end . of :J\une# .

1_1_0 <844 B> ^**I** said :look h\ere#
1_1_0 <845 B> **this ^English L\anguage p/aper#**
1_1_0 <846 B> has ^been be'devilled 'long e"!n\ough#

In Polish, coreference with the subject of the matrix clause is coded only by agreement, as is coreference in the sequential clause:

(35) **Mówił,** że **jest** komunistą.
say:PAST:3M COMP be:3SG communist:M
'He was saying that he was a communist.'

(36) **Mówi,** że **jest** apostołem. a potem się **usprawiedliwia.**
say:3M COMP be:3SG apostle CONJ later REFL apologize:SG
'He says that he is an apostle and later apologizes.'

Polish differs from English in that a pronoun must be used to code switch reference even if the subject of the complement clause differs from the subject of the matrix clause in person, gender or number. This pronoun is of the series *on* (3M), *ona* (3F), *oni* (3PL):

(37) **Mówią,** że **on** nawet nie mógł pomyśleć o czymkolwiek.
say:3PL:PRES COMP 3M even NEG can think:PRF about anything
'They say that he was not able to think about anything.' (Sources)

Even if the pronoun in the complement clause has the same gender, person, and number as the subject of the embedded clause, it must be interpreted as having a different referent:

(38) **Mówi** że **on** nawet nie mógł pomyśleć o czymkolwiek.
say:3M:SG:PRES COMP 3M even NEG can think about anything
'He$_i$ says that he$_j$ was not able to think about anything.'

5. The *de dicto* and *de re* domains

Languages that code the subdomains *de dicto* and *de re* distinguish between referents that have their existence only in the domain of speech and those that have their existence in the domain of reality. The domain of speech includes those referents whose existence is only hypothetical. In English, a proximate object in the domain *de re* is coded by the demonstrative 'this':

1_1_0 <32 A> *is ^**this** a spare p/aper#*
1_1_0 <33 B> (([@] ^y\eah#
1_1_0 <34 B> I actually ^got it for y/ou#))
1_1_0 <35 A> ^thank you very m/uch#
1_1_0 <36 A> ((1 syll)) *^thanks very much in:d\eed#*
1_1_0 <37 B> *I've ^probably got some :m\ore#*
1_1_0 <38 B> [F@:] ^further b\ack# .

In English, the *de dicto* category is coded by the demonstrative 'that'.

1_1_0 <50 B> ^you give* them the :l\ot {^you s=ee#}# *.*
1_1_0 <51 B> ^**that**'s the **p/oint#**
1_1_0 <52 B> ((and)) ^make sure that there's :s\/omething#

The following fragment of conversation concerns graphology papers. The demonstrative 'that' (bolded) explicitly refers to the paper as a general category (e.g., a paper required for a course) rather than to the specific paper most recently mentioned in discourse:

1_1_0 <1 B> ((of ^Spanish)) . graph\ology#
1_1_0 <2 A> ^w=ell# .
1_1_0 <3 A> ((if)) did ^y/ou _set _that# -
1_1_0 <4 B> ^well !J\oe and _I#
1_1_0 <5 B> ^set it betw\een _us#
1_1_0 <6 B> ^actually !Joe 'set the :p\aper#
1_1_0 <7 B> and *((3 to 4 sylls))*
1_1_0 <8 A> *^w=ell# .
1_1_0 <9 A> "^m/\ay* I _ask#
1_1_0 <10 A> ^what goes !\into **that** paper n/ow#

Some languages code a distinction in specific interrogative clauses between a hypothetical, unknown referent and a real referent belonging to a specific group. In Polish this distinction is coded by the use of the forms *kto* 'who' or *co* 'what' (*de dicto*) vs. the forms *który, która, które* 'which one' (*de re*).

Domain *de dicto*:

(39) Ciekaw jestem, **kto** zostawił to mydło.
interested:M be:1SG who leave:3M DEM soap:ACC
'I wonder who left this soap.'

Cf. the domain *de re*, in which the existence of the referent is assumed and only its identity is questioned:

(40) **Która** godzina. Szesnasta pięćdziesiąt osiem.
what:F hour sixteen fifty eight
'What time is it? 4:58 p.m.' (Sources)

(41) Franuś. **Którego** to świętego wodziły na pokuszenie
Franus. which:ACC DEM saint:ACC lead:PAST:3PL:F on temptation
diabły w kostiumie z gołego babskiego ciała Świętego
devil:PL:NOM in costume from naked female body Saint:ACC
Marksa.
Marx:ACC
'Franus! Which saint was led into temptation by devils dressed in a costume tailored from a naked female body? Saint Marx.' (Sources)

6. The domain of definiteness

The category definiteness has no reliable functional characterization in linguistic theory. Traditional descriptions, which take English, Latin or some other western Indo-European language as a proto-type for the category of definiteness, do not provide a theoretical description of the category. We begin with a working definition of the function of the category definite as instructing the hearer to identify the referent without indicating a specific subdomain, such as previous mention, 'known', or deixis, in which this identification is to be sought. This characterization subsumes the definition given in Matthews (1997: 89) of definiteness as 'referring to, or characteristically indicating reference to, an identifiable individual or set of individuals.'

6.1. Definiteness in English

The coding of definiteness is the referential function of the definite marker in English. Evidence for this assertion is that the identification of a referent marked by the definite marker may be found in any one of a number of subdomains. The identification of the referent may be in the subdomain of previous mention:

1_1_0 <76 A> ((but)) **the ^damn thing** ((hasn't)) c/ome# -
1_1_0 <77 A> [@:] I ^did get a !p\ostcard fr/om him# — -
1_1_0 <78 A> ^saying that [@:m] **the !thing** is now :r/eady# .(LLC)

The identification of the referent marked definite may be found in the realm of unique objects:

(42) The Times, The Guardian (Quirk et al. 1972: 79)

The referent marked definite may be in the domain of the 'known':

(43) John asked his wife to put on **the kettle** while he looked in **the paper** to see what was on **the radio**. (Quirk et al. 1972: 73)

The definite marker may mark a referent to be identified within the environment of speech:

(44) It is there on **the bookshelf.**

In short, the definite marker in English directs the hearer to identify the referent through any means available.

A similar system exists in Polish, a language usually held not to have the category definiteness.

6.2. Definiteness and topicalization in Polish

Polish is usually said to lack definite articles (but see Bacz 1989). If the term 'definite article' is taken to mean a grammatical morpheme whose function is the same as that of the definite article in English and French, then the statement is true. However, an examination of any natural language text in Polish reveals a great number of instances where determiners occur before all kinds of nouns. These examples do not involve deixis, and yet the conditions in which determiners are used differ significantly from the conditions in which definite articles occur in English. The question to be asked, then, is what is the function of determiners in Polish? In this section, we present a case study of the role of determiners in the coding of topicalization and its connection to definiteness. Our study reveals that Polish has an intriguing system of coding topicalization, a system that has not been described elsewhere for Polish.

Polish has the singular proximate determiners *ten* (m.), *ta* (f.), and *to* (n.) and the plural proximate forms *ci* (masculine human nouns) and *te* (all other nouns). These determiners may precede or follow the noun they determine, with the order Determiner Noun being functionally unmarked. Whenever one of the determiners precedes the noun, such a noun is identifiable on the basis of information from preceding discourse, from the environment of speech (deixis), or through the hearer's cognitive system. The same is true of nouns preceded by the definite article in English, but, as we show below, there are significant differences between the use of determiners in Polish and the use of determiners in English.

The fundamental function of the determiner in Polish is to topicalize the following noun. However, a prerequisite for topicalization is that the noun be identifiable to the hearer. The evidence for the topicalization function consists of the following. First, once the noun has been marked by a determiner, its immediate subsequent mention does not have the determiner. Second, each time the determiner is used, the noun following the determiner is different from the noun in the preceding noun phrase. The structure is thus N_1 DET N_2, where N_2 is the topicalized noun. Any noun phrase, including subject, object, or a noun phrase preceded by a preposition, can be topicalized by means of the determiner. The determiner can be used with nouns that are identifiable through other means, either through inherent lexical properties (e.g. proper names) or through other identifying markers, such as possessive pronouns.

Evidence for the identifiability of the noun preceded by the determiner is provided by natural discourse data, in which every noun preceded by a determiner is identifiable by some means. Consider the following example. The noun *manekiny* 'mannequins' has been mentioned in preceding discourse by a different speaker, and subsequent mentions are linked with the previous mention by the use of proximate determiner:

(45) Wysoki sąd pyta mnie, co się stało z **tym**
high court ask:3SG 1SG:ACC what REL happen with DEM:M:INSTR
manekinem płci żeńskiej.
mannequin:INSTR SEX:GEN feminine:GEN
'Your honor asks me what happened with this mannequin of the female sex.'

A skąd pan mecenas wie, że **ten manekin** był
CONJ where from Mr. counsel know COMP DEM mannequin be:3M
płci żeńskiej.
sex feminine
'And how does counsel know that the mannequin was female?'

Ja tego nie stwierdziłem.
1SG DEM:N NEG establish:1SG:PAST
'I didn't establish this.'

Jest chyba faktem znanym ludziom dojrzałym,
be:3SG probably fact:INSTR known people:DAT mature:PL:DAT
że **te** **manekiny** podobnie jak anioły nie posiadają płci.
COMP DEM:PL mannequin:PL similarly like angels NEG possess sex
'It is probably a fact known to all mature people that mannequins, like angels, are sexless.' (Sources)

Previous mention is not a prerequisite for the use of a determiner before a noun. Rather, the presence of the determiner preceding the noun indicates that the speaker expects the hearer to identify the noun through any means available. The following fragments come from literary Polish. In each case, 'the boy' may or may not have been mentioned previously, but the presence of the determiner indicates that the identify of the boy is known to the hearer. The function of the determiner is to mark 'boy' as the topic:

(46) Czy Pan żąda od nas, że-by-ś-my tak, jak **ten nieszczęśliwy**
Q Sir demand from us COMP:SUBJ:1PL so like DEM unfortunate
chłopak, bez sensu nadstawiali karku.
boy without sense risk:3PL neck
'Do you demand that we senselessly risk our necks, just like that unfortunate boy?' (Sources)

(47) Ciekaw jestem, czy ona jeszcze chce, żeby **ten jej**
wonder be:1SG whether 3F still want:3SG COMP:SUBJ DEM 3F:POSS
chłopak żył.
boy live:PAST
'I wonder whether she still wishes for that boy of hers to be alive.' (Sources)

Proper names are identifiable by virture of their inherent lexical properties and so may be topicalized by the proximate determiner:

(48) A **ta Górecka** pracuje już u was długo.
CONJ DEM:F Gorecka work:3SG already at 2PL long
'And this Gorecka, has she been working long at your place?' (Sources)

(49) **Tego Milusicza** to ja bym nawet nie poznała.
DEM:M:ACC Milusicz DEM 1SG HYP:1SG even NEG recognize:1SG:F
'That Milusicz, I wouldn't have recognized him.' (Sources)

In the following fragment, the determiner precedes a proper name that is also modified by a possessive pronoun:

(50) Tak jest zawsze, kiedy staremu zachciewa się żeniaczki
so be always when old:DAT want:FREQ REFL marriage
z młódką.
with young:DIMIN:F
'It is always like that when old man all of a sudden fancies a marriage to a young girl.'

Ile ona ma lat, **ta twoja Narcyza.**
how many 3F have:3SG years:GEN DEM:F 2SG:POSS:F Narcyza
'How old is she, that Narcyza of yours?'

Pięćdziesiątki doszła.
fifty:GEN reach:PAST:3F:SG
'She has reached fifty.' (Sources)

Evidence that the proximate determiner does not direct the hearer to a specific subdomain, such as previous mention or deixis, is provided by utterances in which the determiner is used but the referent does not occur in the speech environment or in the preceding discourse. In the following fragment, *gotuwka* 'cash' has not been mentioned in the preceding discourse, but because the utterance is produced at a meeting whose goal is to find means for repairing a local school, money is a constant issue at the meeting:

(51) Przecie mówie, chodzi o to, i ze-by tu
indeed say:1SG concern:PRES PREP DEM CONJ COMP-HYP here
troche mni **ty gotufki**.
a little less DEM cash
'That's what I am saying: The aim is to spend a little less cash.' (Nitsch 1960: 226)

Here is an example of the use of determiner with a toponym. The importance of this example is that the determiner is not used with the toponym on first mention because the toponym is not a topic. On second mention the toponym is topicalized and is therefore marked by the determiner:

(52) Potym Janka i mnie odwiyzli do Mysłowic.
afterwards Janek:ACC CONJ 1SG:ACC take away:3PL:M to Myslowice.
'Afterwards they took Janek and me to Myslowice.'

F-Cieszynie my sie cały czas nie widzieli, ale do
In-Cieszyn 1PL REFL all time NEG see:3PL:M but to
tyh-Mysłowic my jechali w jednym aucie.
DEM:PL:GEN-Myslowice 1PL travel:3PL:M in one car
'In Cieszyn we did not see each other at all, but to Myslowice we were travelling in the same car.' (Nitsch 1960: 50)

In the following fragment of narrative from a 23-year-old farmhand, presumably illiterate, the first mentions of *gazda* 'rancher' and *pies* 'dog' do not have determiners. The next mention of *pies* 'dog' has a determiner because it is the topic of the next clause, following the conjunction *i*:

(53) a. Roz u jednego **gazdy**, jeden **gazda** mioł **psa**, i **ton** **pies**
once at one rancher one rancher had dog and DEM:M dog
był straśnie mǫdry.
be:M frightfully wise
'Once, at a ranch, a rancher had a dog. And the dog was very wise.'

In the next sentence, the rancher, the dog and the shepherd are all sentence topics and are marked by determiners:

b. **To** **posoł** **temu** **gazdovi** **ten** **pies**.
DEM herd DEM:M:DAT rancher:DAT DEM:M dog
'And the dog was herding sheep for the rancher.

In the next three examples, the arguments *wilk* 'wolf' and *łofce* 'sheep' each occur without the determiner in (53c–d), because this is the first time they are mentioned. Their subsequent topicalization involves a determiner. The dog appears as topic in two consecutive sentences. In each case, the argument marked by the determiner is identifiable through previous mention:

(53) c. I ftoncas hodziły wilki kie on posoł.
and that time go:FREQ:PL:N wolves where 3M herd
'At that time wolves were roaming where he was herding.

d. Psziset **wilk** do **tego** **psa** kcioł mu wziǫś
come:3M:PAST wolf to DEM:GEN dog:GEN want:3M 3M:DAT take
łofce.
sheep
'A wolf came to the dog and wanted to take a sheep from him.' [The dog, who was big and wise, prevented the wolf from taking the sheep.]

e. Tak potem hycił **ton** **wilk** pytać **tego** **psa** o
so after grab DEM:M wolf ask DEM:ACC dog:ACC about
tǫ **łofcǫ**.
DEM:F:ACC sheep:ACC
'So, afterwards, the wolf started to ask the dog about the sheep.' (Nitsch 1960: 116)

We have observed that a noun preceded by the determiner must be different from the noun of the preceding noun phrase (N_1 DET N_2, where N_2 is the topicalized noun). Additionally, a noun may not be marked by a determiner if it immediately follows another mention of the same noun in the structure DET N. This is consistent with the topicalization function of determiners. The rule is thus DET N_1 X × DET N_1, where X is not a noun. This constraint on the use of the proximate determiner is illustrated in the following narrative from a presumably illiterate 80-year-old speaker:

(54) Paśli my woły i **bydło**, sytkwo i śfinia była pszy
tend:PAST:PL 1PL oxen and cattle all and pig be:PAST:F next
tem bydle.
DEM cattle
'We were tending oxen, and cattle, and everything. And there was a pig with the cattle,

a **wilk** przised do nos pastyz'y.
and wolf came to us shepherds
'and a wolf came up to us shepherds.

jak **ton** **wilk** skocuł do **te** **śfinie**
when DEM:M wolf jump:PAST:M to DEM:F pig:ACC
'The wolf jumped at the pig,'

jak **śfinia** skocyła do **tego** **wilka.**
when pig:NOM jump to DEM:M:LOC wolf:
'and the pig jumped at the wolf.'

Jak **wilk** zacon lecieć, to tag **wilk** rycoł
when wolf start run DEM so wolf scream
na **to** **śfinią a** **śfinia** leciała za nim.
at DEM:F pig CONJ pig run after him
'The wolf started to run, he screamed so at the pig and the pig run after him.' (Nitsch 1960: 115)

Thus, while English and Polish both use a determiner before a noun to code the noun as identifiable, the functions of determiners in the two languages are quite different. In Polish, the determiner codes topicalization of a noun that should be identifiable to the hearer, while in English the determiner does not have this topicalization function. The differences between the functions of determiners in the two languages explain the differences in their distribution.

7. Case marking and the domain of reference

The purpose of the present section is to demonstrate that case marking can be used to code referentiality. The mere presence of a rich case marking system in a language does not necessarily mean that case is used to code reference. The fundamental prerequisite for this function is the option of using different cases in the same environment.

In contemporary Russian as in Polish, the second argument of a clause may be marked by either the genitive or the accusative case. However, the semantic functions coded by the two cases appear to differ from Russian to Polish. While the object of the negative clause in Polish must be marked genitive, in Russian either the genitive or the accusative case may be used with the object in the negative clause. It appears that the two cases code different subdomains of referentiality. The accusative case codes a referent that is known, specific, previously mentioned, or present in the environment of speech, while the genitive case codes a referent that is not identifiable in any of these subdomains. Evidence for the proposed hypothesis is provided by natural discourse data in which nouns without any determiners are marked by the genitive or the accusative case in the negative clause:[15]

Genitive case:

(55) Nu, ja **tonkostej** ne znaju.
well, 1SG fine points:GEN NEG know:1SG:PRES
'Well, I do not know any fine points.' (Russian sources)[16]

Cf. the accusative:

(56) Nu, ja eti **tonkosti** ne znaju.
well, 1SG DET fine points:ACC NEG know:1SG:PRES
'Well, I do not know these fine points.' (Russian sources)

Genitive:

(57) A ischezli sovershenno ne ostaviv **sledov** dazhe
CONJ diasppear:PRF:3PL completely NEG leave trace:PL:GEN even
v literature.
in literature
'And they have completely disappeared without a trace, even in the literature.' (Since no traces were left, the traces cannot be referential.) (Russian sources)

Cf. accusative:

(58) A ischezli sovershenno ne ostaviv eti **sledy**
CONJ diasppear:PRF:3PL completely NEG leave DEM trace:PL:ACC even
dazhe v literature.
even in literature
'And they have completely disappeared, without those traces, even in the literature.'

In the following example, the second argument is referential from the point of view of the speaker and the hearer but unknown to the subject of the clause and so is coded by the genitive case:

(59) Tepeŕ nikto **etogo** **slova** ne znaet.
now nobody DEM:GEN word:GEN NEG know:3SG:PRES
'Nowadays nobody knows this word.'

Here is an example of the use of the accusative case to mark reference to a specific activity just mentioned in speech:

(60) Nu ja dazhe ne delala **eto** po formule, a prosto
well I even NEG do this:ACC according formula:DAT but simply
poschitala.
count:PRF:PAST:3F:SG
'I didn't even do it according to a formula, I just simply counted [them].'

In the next example, the accusative case is used on an argument referring to specific grammatical forms of Russian:

(61) Dazhe v piśmax, dazhe v russkix povestäx ne upotrebl'aet
even in letters even in Russian novellas NEG use:3SG
genitivy, upotrebläet prit'azhatel'nye **prilagatel'nye**,
genitive:ACC use:3SG possessive:PL adjective:PL:ACC
'Even in letters, even in Russian novels he does not use genitives, and instead uses possessive adjectives.' (Russian sources)

In some negative clauses, the genitive case is disallowed and the object must be marked accusative. This is the case when the object is a body-part noun and the subject is the whole of which the object is a part. Because the object is specific from the point of view of the subject, the object is marked accusative:

(62) Eti botinki eschcho tem xoroshi, chto oni ne natirajut
DEM:PL shoes:NOM also DEM:INSTR good:PL COMP 3PL NEG scratch
nogi.
legs:ACC
'The other reason why these shoes are good is because they do not chafe the legs.' (Russian sources)

Use of the genitive case marker in this clause would be unacceptable because it would code as non-specified an entity in a construction whose function is to code a specific entity. The shoes, the subject of the clause, are very much referential and specific, being present in the environment of speech:

(63) Eti botinki eschcho tem xoroshi, chto oni ne natirajut
DEM:PL shoes:NOM also DEM:INSTR good:PL COMP 3PL NEG scratch
***nog.**
legs:GEN
'The other reason why these shoes are good is because they do not chafe legs.'

Further evidence for the functions of the two cases in the negative clause is that while either case may be used with a third-person possessor, only the accusative case may be used with a second-person possessor. This is because the genitive case codes an entity unknown to the hearer:

(64) Ja ne uznal ego **glaz/golosa**
1SG NEG recognize:1SG his eyes/voice:GEN
'I did not recognize his eyes/voice.'

(65) Ja ne uznal ego **glaza/golos**
1SG NEG recognize:1SG his eyes/voice:ACC
'I did not recognize his eyes/voice.'

(66) ja ne uznal tvoi/y **glaza/golos**
3SG NEG recognize:1SG your:PL/SG eyes/voice:ACC
'I did not recognize your eyes/voice.'

Russian also allows different case marking on the subject of the verb 'to be' in the negative clause. Here, the subject can be marked referential or non-referential by the use of the nominative versus the genitive case. The following example illustrates the use of both cases to mark the subject of the negative clause in the same utterance. In the first clause the subject is referential, a member of the family, and is coded by the nominative case. In the second clause the subject is inherently non-referential, 'nobody', and is coded by the genitive case:

(67) U nego **nikto** ne byl iz rodnyx **nikogo**
at 3M:LOC nobody:NOM NEG be from relative:PL:GEN nobody:GEN
ne bylo.
NEG be
'Not a single relative visited him, there was nobody.' (Russian sources)

Proper names are inherently referential and are usually coded by the nominative case in the negative clause. A proper name marked nominative cannot be used with a determiner that explicitly codes the referent as unknown:

(68) Nata ne mozhet zdes' byt' *nekij **Semionov**?
Nata, NEG can:3SG here be some:NOM Semionov:NOM
'Nata, isn't there a Semionov around here?'

If the proper name is modified by a determiner that makes the name non-specific, the genitive rather than the nominative case must be used:

(69) Nata ne bylo li zdes' nekayego **Semionova**?
Nata, NEG be Q here some:GEN Semionov:GEN
'Nata, wasn't there a fellow named Semionov around here?'

In the negative clause, proper names in object function in Russian are marked by the genitive case.

8. A case study of systems interaction in reference: Mina

In this section we provide evidence for the existence in Mina, a Central Chadic language, of various subdomains in the domain of reference by illustrating constraints on the co-occurrence of various types of determiners. Markers of some subdomains may co-occur with markers of other subdomains, and some markers may co-occur with possessive pronouns. If two determiners may co-occur, this is evidence that they belong to two different subdomains. If two determiners belong to the same subdomain, they will not co-occur. Mina has the following subdomains within the domain of reference: deixis; switch reference; known; deduced; and remote previous mention. We provide evidence for the existence of each of the proposed subdomains and illustrate the interactions among coding means in these subdomains.

8.1. Deixis

Mina appears to have only one deictic marker, *wà*, whose phrase-final forms *wàcín* or *wècin* (when vowel harmony applied) and *wàhín*, are used interchangeably. All natural language data indicate that this marker has the function of coding proximate deixis (all data from Frajzyngier et al. Ms.):

(70) **Wècín** kújì.
DEM Kuji
'This is [a story of] Kuji.' (The story of Kuji follows.)

(71) **Wàcín** àládà tə́ kúlí-yíì wàcíŋ tók zà.
DEM custom (Hausa) GEN kuli-PL DEM finish AUX
'That is the tradition of the kuli. It [the story] has ended.'

(72) Hà ndí dzán-á nám skə̀n mə̀ná **wà** tíkì.
2SG HAB find-OBJ 1DU thing like DEM where
'Where do you find us things like this?"'

8.2. The category 'known'

The deictic marker *wà* and its phrase-final form *wàcín/wàhín* may be used to mark a referent that is one of the main topics of paragraph, a story, or a discourse. The function of the deictic marker in this case is to indicate that the referent is to be treated as a known entity, regardless of whether the hearer actually knows the referent. The protagonist of a story often is introduced with the marker *wà*, as in these opening lines of two different stories:

(73) **Hìd-yíì wà** í tə̀tə̀ màkáɗ.
man-PL DEM 3PL 3PL three
'There were these three men.'

(74) **Hìdè wècín** í tə̀tə̀ nfáɗ.
man DEM 3PL 3PL four
'There were these four men.'

In the following fragment, the first mention of noun *kə̀ɗə́m* 'calabash' is not accompanied by *wà* or any other determiner. Later in the narrative the noun 'calabash' is marked by *wà*, indicating that the referent for this noun is to be treated as a known entity:

(75) À à dzàn-á **kəɗə́m**.
ah 3SG find-GO calabash
'She found a calabash.'

(76) Àa ndə ɓə̀t-à nòk skú syì á vàŋgáy.
ah go get-OBJ 1PL NEG COM PRED how
'Ah, go bring it to us, otherwise what can we do?'

(77) À zá hí ɮ-ə́ŋ hìdì.
3SG COMP 2PL send-3SG man
'He [the man] said, "Send somebody."'

(78) ɮə́ŋ íɮə́ŋ hìd-yíì ndə́ɓə̀t í ɓə̀t-á-ŋ **kəɗə́m** **wàcíŋ** dà
send 3PL send man-PL go get 3PL get-OBJ-3SG calabash DEM bring
í dà-há-w.
3PL bring-GO-3SG
'They sent some people and they went and got the calabash for him and brought it.'

(79) Wà kə́ lù-á-ŋ n kəɗə́m tə́ ží vàŋgáy bàháman.
but INF say-OBJ-3SG PREP calabash GEN then how Bahaman
'What do you say to the calabash, Bahaman?'

8.3. The domain of deduced referent

Mina has a subdomain of 'deduced' reference that is marked by the form *tá* (phrase-internal form *tə́*; phrase-final form *táŋ*). This marker instructs the hearer to identify the referent through a process of deduction using knowledge from various domains, including the hearer's cognitive system, the speech environment and previous discourse. The form *tá* may be the only component of a noun phrase or it may modify another noun or a quantifier.

One piece of evidence for the proposed function of the marker *tá* is that its antecedent need not have been mentioned in discourse. In fact, the presence of *tá* explicitly tells the hearer that the referent is not the noun marked by *tá* but some other referent associated with that noun. In the last line of the following fragment, *tá* follows the noun *báy* 'chief', which has been mentioned several times in the preceding discourse. However, the form *tá* does not identify the chief but rather the chief's court, an entity that has not been mentioned in discourse at all:

(80) **Báy** zá ngwáy bàhámàn bákà bá dzàn-á nòk mí.
chief COMP people Bahaman today still find-OBJ 1PL what
'The chief said, "People, what else did Bahaman find for us today?"'

(81) Hí ndə̀ lù-á-ŋ mə́ ndà-hà.
2PL go say-OBJ-3SG SUBJ go-GO
' "Go tell him to come here." '

(82) Ndá yà í y-ù.
go:GO call 3PL call-3SG
'One went to call him.'

(83) Tíl á nd-á ár **báy tàŋ**.
go 3SG go-GO PREP chief DEM
'He went to the chief's [court].'

In the next example, the Koran is the object of the first clause. The meaning of the second sentence is as shown in the English translation. However, the only overt object marker in the second sentence is the marker *táŋ*. Because the reduplication of the verb *náz* 'throw' indicates a repeated action, the antecedent of *táŋ* cannot be the Koran itself but must be some plural object associated with the Koran. This object can only be the pages of the Koran, even though the pages themselves have not been overtly mentioned. The use of *tá* thus instructs the hearer to deduce the referent for the object:

(84) ɓə̀t á ɓə̀t **déftèr** ngə̀n pàts.
take 3SG take Koran (Fula) 3SG took
'He took his Koran.
Ntá náz náz náz náz á náz **táŋ** á nə̀ yə̀m wàhíŋ.
one throw throw throw throw 3SG throw DEM PREP PREP water DEM
'He took one [page] after another and threw them upon the water.'

Here is another example in which the form *táŋ* functions as the head of a noun phrase, the referent for which does not overtly occur anywhere but must be deduced from the first part of the sentence:

(85) À zá ngùl-yíì ghlámbáy tə́ màcíŋ lù-á-ŋ mə̀k.
3SG COMP husband-PL stick GEN DEM say-OBJ-3SG would you
'She said, "My husband, this stick, say to it,

(86) Ghlámbáy nɗ-á-k gí syì à n kə̀ ɗál-á **táŋ**.
stick hit-OBJ-1SG POL COM 3SG PREP INF do-OBJ:2SG DEM
"Stick, hit me,' and it will do it to you.'"

Another piece of evidence for the proposed function of the form *tá* is that it can co-occur with the marker *wà*, whose function is to code a known entity. Here as elsewhere, *tà* instructs the hearer to associate the referent with some other entity:

(87) Zàgíy tíl ndə̀ ɓə̀t í ɓə̀t-áhà-w gáɗ bə̀ **wàl**
courtiers (Fula) go go take 3PL take-GO-3SG push with woman
wà tàŋ.
DEM DEM
'The courtiers went and brought it [the calabash] with the woman [the one associated with the calabash].'

Another piece of evidence for the proposed hypothesis is provided by the fact that the form *tá*, unlike the form *wà*, can co-occur with possessive pronouns to instruct the hearer to interpret the marked noun in connection with some other element. The following is the tail end of a fragment in which the husband has been attempting to find out where his wife is going. The phrase *wàl ngə̀n* 'his wife' is followed by *táŋ*, leading the hearer to interpret the referent not simply as 'the wife' but as 'the wife after her shoes had been filled with ashes':

(88) Híhldìɓ híhldìɓ á híhldìɓ-é-ŋ kràp wàhíŋ.
sew sew 3SG sew-OBJ-3SG shoe DEM
'He sewed and sewed and sewed her the shoes.'

(89) Bə̀k bə̀k á bə̀k-á-ŋ ɓə̀ wírnjìk kə́ nə̀ mə̀ŋ.
fill fill 3SG fill-OBJ-3SG ASSC ash AFF PREP LOC.ANAPH
'He filled them with ashes.'

(90) Séy **wàl ngə̀n táŋ** á nd-rə̀ wàcín syì wírnjìk ɗíy-à bə̀k-áhà
so wife 3SG DEM 3SG go-D.HAB DEM COM ash start-GO pour-GO
cìɗé cìɗé cìɗé cìɗé à kə̀tə́f.
pile pile pile pile PREP road
'As his wife went along, ashes kept pouring out in little piles along the road.'

8.4. Remote previous mention

The category of remote previous mention in Mina is coded by the form *nákáhà*, whose phrase-internal variant is *nákà*. The form *nákáhà* can function as the modifier of a noun or as the head of a noun phrase. It is used when a large number of potential referents intervene between the antecedent and the anaphor.

Evidence that the form *nákáhà* does not code deixis is that it may occur with nouns not present in the speech environment. Evidence that the form codes previous mention rather than the category 'known' is provided by the fact that *nákáhà* can co-occur with possessive pronouns, which mark a noun as known. In the following fragment, the possessive phrase *wàl ngə̀n* 'his wife' was last mentioned by the narrator four sentences earlier. Several other potential referents, including the husband, the stick, and the footprints, have intervened, so *wàl ngə̀n* next occurs with the remote previous mention marker:

(91) Ngàzù wá tú wàl nàŋ ngàzù wá tú wàl nàŋ ngàzù wá tú wàl nàŋ.
foot DEM GEN wife 1SG foot DEM GEN wife 1SG foot DEM GEN wife 1SG
'That is my wife's foot, that is my wife's foot, that is my wife's foot.'

(92) Žèɓ žèɓ á žèɓ-ù ndə̀ dzáŋ **wàl ngə̀n nákáhà**.
follow follow 3SG follow-3SG go find wife 3SG REM
'He followed and followed and found his wife.'

A noun marked by the remote previous mention marker also may be marked 'known' by the marker *wà*. The following sentence occurs in a story in which the husband has killed a guinea fowl, which is the topic of the paragraph:

(93) Ndá zə̀m zə̀m **nákà** **wà zá**.
go eat eat REM.ANAPH DEM AUX
'They returned and ate that one [i.e. the guinea fowl that the man had killed].'

Similarly, in a story about a lost sesame seed, the remote previous mention marker is followed by the marker of the category 'known':

(94) Dzàŋ á dzàn-á mə̀ tə́ gwíɗín **nákà wèhíŋ**.
find 3SG find-GO REL GEN single DEM DEM
'He found that one [the lost sesame seed].'

8.5. Switch reference through special pronouns

Switch reference for subject in Mina is coded by the use of a special third-person pronoun. Mina has two third person pronouns. The pronoun *à* is the default form; it occurs in pragmatically neutral clauses in the indicative affirmative and negative moods:

(95) ɓə̀t á ɓə̀t déftèr ngə̀n.
take 3SG take Koran (Fula) 3SG
'He took out his Koran.'

The form *mbí* (phrase-internal form *mbə́*; phrase-final *form mbə́ŋ*), glossed ANAPH for 'anaphor', is an independent pronoun that always functions as the head of a noun phrase, though it may be preceded by a preposition. The antecedent of *mbí* may be a noun or a proposition. The function of the form *mbí* is to code switch reference to a previously mentioned entity:

(96) Báy wílè á dámù **mbí** nd-á ɓə̀t wə̀dá.
chief still PRED bush ANAPH go-GO eat food
'The chief$_i$ is still in the bush. He$_j$ came to take the food.'

(97) Báy zá gár kà zá **mbə́** gár ábə nd-á ngə̀ŋ.
chief COMP leave AFF be ANAPH stand ASSC go-GO 3SG
'The chief$_i$ said, get out of here. He$_j$ stood up and went back.'

(98) À-ndə̀ r skù **mbí** mì žèɓér tə́ tkóŋ.
3SG-go D.HAB NEG ANAPH REL follow GEN 2SG
'If it does not work, she should follow your [advice].'

(99) káf yà í yà-há-ú ɓə̀t í ɓə̀t zà dzáŋ kə́ á bíŋ
morning call 3PL call-GO-3SG take 3PL take AUX close AFF PREP room
'He$_i$ was called in the morning, he$_i$ was locked in a room.

Tíl á dámù.
leave PREP bush
'He$_j$ [the one who had locked the door] went into the bush.

Séy **mbə́ŋ** ɓə̀t nèwén tə́ díndèm díyà ɓám.
SO ANAPH take salt GEN sweet start eat
'He$_i$ [the one who was locked in] took the sugar and started eating.'

The phrase-final form of the anaphor, i.e. the form with the suffix *-n*, codes the anaphor as topicalized. Like other topicalized nominal subjects, the topicalized anaphor is followed by a coreferential subject pronoun:

(100) Séy pá í vál-á-ŋ jénì.
so give 3pl give-obj-3sg axe
'So, they gave him an axe.

Mbéŋ à tìk-é tàlàŋ káyàk kə jénì.
anaph 3sg tilt-go head earth prep axe
'He inclined his head because of the axe'

(101) Tíl ngə̀n á wtá ván gə̀ɮ gə̀ɮ báy á kətəf **mbə́n** zə́m wə̀də́
leave 3sg pred home rain hit hit chief prep road anaph eat food
tók ván tók zà.
finish rain finish be
'When he$_i$ returned home, the rain$_j$ hit the chief on the road. He$_i$ finished eating and the rain also finished.'

(102) Tséy wə̀ží báy-yíì zá vl-á nènéŋ **mbéŋ** à zá
so children-pl chief-pl comp give-obj 1pl.excl anaph 3sg comp
gwáɗ á bíŋ kàcíŋ.
plenty prep room dem
'The children of the chief said: give [it] to us. He said: there is plenty here in the room.'

The anaphor *mbí* is not marked for number and can refer to either a singular or a plural referent. The referent may actually follow the anaphor:

(103) Báy ábə̀ nd-á ngə̀n séy **mbéŋ gə̀míɮìɗ-yíi** mə̀ nd-á-y zà kə̀
chief assc go-go 3sg so anaph monkey-pl rel go-go-stat be inf
ɓám pày wàcíŋ.
eat tree dem
'The chief went back. Then, the monkeys came to eat the fruit of that tree.'

8.6. Summary of reference coding in Mina

The marker *wà* following a noun codes the noun either for proximate deixis or as belonging to the category 'known'. The form *tá*, which may follow a noun or may serve as the head of a noun phrase, instructs the hearer to deduce the referent either from common knowledge or from the preceding discourse. The form *nákáhà*, when occurring alone or after a noun, codes remote previous mention.

Evidence for the functions of these markers comes in part from co-occurrence restrictions. The form *wà* cannot co-occur with a possessive pronouns, since both *wà* and the possessive construction serve to mark a noun as known. The markers *tá* and *nákáhà* can occur with the possessive construction because these markers code different domains. The remote mention marker *nákáhà* can co-occur with *wà* to code both remote mention and and the category 'known'. The form *wà* may be followed by *tà* to code a referent that is both known and to be deduced. The form *nákáhà* cannot be followed by the form *tá*, because a noun that is marked as having been mentioned previously need not be deduced. The functions of the various forms in Mina, and their co-occurrence restrictions, provide further support for the existence of the postulated functional subdomains within the domain of reference.

9. Conclusions

The coding of reference instructs the hearer to seek the identity of a referent in one or more subdomains within the domain of reference. We have demonstrated that in order to understand the referential function of a coding means in a given language it is necessary to examine the entire system of reference coding in that language. Different languages code different subdomains, and the same type of coding means may code a different subdomain from one language to the next. The subdomain of deixis may exist in all languages, but other domains appear to be less widespread. In this chapter we have described the domains of previous mention, with its possible subdomains of proximate and remote mention; the domain of the known referent; the domain of the deduced referent; the domains of coreference and switch reference; the domains *de dicto* and *de re*; and the domain of definiteness. Describing reference coding by examining language-specific subdomains allows us to explain why certain determiners can co-occur in some languages but cannot co-occur in others.

CHAPTER 12

Conclusions, implications, and open questions

1. Introduction

The present work has implications for (1) the theory of the functions of phonology; (2) the theory of the organization of the lexicon (3) the theory of linear order as a coding means; (4) the phrase structure theory; (5) the methodology of discovering the function of a linguistic form; and (6) the theory of grammaticalization. The work also contributes to a better understanding of the category of agreement, the functions of matrix clause coding, the functions of nominal classification, and the organization of the reference system. Since most of these elements have been described in the body of the work, we provide here only brief summaries of the most important findings and conclusions. With respect to the theory of grammaticalization, which has not been touched in the body of the work, we provide a more complete discussion.

2. The functions of phonology

The well-known functions of phonological systems include coding specific semantic functions, such as the interrogative and other modalities, and enabling differentiation among lexical items and grammatical morphemes, and various functions in conversations, allowing the interaction between the speaker and hearer, as postulated by Local et al. (1986). To these functions of phonology we add that of indicating the internal organization of an utterance. Specifically, phonology indicates which elements in a sequence form a single constituent and which belong to different constituents. Phonology thus enables the interpretation of various elements of the utterance in connection with other elements. This is the function of final vowel retention and vowel deletion in several Chadic languages; of the nasal variant of pronouns after prepositions in Polish; and of consonant alternation in Welsh.

3. The organization of the lexicon

The lexicon of a given language is organized according to the needs of the fundamental functional domains encoded in the grammar of that language. In a language that has grammaticalized the domain of the proposition, for example, one would expect to find a distinction between the functions of predicate and argument, as realized through the lexical categories verb and noun. In a language organized around the notions of topic and comment, one would expect to find some formal indicators of these two categories. If a language has different domains for the modification of nouns and verbs, one expects to find the categories adjective and adverb, as is the case in many Indo-European languages. A language may have a single functional category for the modification of both nouns and verbs. This is the case in many Chadic languages, where the modifiers of nouns and modifiers of verbs have the same form.

The set of lexical categories is theoretically open, and different languages have different sets of lexical categories. Such differences reflect the functional domains encoded in different grammatical systems.

4. Implications for linear order as a coding means

The present work formulates the necessary prerequisites for coding through linear order, viz. the existence and nature of the reference point. Coding possibilities are severely constrained when linear order is the only means of coding available. A language with inflectional as well as linear order coding offers far more coding possibilities, in part because the presence of inflectional markers allows for more lexical categories to function as reference points. It remains an open question whether there are default linear orders in languages with inflectional coding and how these may be discovered.

5. Implications for phrase structure rules

Since Frege 1879, and perhaps earlier, the language of mathematical logic has relied on the principle of well-formedness. This principle was at the basis of early transformational grammar and survives today in the theory of phrase structure rules. These rules have been formulated in terms of the arrangement of formal categories within some syntactic unit such as phrase, clause, sentence. In our approach there is no place for phrase-structure rules as a means of forming structures. Instead, the principle of well-formedness refers to the principle of functional transparency, restated here:

1. Every utterance must have a transparent function within the discourse.
2. Every constituent must have a transparent function within the utterance.

Transparency refers to the functional domains coded through grammatical means in the language rather than to the hearer's need to understand the role of the elements in some real world. If a language codes functional transparency through linear order, specifically juxtaposition, the well-formedness principle as postulated above may well be stated in terms resembling phrase-structure rules. But even here the similarity is only apparent, since what we have is the means of coding a given function rather than a means of forming a given structure. But if a language assures well-formedness through a variety of means, such as inflection on nouns and verbs, phonological means, and linear order, well-formedness can be stated in terms of phrase-structure rules only for those functions that are coded by linear order alone.

6. Methodology regarding the function of linguistic form

Traditional semantics and formal semantics take the meaning of a linguistic form to be something intuitively known. Accordingly, efforts within these frameworks have been directed towards representing meaning in such a way that a given representation will be interpreted in the same way by any reader familiar with the representation system.

Within the proposed framework, a prerequisite to the representation of meaning is the discovery of the meaning of a linguistic form. This discovery cannot be based, as it has been traditionally, on the connection between a linguistic form and inferences about a segment of extra-linguistic reality, but rather on the relationships among the linguistic forms of a given language. The discovery of these relationships must be based on facts concerning the co-occurrence of various forms. If two forms can co-occur, they belong to different functional domains. If two forms cannot co-occur, they belong to the same functional domain. Once the functional domain of a given form has been established, one must establish the role of that form within a given functional domains. Once this role has been discovered, the description of the function of the form is complete.

The relationship between language and communication, i.e. the explanation for how the speaker communicates with the hearer, is that the hearer knows the functional domains of the language of interaction and can reconstruct all of the functions being communicated. The relationship between these functions and any reality is at best oblique, i.e. there is no one to one relationship between any linguistic form and a specific element of the reality.

7. Implications for the theory of language evolution

Implications for the theory of language evolution pertain to two related aspects: (1) motivation for grammaticalization and (2) restructuring of the grammatical system.

7.1. Motivation for grammaticalization

The term 'grammaticalization' as used in the present work refers to the emergence of grammatical structures in general rather than to the narrowly understood emergence of grammatical morphemes from lexical items. Hopper and Traugott (1993) give a summary of proposed motivations for grammaticalization, including various aspects of speaker-hearer relations, economy, simplification, communicative need, routinization, and conventionalization of implicatures. Heine, Claudi and Hünnemeyer (1991) attribute one of the main motivations of grammaticalization to human creativity and propose metaphor as the main force in grammaticalization.

The principle of communicative need is not sufficient in itself to account for the emergence of specific grammatical constructions or morphemes. In particular, communicative need does not account for the existence of different grammatical constructions and for the fact that such constructions code different functions. Communicative need may be useful for explaining similarities between languages, but it does not provide a viable explanation for their differences. To the motivations that have been proposed so far, we add the principle of functional transparency.

The principle of functional transparency is not only the chief motivation in the development of grammatical systems but also provides the motivation for the continuing evolution of syntactic structures. This is because the addition of any element to an utterance requires coding means that make the function of that element transparent. This transparency may be inherent to the lexical form itself, as the inherent function of a verb is that of predicate and the inherent function of a noun is that of argument, or it may be marked by any of various coding means.

The role of the principle of functional transparency in the evolution of syntactic structures is not teleological in the sense of being motivated by the language's tendency to achieve some stage in its development. The role of functional transparency also is not as arbitrary or difficult to define as the principles of economy, simplification, or creativity.

Evidence for the existence of the principle of functional transparency is provided by the phenomena involved in language change. If phonological or other changes result in the elimination of some coding means in the language, there are two possible outcomes: (1) the functions coded by that means will cease to exist in the language; or (2) some other coding means will take over the functions previously coded by the no longer present coding means. The first case is widely attested in languages of the world. Klemensiewicz et al. (1965) is a systematic study of lost grammatical constructions in Polish.

The second case, in which the functions of one coding means are taken over by another coding means, is exemplified by the coding of grammatical relations through linear order after phonological changes have led to the elimination of nominal and/or verbal inflection. Cases in point are English and Palestinian Arabic, both of which at one stage had case inflection on nouns and a rich system of inflection for person and number on verbs. As a result of phonological changes affecting all classes of morphemes, English came to rely solely on linear order to code relations between the predicate and arguments. Palestinian Arabic has retained the coding of person, gender, and number on the verb but has completely lost nominal inflection, and it too relies on word order to code relationship between the verb and arguments.

Finally, synchronic evidence for the proposed motivation for grammaticalization comes from Polish. In the class of neutral nouns, the distinction between nominative and accusative case has been neutralized for both singular and plural nouns. In a clause containing two such arguments, the relationship between the arguments and the predicate is coded through the linear order SVO.

7.2. Restructuring of grammatical systems

The restructuring of a grammatical system is also very much linked with the principle of functional transparency. The process of grammaticalization never starts *ex nihilo*; in any language at any stage there is a certain grammatical system consisting of some formal means that enable the realization of some pragmatic, semantic or discourse functions. In the process of language change, a formal means may be affected to the extent that it cannot carry the functions that it used to carry. The language is faced with either losing these functions or grammaticalizing new means to carry them. Whether a given formal means is replaced by another means depends very much on the usefulness of the means for the whole system of the language. If the function carried by a formal means is very narrow, the means carrying this function may not be replaced. If the function is very broad or feeds into other functions, it will very likely be replaced by other means. We first illustrate the case of a grammatical means that has been lost and has not been replaced.

The grammatical systems of many Indo-European languages used to code the category 'dual' on both nouns and verbs. Some Polish dialects still have dual marking in the verbal system, but literary Polish has lost the category entirely. The concept of 'dual' can be conveyed relatively easily through the use of the numeral 'two', if necessary. No other means of coding the dual has been grammaticalized. A similar situation obtains in many other Indo-European languages.

Consider now the gender system in French. The language at one time had a system of gender marking on nouns, markers that are still fully present in Latin. The loss of final vowels and the weakening of final consonants in French resulted in the loss of these gender markers. According to Jensen (1990), French began using definite and indefinite articles in the 11th century. Latin does not have articles. One may use the numeral 'one' or a demonstrative to code such categories as 'unknown', 'referential', 'specific', or 'one of a group', but the use of such forms in Latin is not obligatory. What could have been the motivation for the development of definite and indefinite articles in French, when Latin existed without such articles? It is likely that definite articles in French replaced gender markers, thereby assuming the function of overtly marking each noun for gender. The motivation for the development of gender markers, in turn, was to enable the use of a system of reference using such gender-marked forms as *il* and *elle* and, in written French, *ils* and *elles*. The motivation for the grammaticalization of articles in German was probably very similar. Thus, a language may replace one formal means with another in order to continue coding a major function in the language, in this case the coding of reference in discourse.

It cannot be predicted which coding means will replace another, and similar coding means may develop in different languages for very different reasons. The motivation for the development of English definite and indefinite articles, superficially similar to articles in French and German, has yet to be explained. The principles of functional transparency and systems interaction provide a basis for seeking explanations for this and other phenomena in the development of grammatical systems.

Notes

1. There are many reasons why a speaker would produce a form not attested in natural discourse. Chief among these is that the speaker may simply translate a form from the language of interaction between the linguist and the native speaker. It also often happens that the speaker somehow considers the forms of the language of the interaction to represent a better model and tries to provide forms that fit that model as closely as possible. A linguist can produce forms not attested in his/her native language while trying to test the limits of grammaticality. Data obtained in this way cannot serve as a basis for linguistic analysis.

2. Data from the London–Lund Corpus of spoken English are given in the form in which they appear in the corpus, including the numbering system adopted there. This allows the reader to check the larger context in the corpus and also to see the change of speaker notation. The letters A and B and a and b indicate two different speakers. Later in this work, the London–Lund Corpus is referenced in examples as (LLC).

3. Polish examples marked as (Sources) come from an electronic version of sources to Kurcz et al. (1990), *Słownik frekwencyjny współczesnej polszczyzny* (Polish Frequentative Dictionary). We are very grateful to Zygmunt Saloni for providing us with an electronic copy of the sources, which made the search for various examples so much easier.

4. The noun *gnat* 'large bone' at one time was used metaphorically to mean 'handgun'.

5. Sources for the languages in the table are given in references.

6. Those few exceptions involving the use of the feminine gender to refer to countries and to ships do not contradict the postulated productive system.

7. The a.c.i. construction has often been considered an instance of raising (cf. Pepicello 1977).

8. Givón (1990) rightly points out how little space Postal (1974) devotes to the functions of raising. Dik (1979) discusses only how raising can be incorporated into his version of functional grammar; he does not discuss the functions of raising.

9. Similarly, in Modern Hebrew the subject may be encoded in the embedded clause and as a suffix to the complementizer (Immanuel Barshi, p.c.).

10. The proposed hypothesis concerns only the inflectional coding of the dative case. In some languages the indirect object is coded by a preposition, and this preposition may also be used to code the direct object under certain conditions. This is the case of the Spanish preposition *a*.

11. Why body-part terms and kinship terms can occur without a possessor in Polish but not in English is a fundamental question concerning the forms of noun phrases in various languages and deserves separate study.

12. The notion of location was suggested by Vera Podlesskaya.

13. Written sources are texts transcribed by Adrian Edwards. These texts do not have tonal notation. Other texts are transcribed by Zygmunt Frajzyngier and Eric Johnston.

14. For the notion of 'default' with respect to reference, cf. Comrie (1998).

15. We are grateful to Valentin and Olga Okorokov for grammaticality judgments concerning various clauses in Russian.

16. Russian examples are taken from an electronic corpus of spoken contemporary Russian.

References

Agud, Ana. 1980. *Historia y teoria de los casos*. Madrid: Gredos.

Aikhenwald, Aleksandra. 2000. *Classifiers*. Oxford: Oxford University Press.

Aikhenvald, Alexandra Y., R.M.W Dixon, and Masayuki Onishi (eds). 2001. *Non-canonical marking of subjects and objects*. Amsterdam/Philadelphia: Benjamins.

Armbruster, Hubert Charles. 1960. *Dongolese Nubian. A grammar*. Cambridge: The University Press.

Awbery, G.M. 1976. *The syntax of Welsh*. Cambridge: Cambridge University Press.

Bacz, Barbara. 1989. Do cases define? On expressing the definite/indefinite opposition in Polish. Linguistic Association of Canada and the United States (*LACUS*) *Forum* 16: 81–9.

Baker, Mark C. 1988. *Incorporation: A theory of grammatical function change*. Chicago: University of Chicago Press.

Barlow, Michael. 1992. *A situated theory of agreement*. New York: Garland.

Barnes, Janet. 1986. Evidentials in the Tuyuca verb. *International Journal of American Linguistic* 50: 255–71.

Barreteau, Daniel. 1988. *Description du Mofu-Gudur* vols. 1 & 2. Paris: ORSTOM.

Barreteau, Daniel, and Yves le Bléis. 1990. *Lexique Mafa*. Paris: Geuthner and ORSTOM.

Beyer, Stephan V. 1992. *The classical Tibetan language*. Albany, N.Y.: State University of New York Press.

Bhat, D.N.S. 1994. *The adjectival category. Criteria for differentiation and identification*. Amsterdam/Philadelphia: Benjamins.

Bills, Garland D., Bernardo Vallejo C., and Rudolph C. Troike. 1969. *Introduction to spoken Bolivian Quechua*. Austin and London: University of Texas Press.

Blake, Barry J. 1995. *Case*. Cambridge: Cambridge University Press.

Bok-Bennema, Reineke. 1991. *Case and agreement in Inuit*. Berlin/New York: Foris.

Bolkestein, A. Machtelt. 1976a. The relation between form and meaning of Latin subordinate clauses governed by *verba dicendi*. *Mnemosyne* 29.2: 55–175 and *Mnemosyne* 29.3: 68–300.

Bolkestein, A. Machtelt. 1976b. A.c.i.-and *ut*-clauses with *verba dicendi* in Latin. *Glotta* 54.1/2 :63–291.

Bolkestein, A. Machtelt. 1977. Part II. The difference between free and obligatory *ut*-clauses. *Glotta* 55.1/2: 231–50.

Bolkestein, A. Machtelt. 1979. Subject-to-object raising in Latin? *Lingua* 48: 5–34.

Boniewicz, Alina. 1982. Properties of raised constructions in English and Polish. *Papers and Studies in Contrastive Linguistics* 15: 5–110.

Borsley, Robert D., and Ian Roberts 1996. *The syntax of Celtic languages*. Cambridge: Cambridge University Press.

Bosch, Peter. 1983. *Agreement and anaphora: A study of the role of pronouns in syntax and discourse*. London/New York: Academic Press.

Chao, Yuen Ren. 1968. *A grammar of spoken Chinese*. Berkeley: University of California Press.

Chomsky, Noam. 1992. *A minimalist program for linguistic theory*. Cambridge, Mass.: MIT Occasional Papers in Linguistics 1.

Chomsky, Noam. 1995. *The minimalist program*. Cambridge, Mass.: MIT Press.
Chomsky, Noam. 2000. *The architecture of language*. New Delhi: Oxford University Press.
Clements, George N. 1975. The logophoric pronoun in Ewe: Its role in discourse. *Journal of West African Languages* 10.141–77.
Cohen, Albert 1965 (1938). *Mangeclous*. Paris: Gallimard.
Cohen, Marcel. 1936 (1970). *Grammaire de language amharique*. Paris: Klincksieck.
Comrie, Bernard. 1998. Reference tracking: Description and explanation. *Sprachtypologie und Universalienforschung (STUF)* 51.1:335–46.
Corbett, Greville. 1991. *Gender*. Cambridge: Cambridge University Press.
Corbett, Greville. 2000. *Number*. Cambridge: Cambridge University Press.
Corbett, Greville. 2001. Agreement: Canonical instances and the extent of the phenomenon. In: Geert Booij, Janet DeCesaris, Angela Ralli, and Sergio Scalise, eds, *Studies in theoretical morphology: Selected papers from the Third Mediterranean Morphology Meeting*, Barcelona, 2001.
Craig, Colette. 1986. Introduction. In: Colette Craig, ed., *Noun classes and categorization*. Amsterdam/Philadelphia: Benjamins, 1–10.
Croft, William. 2000. Parts of speech as language universals and language-particular categories. In: Petra Vogel and Bernard Comrie, eds, *Approaches to the Typology of Word Classes*. Berlin: Mouton de Gruyter, 65–102.
Croft, William. 2001. *Radical construction grammar: Syntactic representation in typological perspective*. Oxford: Oxford University Press.
Dąbrowska, Ewa. 1997. *Cognitive semantics and the Polish dative*. Berlin/New York: Mouton de Gruyter.
Davies, William D. 1986. *Choctaw verb agreement and universal grammar*. Dordrecht/Boston: Reidel.
de Jong, Daan. 1990. The syntax-phonology interface and French liaison. *Linguistics* 28:57–88.
Demuth, Katherine. 2000. Bantu noun class systems: Loan word and acquisition evidence. In: Gunter Senft, ed., *Systems of nominal classification*. Cambridge/New York: Cambridge University Press.
Denny, J. Peter. (1986). The semantic role of noun classifiers. In: Colette Craig, ed., *Noun classes and categorization*, 297–308. Amsterdam/ Philadelphia: Benjamins.
Diessel, Holger. 1999. *Demonstratives. Form, function, and grammaticalization*. Amsterdam/ Philadelphia: Benjamins.
Dik, Simon. 1979. Raising in a functional grammar. *Lingua* 47:119–40.
Dik, Simon C. 1989. *The theory of functional grammar*. Dordrecht: Foris.
Dimmendaal, Gerrit Jan. 1983. *The Turkana language*. Dordrecht: Foris.
Dixon, R.M.W. 1977. Where have all the adjectives gone? *Studies in Language* 1.1:19–80.
Dixon, R.M.W. 2000. A-constructions and O-constructions in Jarawara. *International Journal of American Linguistics* 66.1:22–56.
Downing, Pamela. 1996. *Numeral classifier systems: The case of Japanese*. Amsterdam/ Philadelphia: Benjamins.
Downing, Pamela, and Michael Noonan, eds 1995. *Word order in discourse*. Amsterdam/ Philadelphia: Benjamins.
Dryer, Matthew. 1992. The Greenbergian word order correlations. *Language* 68.1:81–138.
DuBois, John. 1987. The discourse basis of ergativity. *Language* 63.4:805–55.

Ebert, Karen. 1971. *Referenz, Sprachsituation und die bestimmten Artikel in einem nordfriesischen Dialekt*. Bredstedt: Nordfriisk Instituut, Studien und Materialen 4.

Edgar, John. 1989. *A Masalit grammar*. *Sprache und Oralität in Afrika* 3. Berlin: Reimer.

Elliott, W. Neil. 1981. *Grammatical number*. Ph.D. dissertation, City University of New York. Ann Arbor, Mich.: University Microfilms International.

Ernout, Alfred, and François Thomas. 1972. *Syntaxe latine*. Paris: Klincksieck.

Evans, Nicholas. 2000. Kinship verbs. In: Petra Vogel and Bernard Comrie, eds, *Approaches to the typology of word classes*. Berlin/New York: Mouton de Gruter, 103–72.

Frajzyngier, Zygmunt. 1965. An analysis of intensive forms in Hausa verbs. *Rocznik Orientalistyczny* 29.2: 31–51.

Frajzyngier, Zygmunt. 1977. The plural in Chadic. In Paul Newman and Roxanna Ma Newman, eds, *Papers in Chadic linguistics*. Leiden: Afrika-Studiecentrum, 37–56.

Frajzyngier, Zygmunt. 1985a. 'Causative' and 'benefactive' in Chadic. *Afrika und Übersee* 68: 23–42.

Frajzyngier, Zygmunt. 1985b. Ergativity, number, and agreement. In: Mary Niepokuj, Mary VanClay, Vassiliki Nikiforidou, and Deborah Feder, eds, *Proceedings of the eleventh annual meeting of the Berkeley Linguistic Society*, 96–106.

Frajzyngier, Zygmunt. 1985c. Logophoric systems in Chadic. *Journal of African Languages and Linguistics* 7: 23–37.

Frajzyngier, Zygmunt. 1985d. Truth and the indicative sentence. *Studies in Language* 9.2: 243–54.

Frajzyngier, Zygmunt. 1986. Propositional characterization of categories. In: Scott DeLancey and Russell S. Tomlin, eds, *Proceedings of the first Annual Meeting of the Pacific Linguistic Conference*, 108–19.

Frajzyngier, Zygmunt. 1988. Semantic determinants of syntactic frames. In: Herrmann Jungraithmayr, and Henry Tourneux, eds, *Etudes Tchadiques, transitivité et diathèse*. Paris: Geuthner, 97–116.

Frajzyngier, Zygmunt. 1989a. *A grammar of Pero*. Berlin: Reimer.

Frajzyngier, Zygmunt. 1989b. Non-propositional addressees. *Chicago Linguistic Society* 25.2: 41–9.

Frajzyngier, Zygmunt. 1989c. Three kinds of anaphors. In: Isabelle Haïk, and Laurice Tuller, eds, *Current Progress in African Linguistic*. Dordrecht: Foris, 194–216.

Frajzyngier, Zygmunt. 1991. The *de dicto* domain in language. In: Elizabeth C. Traugott and Bernd Heine, eds, *Approaches to grammaticalization* 1. Amsterdam/Philadelphia: Benjamins, 219–51.

Frajzyngier, Zygmunt. 1993. *A grammar of Mupun*. Berlin: Reimer

Frajzyngier, Zygmunt. 1995a. Functional theory of complementizers. In: Joan Bybee and Suzanne Fleischman, eds, *Mood and modality*. Amsterdam/Philadelphia: Benjamins, 473–502.

Frajzyngier, Zygmunt. 1995b. Two complementizers of Lele. In: Dymitr Ibriszimow and Rudolf Leger with Gerald Schmitt, eds, *Studia Chadica et Hamitosemitica: Akten der internationalen Symposions zur Tschadsprachenforschung*, Johann Wolfgang Goethe-Universität, Frankfurt am Main, 6.-8. Mai 1991, 163–70.

Frajzyngier, Zygmunt. 1996. *Grammaticalization of the complex sentence. A case study from Chadic*. Amsterdam/Philadelphia: Benjamins.

Frajzyngier, Zygmunt. 1997a. Grammaticalization of number: From demonstratives to nominal and verbal plural. *Linguistic Typology* 1: 193–242.

Frajzyngier, Zygmunt. 1997b. Pronouns and agreement: Systems interaction in the coding of reference. In: Hans Benis, Pierre Pica, and Johan Rooryck, eds, *Atomism and binding*. Dordrecht: Foris, 115–40.

Frajzyngier, Zygmunt. 1999. Domains of point of view and coreferentiality: Systems interaction approach to the study of reflexives. In: Zygmunt Frajzyngier and Traci S. Curl, eds, *Reflexives*. Amsterdam/Philadelphia: Benjamins.

Frajzyngier, Zygmunt. 2001. *A grammar of Lele*. Stanford Monographs in African Languages. Stanford: CSLI.

Frajzyngier, Zygmunt. In press. Tense and aspect as coding means. In: Ekkehard Wolff and Bernard Comrie, eds, *West African Language Typology: Papers from the International Symposium on Areal Typology of West African Languages*.

Frajzyngier, Zygmunt. In press. The principle of functional transparency and dative predication: A case study in Chadic. In: E. Voeltz, ed., *Dative in African languages*. Amsterdam/Philadelphia: Benjamins.

Frajzyngier, Zygmunt. *A grammar of Gidar*. MS.

Frajzyngier, Zygmunt, and Robert Jasperson. 1991. *That*-clauses and other complements. *Lingua* 83.133–53.

Frajzyngier, Zygmunt, Eric Johnson, with Adrian Edwards. Ms. *A grammar of Mina*.

Frajzyngier, Zygmunt, Holly Krech, and Armik Mirzayan. 2002. Motivation for copula in equational clauses. *Linguistic Typology*, 6.2, 155–98.

Frajzyngier, Zygmunt, and Jan Mycielski. 1998. On some fundamental problems of mathematical linguistics. In: Carlos Martin-Vide, ed., *Mathematical and computational analysis of natural language*. Amsterdam/Philadelphia: Benjamins.

Frajzyngier, Zygmunt, with Erin Shay. 2002. *A grammar of Hdi*. Berlin: Mouton de Gruyter.

Frege, Gottlob. 1879. Begriffsschrift. English translation in J. van Heijenoort, ed., *From Frege to Gödel: A source book in mathematical logic*, 1879–1931. Cambridge. Mass.: Harvard University Press.

Gary, Romain. 1980. *Les cerfs-volants*. Paris: Gallimard.

Gil, David. 1994a. Adjectives without nouns: an e-mail conversation. Conversations on noun phrases, 31–48. *EUROTYP Working Papers* VII/20. European Science Foundation.

Gil, David. 1994b. The structure of Riau Indonesian. *Nordic Journal of Linguistics* 17:179–200.

Gil, David. 1999. Riau Indonesian as a pivotless language. In: Ekaterina V. Rachilina and Yakov G. Testelec, eds, *Tipologija i teorija jazyka: Ot opisanija k objasneniju. K 60-letiju Aleksandra Evgen'eviča Kibrika*. Moskva: Jazyki Russkoj Kul'tury.

Gildersleeve, B.L., and Gonzalez Lodge. 1971 (1895). *Gildersleeve's Latin grammar*. London: Macmillan; New York: St Martin's Press.

Givón, Talmy. 1984. *Syntax: A functional-typological introduction*. Vol. 1 Amsterdam/ Philadelphia: Benjamins.

Givón, Talmy. 1990. *Syntax. A functional-typological introduction*. Vol. 2. Amsterdam/ Philadelphia: Benjamins.

Givón, Talmy, and S. Wright. 1987. The pragmatics of indefinite reference: Quantified text-based studies. *Studies in Language* 11.1:1–33.

Greenberg, Joseph H. 1963. Some universals of grammar, with particular reference to the order of meaningful elements. In: J.H. Greenberg, ed., *Universals of Language*. Cambridge, Mass.: MIT, 58–90.

Greenberg, Joseph H. Greenberg, Charles A. Ferguson and Edith Moravcsik, eds 1978. *Uni-*

versals of human language, Volume IV: Syntax. 249–8. Stanford: Stanford, University Press

Grinevald, Colette. 1995. Paper read at the at the Session on Functionalist Methodology of the Conference on Functional Approaches to Grammar, University of Albuquerque.

Haegeman, Liliane. 1991. *Introduction to government and binding theory.* Oxford: Blackwell.

Haegeman, Liliane. 1994. *Introduction to government and binding theory,* 2nd edition. Oxford: Blackwell.

Hagège, Claude. 1974. Les pronoms logophoriques. *Bulletin de la Société de Linguistique de Paris* 69.1:287–310.

Hagège, Claude. 1982. *La structure des langues.* Paris: Presses Universitaires de France.

Hale, Kenneth. 1992. Basic word order in two "free word order" languages. In D.L. Payne, ed., *Pragmatics of word order flexibility. Typological Studies in Language* 22:63–82. Amsterdam/Philadelphia: Benjamins.

Harlow, Steve. 1989. The syntax of Welsh soft mutation. *Natural Language and Linguistic Theory* 7:289–316.

Haspelmath, Martin. 1993. *A grammar of Lezgian.* Berlin: Mouton de Gruyter.

Haspelmath, Martin. 1999. Explaining article-possessor complementarity: Economic motivation in noun phrase syntax. *Language* 75.2.

Hawkins, John A. 1994. *A performance theory of order and constituency.* Cambridge: Cambridge University Press.

Heath, Jeffrey. 1978. *Ngandi grammar, texts and dictionary.* Canberra: AIAS.

Heath, Jeffrey. 1999a. *A grammar of Koyra Chiini: The Songhay of Timbuktu.* Berlin/New York: Mouton de Gruyter.

Heath, Jeffrey. 1999b. *A grammar of Koyraboro (Koroboro) Senni: The Songhay of Gao, Mali.* Köln: Rüdiger Köppe.

Heine, Bernd, Ulrike Claudi and Friederike Hünnemeyer. 1991. *Grammaticalization.* Chicago: Chicago University Press.

Hengeveld, Kees. 1992. *Non-verbal predication: Theory, typology, diachrony.* Functional Grammar Series 15. Berlin: Mouton de Gruyter.

Hockett, Charles F. 1955. *A course in modern linguistics.* New York: MacMillan.

Hoffmann, Carl. 1963. *A grammar of the Margi language.* Oxford: Oxford University Press.

Holland, Gary B. 1982. A note on raising in Indo-European. In: Monica Maccaulay, Orin D. Gensler, Claudia Brugman, Inese Civkulis, Amy Dahlstrom, Katherine Krile, Rob Sturm, eds, *Proceedings of the Eighth Annual Meeting of the Berkeley Linguistics Society.* Berkeley: Berkeley Linguistics Society.

Hopper, Paul J., and Sandra A. Thompson. 1980. Transitivity in grammar and discourse. *Language* 56.2:251–99.

Hopper, Paul J. and Sandra A. Thompson. 1984. The discourse basis for lexical categories in universal grammar. *Language* 60.4:703–52.

Hopper, Paul J. and Sandra A. Thompson. 1985. The iconicity of the universal categories 'noun' and 'verb'. In: J. Haiman, ed., *Iconicity in syntax.* Amsterdam/Philadelphia: Benjamins, 151–83.

Hopper, Paul J. and Elizabeth Closs Traugott. 1993. *Grammaticalization.* Cambridge: Cambridge University Press.

Horn, George M. 1985. Raising and complementation. *Linguistics* 23.6 (280): 13–850.

Hutchison, John P. 1981. *The Kanuri language: A reference grammar.* Madison, Wisconsin: African Studies Program.

Hyman, Larry M., and Bernard Comrie. 1981. Coreference and logophoricity in Gokana. *Studies in African Linguistics*, Supplement 8. 69–72.

Inkelas, Sharon, and Draga Zec. 1990. *The phonology-syntax connection*. Chicago and London: University of Chicago Press.

Jackendoff, Ray. 2001. *Foundations of Language*. Oxford: Oxford University Press.

Jake, Janice Lynn. 1985. *Grammatical relations in Imbabura Quechua*. New York: Garland.

Jakobson, Roman. 1966 (1963). Implications of language universals for linguistics. In: J.H. Greenberg, ed., *Universals of Language*, 2nd edition. Cambridge, Mass: MIT, 263–78.

Jarvis, Elizabeth. 1989. Esquisse grammaticale du Podoko. In: Daniel Barreteau and Robert Hedinger, eds, *Descriptions de languages Camerounaises*. Paris: Agence de coopération culturelle et technique and ORSTOM, 39–127.

Jelinek, Eloise. 1993. Ergative 'splits' and argument type. In: Jonathan D. Bobaljik and Colin Phillips, eds, *Papers on Case and Agreement*. MIT Working Papers in Linguistics 18.15–42.

Jensen, Frede. 1990. *Old French and comparative Gallo-Romance syntax*. Tübingen: Niemeyer.

Karolak, Stanisław. 1984. Składnia wyrażeń predykatywnych. In: Zuzanna Topolińska, ed., *Gramatyka współczesnego języka polskiego. Składnia*. Warsaw: Państwowe Wydawnictwo Naukowe, 11–212.

Kautzsch, E., ed. 1910. *Gesenius' Hebrew Grammar*. Oxford: Clarendon Press.

Kidima, Lukowa. 1987. Object agreement and topicality hierarchies in Kiyaka. *Studies in African Linguistics* 18.2: 175–209.

Kim, Won-ho. 1994. *Grammatical relations and anaphora in Korean*. Ph.D. dissertation, University of Colorado.

Klemensiewicz, Zenon, Janina Konieczna-Twardzikowa, and Krystyna Pisarkowa. 1965. *Zapomniane konstrukcje składni staropolskiej*. Wrocław/Warszawa/Kraków: Zakład Narodowy im. Ossolińskich.

König, Ekkehard, and Martin Haspelmath. 1998. Les constructions à possesseur externe dans les langues de l'Europe. In: Jack Feuillet, ed., *Actance et valence dans les langues d'Europe*. Berlin: Mouton de Gruyter, 525–606.

Kononov, A.N. 1960. *Grammatika sovremennogo uzbekskogo literaturnogo jazyka*. Moscow/ Leningrad: Akademia Nauk.

Kortmann, Bernd. 2002. New prospect for the study of English dialect syntax. In: Sjef Barbiers, Leonie Cornips and Susanne der Kleij, eds, *Syntactic Microvariation*. Amsterdam: Meertens Institute, Meertens Institute Electronic Publications in Linguistics (MIE-PiL).

Kraft, Charles H. 1963. *A study of Hausa syntax*. Hartford, Conn.: Hartford Seminary Foundation.

Kuno, Susumu. 1973. *The structure of the Japanese language*. Cambridge, Mass.: MIT Press.

Kurcz, I., A. Lewicki, J. Sambor, K. Szafran, and J. Woronczak. 1990. *Słownik frekwencyjny polszczyzny współczesnej*. Cracow: Polska Akademia Nauk, Instytut Języka Polskiego.

Kuryłowicz, Jerzy. 1964. *The inflectional categories of Indo-European*. Heidelberg: Winter.

Lafitte, Pierre. 1942. *Grammaire basque*. Bayonne: Editions des Amis du Musée basque et 'IKAS'.

Lakoff, George. 1987. *Women, fire, and dangeraous things*. Chicago: University of Chicago Press.

Lang, Adrianne. 1975. *The semantics of classificatory verbs in Enga (and other Papua New*

Guinea languages). Pacific Linguistics Series B, No. 39. Canberra: Australian National University.

Lapointe, Steven. 1985. *A theory of grammatical agreement*. New York: Garland.

Lazard, Gilbert. 1999. La question de la distinction entre nom et verbe en perspective typologique. *Folia Linguistica* 33.3–4: 389–418.

Legendre, Geraldine. 1986. Object raising in French: A unified account. *Natural Language and Linguistic Theory* 4.2: 37–183.

Lehmann, Christian. 1982. Universal and typological aspects of agreement. In: Hansjakob Seiler and F. J. Stachowiak, eds, *Apprehension. Das sprachliche Erfassen von Gegenständen. II. Die Techniken und ihr Zusammenhang in Einzelsprachen*. 201–167. Tübingen: Narr.

Lehmann, Christian. 1988. On the function of agreement. In: Michael Barlow and Charles A. Ferguson, eds, *Agreement and natural language: Approaches, theories, descriptions*. Stanford: CSLI.

Leslau, Wolf. 1995. *Reference grammar of Amharic*. Wiesbaden: Harrassowitz.

Li, Charles N., ed. 1975. *Word order and word order change*. Austin and London: University of Texas Press.

Li, Charles N. and Sandra A. Thompson. 1989. *Mandarin Chinese: A functional reference grammar*. Berkeley: University of California Press.

Lindenfeld, Jacqueline. 1973. *Yaqui syntax*. Berkeley: University of California Publications.

Local, John, J. Kelly and W. Wells. 1986. Towards a phonology of conversation: Turn-taking in urban Tyneside speech. *Journal of Linguistics* 22.2: 411–37.

Lyons, Christopher. 1999. *Definiteness*. Cambridge: Cambridge University Press.

Magomedbekova, Z. M. 1967. *Axvaxskij jazyk*. Tbilisi: Metsniereba.

Magometov, A. A. 1970. *Agulskij jazyk*. Tbilisi: Metsniereba.

Mallinson, Graham, and Barry J. Blake. 1981. *Language typology: Cross-linguistic studies in syntax*. Amsterdam/New York: North Holland.

Marouzeau, Jean. 1951. *Lexique de la terminologie linguistique*. Paris: Geuthner.

Martinet, André. 1967. Que faut-il entendre par 'fonction des affixes de classe'? *La classification nominale dans les langues négro-africaines*. Paris: CNRS, 15–25.

Matthews, Peter. 1997. *The concise Oxford dictionary of linguistics*. Oxford: Oxford University Press.

McConell, Frank D., ed. 1978. *Byron's poetry*. New York: Norton.

Meillet, Antoine. 1937. *Introduction à l'étude comparative des langues indo-européennes*, 8th edition. Paris: Librairie Hachette.

Milewski, Tadeusz. 1950. La structure de la phrase dans les langues indigènes de l'Amérique du Nord. In: Tadeusz Milewski, ed. (1967), *Études typologiques sur les langues indigènes de l'Amérique*. Kraków: Polska Akademia Nauk, 7–101.

Miller, Philip H., Geoffrey K. Pullum, Arnold M. Zwicky. 1997. The principle of phonology-free syntax: Four apparent counterexamples in French. *Journal of Linguistics* 33: 67–90.

Miller, J. and R. Weinert. 1998. *Spontaneous spoken language: Syntax and discourse*. Oxford: Oxford University Press.

Mithun, Marianne, with Reginald Henry. 1982. *A Cayuga grammar*. Brantford, Ontario: Woodland Indian Cultural and Educational Centre.

Mithun, Marianne. 1991. Active/agentive case and its motivations. *Language* 67: 510–46.

Mithun, Marianne. 1992. Is basic word order universal? In: Doris L. Payne, ed., *Pragmatics of word order flexibility*. Amsterdam/Philadelphia: Benjamins.

Miyagawa, Shigeru. 1989. Structure and case marking in Japanese. *Syntax and Semantics* 22. San Diego: Academic Press.
Moravcsik, Edith. 1978. Agreement. In: Greenberg et al., 371–4.
Moravcsik, Edith. 1978. On the case marking of objects. In: Greenberg et al., 249–8.
Moreno, Mario Martino. 1938. *Introduzione alla lingua Ometo*. Rome: Mondadori.
Najlis, Elena. 1973. *Lengua selknam*. Filolologia y linguistica 3. Buenos Aires.
Newman, Paul. 1982. Grammatical restructuring in Hausa: Indirect objects and possessives. *Journal of African languages and Linguistics* 4: 59–73.
Newman, Paul. 1990. *Nominal and verbal plurality in Chadic*. Dordrecht: Foris.
Nichols, Johanna. 1986. Head marking and dependent-marking grammar. *Language* 62.1: 56–119.
Nichols, Johanna. 1992. *Linguistic diversity in space and time*. Chicago: University of Chicago Press.
Nichols, Johanna, and Joe Schallert. 1983. The pragmatics of raising in Old Russian and Common Slavic. In: Michael S. Flier, ed., *American Contributions to the Ninth International Congress of Slavists*. Columbus: Slavica, 221–46.
Nitsch, Kazimierz. 1960. *Wybór polskich tekstów gwarowych*, 2nd edition. Warsaw: Państwowe Wydawnictwo Naukowe.
Noonan, Michael. 1992. *A grammar of Lango*. Berlin: Mouton de Gruyter.
Owens, Jonathan. 1993. *A grammar of Nigerian Arabic*. Wiesbaden: Harrassowitz Verlag.
Payne, Doris L., ed. 1992. *Pragmatics of word order flexibility*. Amsterdam/Philadelphia: Benjamins.
Pepicello, W. J. 1977. Raising in Latin. *Lingua* 42: 09–218.
Pisarkowa, Krystyna. 1959. Przypadek dopełnienia w polskim zdaniu zaprzeczonym. *Język Polski* 39.9–32.
Postal Paul. 1974. *On raising: One rule of English grammar and its theoretical implications*. Cambridge, Mass: MIT Press.
Quirk, Randolph, et al. 1972. *A grammar of contemporary English*. London: Langman.
Reh, Mechthild. 1985. *Die Krongo-Sprache*. Kölner Beiträge zur Afrikanistik 12. Berlin: Reimer.
Riemsdijk, Henk van, and Edwin Williams. 1986. *Introduction to the theory of grammar*. Cambridge, Mass: MIT Press.
Rijkhoff, Jan. 2002. *The noun phrase*. Oxford: Oxford University Press.
Rosch, Eleanor. 1973. On the internal structure of perceptual and semantic categories. In: T. T. Moore, ed., *Cognitive development and the acquisition of language*. New York: Academic Press, 111–44.
Rosenbaum, Peter S. 1967. *The grammar of English predicate complement constructions*. Cambridge, Mass.: MIT Press.
Schachter, Paul and Fe T. Otanes. 1972. *Tagalog reference grammar*. Berkeley: University of California Press.
Schwartz, Linda. 1989. Thematic linking in Hausa asymmetric coordination. *Studies in African Linguistics* 20.1: 29–62.
Seiler, Hansjakob. 1986. *Apprehension. Language, object and order*. Tübingen: Narr.
Sells, Peter. 1990. Is there subject-to-object raising in Japanese? In: Katarzyna Dziwirek et al., eds, *Grammatical relations*. Stanford: CSLI.
Senft, Gunter, ed. 2000. *Systems of nominal classification*. Cambridge/New York: Cambridge University Press.

Shay, Erin. 1999. *A grammar of East Dangla: The simple sentence.* Ph.D. dissertation, University of Colorado. Ann Arbor, Mich.: University Microfilms International.

Shibatani, Masayoshi. 1990. *The languages of Japan.* Cambridge: Cambridge University Press.

Siewierska, Anna, ed. 1998. *Constituent order in the languages of Europe.* Berlin/New York: Mouton de Gruyter

Smith, Michael Brockman. 1987. *The semantics of dative and accusative in German: An investigation in Cognitive Grammar.* Ph.D. Dissertation, University of California, San Diego.

Sproat, Richard. 1985. Welsh syntax and VSO structure. *Natural language nad linguistic theory* 3.173–216.

Stassen, Leon. 1997. *Intransitive predication.* Oxford: Clarendon Press.

Steele, Susan. 1978. Word order variation: a typological study. In: Joseph H. Greenberg, ed., *Universals of human language, Volume IV; Syntax.* 585–623. Stanford: Stanford University Press.

Steele, Susan. 1990. *Agreement and anti-agreement: A syntax of Luiseno.* Dordrecht/Boston: Kluwer Academic Publishers.

Svartvik, Jan, and Randolph Quirk, eds. 1980. *A corpus of English conversation.* Lund: Gleerup.

Szczypiorski, Andrzej. 1971. *Msza za miasto Arras.* Warsaw: Państwowy Instytut Wydawniczy.

Talmy, Len. 1992. Nouns. In William Bright (ed.), *International Encyclopedia of Linguistics,* vol. 3. New York: Oxford University Press, 130–1.

Taylor, Karen. 1991. Proto-Chadic sentential complementation after verbs of perception. In: Herrmann Jungraithmayr and Henry Tourneux, eds, *Etudes Tchadiques: La phrase complexe.* Paris: Geuthner, 73–84.

Thomas, Peter Wynn. 1984. Variation in South Glamorgan consonant mutation. In: Martin Ball and Glyn E. Jones, eds, *Welsh Phonology.* Cardiff: University of Wales Press, 208–36.

Thompson, Sandra A. 1988. A discourse approach to the cross-linguistic category 'adjective'. In: John Hawkins, ed., *Explanations for language universals.* London: Blackwell, 167–85.

Timberlake, A. 1975. Hierarchies in the genitive of negation. *Slavic and East European Journal* 19.123–38.

Tosco, Mauro. 1991. *A grammatical sketch of Dahalo.* Cushitic Language Studies 8. Hamburg: Buske.

Van Valin, Robert D. 1985. Case marking and the structure of the Lakhota clause. In: Johanna Nichols and Anthony Woodbury, eds, *Grammar inside and outside the clause: Some approaches to theory from the field.* Cambridge: Cambridge University Press, 363–413.

Van Valin, Robert D. 1993. A synopsis of role and reference grammar. In: Robert D. Van Valin, ed., *Advances in role and reference grammar.* Amsterdam/Philadelphia: Benjamins, 1–158.

Van Valin, Robert D. and Randy J. LaPolla. 1997. *Syntax: Structure, meaning, and function.* Cambridge: Cambridge University Press.

Voeltz, F. K. Erhard, and Christa Kilian-Hatz, eds 2001. *Ideophones.* Amsterdam/Philadelphia: Benjamins.

Wells, Margaret A. 1979. *Siroi grammar.* Pacific Linguistics Series B, No. 51. Canberra: Australian National University.

Wierzbicka, Anna. 1980. *The case for surface case.* Ann Arbor: Karoma.

Wierzbicka, Anna. 1992. *Semantics, culture, and cognition. Universal human concepts in culture-specific configuratioons*. Oxford: Oxford University Press.

Williams, Stephen J. 1980. *A Welsh grammar*. Cardiff: University of Wales Press.

Xu, Deboa. 1992. Mandarin tone sandhi and the interface study between phonology and syntax. Ph.D. dissertation, University of Illinois, Urbana-Champaign.

Zwicky, Arnold M. and Geoffrey Pullum. 1986. The principle of phonology-free syntax: Introductory remarks. *Working Papers in Linguistics*. The Ohio State University 32, 63–91.

Index of authors

Index of languages

Index of subjects

In the series TYPOLOGICAL STUDIES IN LANGUAGE (TSL) the following titles have been published thus far:

1. HOPPER, Paul J. (ed.): *Tense-Aspect: Between semantics & pragmatics.* 1982.
2. HAIMAN, John & Pamela MUNRO (eds): *Switch Reference and Universal Grammar. Proceedings of a symposium on switch reference and universal grammar, Winnipeg, May 1981.* 1983.
3. GIVÓN, T.: *Topic Continuity in Discourse. A quantitative cross-language study.* 1983.
4. CHISHOLM, William, Louis T. MILIC & John A.C. GREPPIN (eds): *Interrogativity: A colloquium on the grammar, typology and pragmatics of questions in seven diverse languages, Cleveland, Ohio, October 5th 1981-May 3rd 1982.* 1984.
5. RUTHERFORD, William E. (ed.): *Language Universals and Second Language Acquisition.* 1984 (2nd ed. 1987).
6. HAIMAN, John (Ed.): *Iconicity in Syntax. Proceedings of a symposium on iconicity in syntax, Stanford, June 24-26, 1983.* 1985.
7. CRAIG, Colette (ed.): *Noun Classes and Categorization. Proceedings of a symposium on categorization and noun classification, Eugene, Oregon, October 1983.* 1986.
8. SLOBIN, Dan I. & Karl ZIMMER (eds): *Studies in Turkish Linguistics.* 1986.
9. BYBEE, Joan L.: *Morphology. A Study of the Relation between Meaning and Form.* 1985.
10. RANSOM, Evelyn: *Complementation: its Meaning and Forms.* 1986.
11. TOMLIN, Russel S.: *Coherence and Grounding in Discourse. Outcome of a Symposium, Eugene, Oregon, June 1984.* 1987.
12. NEDJALKOV, Vladimir (ed.): *Typology of Resultative Constructions. Translated from the original Russian edition (1983). English translation edited by Bernard Comrie.* 1988.
14. HINDS, John, Shoichi IWASAKI & Senko K. MAYNARD (eds): *Perspectives on Topicalization. The case of Japanese WA.* 1987.
15. AUSTIN, Peter (ed.): *Complex Sentence Constructions in Australian Languages.* 1988.
16. SHIBATANI, Masayoshi (ed.): *Passive and Voice.* 1988.
17. HAMMOND, Michael, Edith A. MORAVCSIK and Jessica WIRTH (eds): *Studies in Syntactic Typology.* 1988.
18. HAIMAN, John & Sandra A. THOMPSON (eds): *Clause Combining in Grammar and Discourse.* 1988.
19. TRAUGOTT, Elizabeth C. and Bernd HEINE (eds): *Approaches to Grammaticalization, 2 volumes (set)* 1991
20. CROFT, William, Suzanne KEMMER and Keith DENNING (eds): *Studies in Typology and Diachrony. Papers presented to Joseph H. Greenberg on his 75th birthday.* 1990.
21. DOWNING, Pamela, Susan D. LIMA and Michael NOONAN (eds): *The Linguistics of Literacy.* 1992.
22. PAYNE, Doris (ed.): *Pragmatics of Word Order Flexibility.* 1992.
23. KEMMER, Suzanne: *The Middle Voice.* 1993.
24. PERKINS, Revere D.: *Deixis, Grammar, and Culture.* 1992.
25. SVOROU, Soteria: *The Grammar of Space.* 1994.
26. LORD, Carol: *Historical Change in Serial Verb Constructions.* 1993.
27. FOX, Barbara and Paul J. Hopper (eds): *Voice: Form and Function.* 1994.
28. GIVÓN, T. (ed.) : *Voice and Inversion.* 1994.
29. KAHREL, Peter and René van den BERG (eds): *Typological Studies in Negation.* 1994.

30. DOWNING, Pamela and Michael NOONAN: *Word Order in Discourse.* 1995.
31. GERNSBACHER, M. A. and T. GIVÓN (eds): *Coherence in Spontaneous Text.* 1995.
32. BYBEE, Joan and Suzanne FLEISCHMAN (eds): *Modality in Grammar and Discourse.* 1995.
33. FOX, Barbara (ed.): *Studies in Anaphora.* 1996.
34. GIVÓN, T. (ed.): *Conversation. Cognitive, communicative and social perspectives.* 1997.
35. GIVÓN, T. (ed.): *Grammatical Relations. A functionalist perspective.* 1997.
36. NEWMAN, John (ed.): *The Linguistics of Giving.* 1998.
37. RAMAT, Anna Giacalone and Paul J. HOPPER (eds): *The Limits of Grammaticalization.* 1998.
38. SIEWIERSKA, Anna and Jae Jung SONG (eds): *Case, Typology and Grammar. In honor of Barry J. Blake.* 1998.
39. PAYNE, Doris L. and Immanuel BARSHI (eds.): *External Possession.* 1999.
40. FRAJZYNGIER, Zygmunt and Traci S. CURL (eds.): *Reflexives. Forms and functions.* 2000.
41. FRAJZYNGIER, Zygmunt and Traci S. CURL (eds): *Reciprocals. Forms and functions.* 2000.
42. DIESSEL, Holger: *Demonstratives. Form, function and grammaticalization.* 1999.
43. GILDEA, Spike (ed.): *Reconstructing Grammar. Comparative Linguistics and Grammaticalization.* 2000.
44. VOELTZ, F.K. Erhard and Christa KILIAN-HATZ (eds.): *Ideophones.* 2001.
45. BYBEE, Joan and Paul HOPPER (eds.): *Frequency and the Emergence of Linguistic Structure.* 2001.
46. AIKHENVALD, Alexandra Y., R.M.W. DIXON and Masayuki ONISHI (eds.): *Non-canonical Marking of Subjects and Objects.* 2001.
47. BARON, Irene, Michael HERSLUND and Finn SORENSEN (eds.): *Dimensions of Possession.* 2001.
48. SHIBATANI, Masayoshi (ed.): *The Grammar of Causation and Interpersonal Manipulation.* 2002.
49. WISCHER, Ilse and Gabriele DIEWALD (eds.): *New Reflections on Grammaticalization.* 2002.
50. FEIGENBAUM, Susanne and Dennis KURZON (eds.): *Prepositions in their Syntactic, Semantic and Pragmatic Context.* 2002.
51. NEWMAN, John (ed.): *The Linguistics of Sitting, Standing and Lying.* 2002.
52. GÜLDEMANN, Tom and Manfred von RONCADOR (eds.): *Reported Discourse. A meeting ground for different linguistic domains.* 2002.
53. GIVÓN, T. and Bertram MALLE (eds.): *The Evolution of Language from Pre-language.* 2002.
54. AIKHENVALD, Alexandra Y. and R.M.W. DIXON (eds.): *Studies in Evidentiality.* 2003.
55. FRAJZYNGIER, Zygmunt and Erin SHAY: *Explaining Language Structure through Systems Interaction.* 2003.
56. SHAY, Erin and Uwe SEIBERT (eds.): *Motion, Direction and Location in Languages. In honor of Zygmunt Frajzyngier.* 2003.